A COMPLETE GUIDE TO THE HISTORY AND INMATES OF THE U.S. PENITENTIARY DISTRICT OF COLUMBIA 1829-1862

Mary C. Thornton

HERITAGE BOOKS
2012

HERITAGE BOOKS
AN IMPRINT OF HERITAGE BOOKS, INC.

Books, CDs, and more—Worldwide

For our listing of thousands of titles see our website at
www.HeritageBooks.com

Published 2012 by
HERITAGE BOOKS, INC.
Publishing Division
100 Railroad Ave. #104
Westminster, Maryland 21157

Copyright © 2003 Mary C. Thornton

All rights reserved. No part of this book may be reproduced or transmitted in any form or by any means, electronic or mechanical, including photocopying, recording or by any information storage and retrieval system without written permission from the author, except for the inclusion of brief quotations in a review.

International Standard Book Numbers
Paperbound: 978-0-7884-2294-2
Clothbound: 978-0-7884-9416-1

TABLE OF CONTENTS

Introduction

Chapter One: Pre-Penitentiary   1

Chapter Two: The Washington County Jail   5

Chapter Three: Courts and Laws   9

Chapter Four: The U. S. Penitentiary   15

Chapter Five: Prison Operations   19

Chapter Six: The Wardens   21

Chapter Seven: Stories from the Inside   41

Chapters Eight through Thirty-nine:
   Intake 1831 through Intake 1862   55-183

Chapter Forty: Perpetrators Who Never Made
   It To The Penitentiary   185

Chapter Forty-one: Conclusion   199

Notes   203

Bibliography   257

Index   263

Dedicated To

Tom

without whose patience and computer expertise, I might never have completed this book.

Introduction

Crime and punishment—a dark side of human history. Yet, we are intrigued by criminals and the crimes they commit as we explore the "hows," imagine the "whys," and join the jurors in judging innocence or guilt.

My intrigue with nineteenth century penitentiaries began as I researched my own ancestry in the 1850 census records for Kentucky. Among the listings were several pages of names of persons employed by, or incarcerated in, the penitentiary at Frankfort, KY. Compared to states along the eastern seaboard, Kentucky was newly-inhabited, and the large number of criminals serving time there in 1850 amazed me. What crimes were being committed, why were they being committed, and by whom were they being committed?

My curiosity led me to look at later censuses for Kentucky and to do some preliminary research on other penitentiaries in operation during the 1800s. As I looked through the records, I wondered how many genealogists like myself might have discovered a long-lost relative had they checked the penitentiary listings. I also wondered how a researcher would feel to find an ancestor on a list of convicts? How would I feel?

I really wanted to know about these old penitentiaries. The prison population at Frankfort grew tremendously between 1850 and 1860, and I decided that for the time being, doing a study on the penitentiary in Kentucky was too large a project for me to pursue. About the same time I started looking into the subject of penitentiaries, my husband and I moved to Washington, DC. I wondered where criminals from this area served their time. As I perused the census records for the District of Columbia, I found a listing for the Penitentiary for the District of Columbia. I was intrigued enough to look around for any records that might pertain to this penitentiary, and when I discovered that the Penitentiary for the District of Columbia was only open for thirty-three years, I decided that researching it might be both interesting and manageable.

I had moments when I wondered if anyone would really want to know about an ancestor who had been a criminal. When I spoke with a fellow genealogist about this, however, we both agreed that ancestors and the crimes perpetrated by those ancestors in no way reflect on us. Who they were and what they did is history.

And so, I proceeded with my research. Initially, I was surprised how many people, even Archives' personnel, did not know that there had ever been a penitentiary within the boundaries of the District of Columbia. My initial findings were solely initials—no names. After many, many hours of research, I was able to attach names and often stories to most of these initials.

Most of my information came from records stored at the National Archives in Washington, D.C. and in College Park, MD. Some information came from old issues of the *Evening Star*, stored on microfilm in the Washingtonia Division of the Main Library in Washington, D.C.

As I have uncovered names and stories about these individuals, I have come to know them and to appreciate their place, as well as my own, in the history of the nation's capital.

In addition to the names of the convicts, numerous other names appear throughout the text. These include the names of people who were victims, judges, law enforcement personnel, Civil War soldiers, doctors, ministers, etc.

No matter what it entails, each of us has a story that is unique. We are all a part of history, and it is the stories we leave behind that will allow future generations to know us and to know themselves. Where have we come from and where are we headed? Discover in the following pages your own place in history as you explore the "hows," imagine the "whys," and join the jurors in examining those ancestors whose lives were somehow touched by the Penitentiary for the District of Columbia.

Chapter One

PRE-PENITENTIARY

Once America gained its independence from England in 1776, its cities and towns began to grow. Increasing numbers of immigrants arrived on its shores, and the nation began to branch out toward the South and the West. In response to this expansion, government representatives quickly and unanimously agreed that there was a need to establish a central seat of government.

Determining just where "central" might be, however, was neither quick nor unanimous. Since the population was concentrated in the northeastern part of the country, centralizing the seat of government according to population would slight those living in the West. Were the capital to be located in any one particular state, surely it would create friction among the other states that might feel the "chosen state" somehow would have more influence than the rest. There did not seem to be any equitable solution. After seven long years of arguing, Congress finally decided to create a federal district.

The location of the district was a decision primarily based on politics rather than on geographic or demographic centrality. Maryland and Virginia agreed to cede land to create the new district. On 3 December 1789, Virginia ceded its share, and on 19 December 1791, Maryland ceded the rest. Initially called the District of Potomac, the ten-mile square territory was made up of two counties—Alexandria County and Washington County. Washington City and Georgetown were part of Washington County, and Alexandria City, a part of Alexandria County. Shortly after it was formed, the area was renamed the District of Columbia.

The question then was where, specifically, to put the capital. The answer: somewhere on the Potomac River. But where? Through a congressional act passed in 1790, President George Washington became responsible for choosing the site for the new capital city and for appointing commissioners to plan and build the new seat of government. Washington's choice was Washington City. Until the actual move took place, however, Philadelphia served as the country's capital.

Washington City was just a small village in 1800 when the government moved in. Though several government buildings had been erected, there was little housing available for incoming officials, and they found a city wanting in services. Dissatisfaction ruled, and for several years, the issue of moving the capital often arose.

The War of 1812 didn't help matters. Burned by the British in 1814, Washington fell into disrepair. Post-war Washington faced total overhaul, and while the federal government undertook major financial responsibility for rebuilding the District, reconstruction was slow as the federal government was very "frugal in appropriating funds."[1]

As the city began to recover and rebuild, people flocked into its emerging neighborhoods. Seeking work and bringing a host of skills with them, many took advantage of the opportunities the growing city had to offer. Some, however, unable or unwilling to find work to support themselves, spent their days in idle repose and resorted to crime as a means of survival. As the population increased, so did the crime rate.

There was no established police force in the District until 1861. In the early 1800s, constables, appointed by the District Circuit Court, were responsible for policing, though they were not highly valued for their ability to control crime. Local justices of the peace, appointed by the President, handled minor contractual cases that involved not more than $50. Both constables and magistrates were paid commissions on the fees each collected. Most operated primarily for their own personal gain rather than for the good of the community. In a report to Congress, it was noted that "a single magistrate, and one of the most respectable, during last year [1829] issued 4000 warrants.[2] Many supposed peacemakers went in search of trouble or even went as far as instigating it in order collect commission.

Persons arrested in the District for committing crimes were confined to one of two jails—the Alexandria jail or the Washington jail. These jails were under the control of a federal marshal.[3] The jail in Alexandria City was an old house that, in 1825, was rented by the United States for $150 per year.[4] The old house was converted into a four-room jail that was "not fit for swine."[5] The Washington jail was not much better.

Searching for a viable solution to their crime problems, Washingtonians looked to other areas of the country for suggestions. Supporters of prison reform hailed the penitentiary as the best answer to crime. Seen as places for reform, penitentiaries exposed the inmates to religious training and also taught them to read and write. Additionally, each prisoner was taught a job skill so that he could contribute, while imprisoned, to the cost of his imprisonment and would have the means of earning a living upon discharge. Many of the early penitentiaries ran prison industries in an effort to make themselves self-supporting, lightening the cost to the government.

Encouraged by the performance of successful penitentiaries around the nation and convinced that a penitentiary was just what Washington needed, the Board of Commissioners petitioned Congress to provide the capital city with its very own penitentiary—the U.S. Penitentiary.

Charles Bulfinch, Architect of the Capitol, was assigned the task of evaluating various penitentiaries to determine which might be the most appropriate model for the U.S. Penitentiary. After visiting prisons in Pennsylvania and New York, Bulfinch reported his findings. In his report to the 19th Congress,[6] he noted the preliminary action taken by both states was the establishment of a penal code. Old laws favoring the death penalty were replaced with new ones establishing guidelines for sentencing criminals to the penitentiary. Once those guidelines were in place, construction of penitentiaries in New York and Pennsylvania began.

One of the penitentiaries Bulfinch visited during its construction was Sing Sing, a large prison thirty miles from New York City, built to house 800. Each of its four floors had two rows of cells. Each cell measured 7'x7'x 3½', was built of stone, and was closed off with an iron door that was grated at the top. A four-inch pipe at the back of each cell provided ventilation. Bulfinch liked what he saw. A penitentiary so designed was economical and efficient, allowing prison personnel to see and hear all that was going on within the prison walls.

Bulfinch returned to Washington, drew up his plans for the U.S. Penitentiary, and submitted them to Congress. The new penitentiary was estimated to cost $40,000 to build. Along with his plans for the new penitentiary, Bulfinch presented plans for a $10,000 jail in Alexandria, and $5,000 worth of improvements to the Washington jail. Congress authorized the total package in 1826.

Construction of the new penitentiary was complete and the new warden had taken up residence there by 1829. Technically, the prison was ready for business, except for one minor detail. The courts still ran under the old laws. There were no guidelines for sentencing criminals to the penitentiary. Two years later, in 1831,Congress enacted a new criminal code for the District of Columbia, and the penitentiary received its first convict.

Chapter Two

THE WASHINGTON COUNTY JAIL

Built in 1802 on Judiciary Square, the Washington jail was a two-story brick building with sixteen, 8'x10' cells on the first floor and three rooms for imprisoning debtors on the second floor. Cells on the first floor held those awaiting trial, witnesses waiting to testify in those trials, pauper lunatics awaiting transfer to the asylum at Baltimore, and hard core criminals serving time for crimes that had already come to court.

Fifteen years later in 1817, however, as the crime rate increased, the jail became too crowded to hold everyone. Poor ventilation and an inadequate sewer system contributed to illness among the inmates. The Washington County jail was no longer sufficient to meet the needs of Washington.

By the 1820s, sixty to seventy prisoners were crammed into 16 cells. The overcrowding was not only unhealthy but allowed for the corruption, by association, of those debtors, juveniles, witnesses, or mental cases imprisoned, sometimes for up to six months, together with hardcore criminals. The Washington jail was seen as a "school of vice."[7] Something had to be done.

Noted in a report to Congress by the Committee on the District of Columbia on the subject of Prisons in the District, dated 1 February 1825, the roof on the Washington jail was so bad that rain came through everywhere. Initially, the committee had intended to request improvements to the jail but decided to request a new jail instead. Unwilling to appropriate funds for a new penitentiary and a new jail, Congress approved a $5000 outlay for making improvements to the Washington jail. By 1834, however, the improved Washington jail was rotting and in danger of falling down.

In February 1839, after being ignored by Congress for several years, the grand jury of the Criminal Court went directly to President Van Buren and requested a new jail. At the president's request, Congress appropriated $31,000 to build a new jail at Judiciary Square (4th and G Streets NW). The new jail, nicknamed the "Blue Jug" because of its exterior blue plaster, opened in 1841.

Designed by architect Robert Mills, the jail was poorly designed for its purpose of housing 126 inmates. There were 22 cells on one floor, each 8 ft. x 10 ft., designed to hold a maximum of 3 prisoners each.[8] Ten debtors rooms, intended to hold sixty, were on the upper floor.

During the 1840s and 1850s, the area around the jail was becoming residential. At first, the neighborhood residents were not too bothered by having the jail nearby, but as time wore on, they began to complain. The inmates of the jail often jeered at passersby and harassed them with profanity or other foul language. The building itself began to deteriorate and as it did so, became insecure, so that the residents of the neighborhood feared some criminal might escape and bring harm to them and their families. They wanted the jail moved.

Congress was repeatedly petitioned for a new jail, but it wasn't until 1866, when a typhus epidemic made the jail "a nest for disease,"[9] that Congress finally agreed. The new jail, designed by Ebon Faxon, was to house at least 300 and have a hospital. The $200,000 price tag was to be split between the federal and District governments.

No sooner had construction begun on the new jail in 1867 than it was halted due to some problems with the plans. Problems resolved, construction resumed, only to be halted again when it was discovered that bribes had been made in conjunction with assigning contracts. When work finally got underway again, the foundation was deemed too poor to continue. The whole project had to be scrapped and restarted.

Architect A. B. Mullet drew up new plans, but it took until 1871 for Congress to approve them. Mullet was allotted $300,000 to build the new jail. In June 1874, an additional $50,000 was requested, and in March 1875, the project needed $140,000 more. The new jail ended up costing $545,000! At its new site on the Anacostia River, the new jail opened in December 1875. It had 292 cells—256 designed to hold a single prisoner, and 36 designed to hold two or more prisoners.[10] The jail was used until a new jail at 19th and Massachusetts Avenue SE replaced it in April 1976.

Additionally in 1871, Congress funded the District Reform School, a reformatory for boys. Boys under sixteen were taken in to the school and remained there until they were reformed or became 21. In a city plagued for years by young boys running wild in its streets, the reform school was enthusiastically welcomed by all.

*****

Happenings at the Jail

"Marriage in Jail,"
Evening Star, 12 March 1858.

A trial was no longer necessary for Conrad Sohl, committed to jail on the charge of raping Charlotte Gerholdt, when Rev. Mr. Finkle married him and Charlotte in the jail. Though the couple was young, the groom seemed industrious and "in tolerable circumstances as to finances." The bride was reportedly "a very good looking young woman."

*****

In July 1851, the grand jury of the Criminal Court visited the jail and reported on one of the inmates, a deaf, dumb colored idiotic boy of about sixteen "left by some unfeeling wretch, in one of the streets of this city nearly two years since"[11] who had been kept in jail in an attempt to discover his identity. Since the first part of 1851, this boy was unable to eat solid food and in June, the grand jury noted that he was wasting away even though he was being well cared for by jail personnel. His identity was never known.

*****

In May 1859, the jail was located in a thickly populated area of dwellings and churches. The grand jury reported it to be an insecure eyesore, whose walls had been cut through in four or five places by escaping prisoners.

*****

"A Visit to the Blue Jug"
Evening Star, 28 August 1861

"A nursery of vice." "An architectural abortion." These were the words reporters used to describe the Washington County Jail in August 1861. Just inside the entrance on 4th Street was a guardroom. At the end of that room were iron-grated doors, behind which were steps to the cells. A curved bar was in front of the grated doors, and visitors were required to stand behind that bar during their visitations so that there would be no possibility for touching between visitor and inmate.

The office, on the west side of the guardroom, held an array of muskets, sabers, and pistols, as well as medicine. Off to one side of the office was a bedroom, which on 28 August 1861 was occupied by a Confederate POW, Dr. Fleming, who had been captured in June 1861, and was being temporarily held at the Washington Jail. A room off the other side of the office was used to store food.

Star reporters were escorted through the jail, noting several awaiting trial. There were two prisoners confined in cells on the first floor and several more, including two white women, on the second floor. Rooms on the third floor held a variety of prisoners—a few secessionists, 18-20 runaway slaves, other Negroes jailed for petty offences, and twelve men confined for disloyalty.

Improvements to the windows on the second and third stories were pointed out to the touring reporters. Each window had been fitted with upward tilting slats so that the only thing visible from the windows was the sky. No longer could prisoners look out and see the street. Before the new slats were put in place, prisoners used to spend their time gazing out the windows and yelling lewd remarks at those who passed along the street below.

Chapter Three

COURTS AND LAW

As construction of the Penitentiary got underway, it became necessary to rethink the existing laws. Initially, punishment was meted out according to the laws of the county wherein the crime was committed. One set of laws pertained to Alexandria County (under Virginia law) and another to Washington County (under Maryland law). These laws had been in effect since colonial times and carried harsh punishment for those who broke them. The death penalty was most common. Whipping or branding was next.

In Alexandria County, there were thirty crimes punishable by the death penalty, and in Washington County, eighteen. For example, under Maryland law, the following crimes committed in Washington County before Maryland designed its new criminal code in 1810, resulted in death: burning a court house; arson of a mansion house; petit treason; murder or arson by blacks; breaking, entering, and stealing goods to a value of five shillings; breaking into a tobacco or other out house and stealing up to the value of five shillings; stealing a boat or a Negro; burning tobacco or tobacco house with tobacco in it; horse stealing; burning a ship, sloop, or boat; "consultation" among slaves to create insurrection, murder or poison anyone or burn a house; attempt by slaves to burn any house or out house in which there was any person, goods, tobacco, Indian corn, or fodder; destroying or burning, or conspiring to do so, military or naval stores of the United States or a state; and mayhem.[12] Punishment under Virginia law was very similar.

On 25 June 1801, Samuel Baker was found guilty of a felony. As punishment, Baker was burned with a hot iron on the thumb of his left hand and required to give security of $100 in promise that he would behave himself in the future.[13] Charles Houseman was found guilty on 27 June 1801 of stealing a handsaw. He was sentenced to return the saw, pay a fourfold fine of $2, and receive 20 stripes.[14] In August 1802, Nancy Swann was found guilty of receiving stolen goods, knowing them to be stolen, and ordered to pay a $2 fine and receive 10 stripes.[15] However, with the advent of the penitentiary, support for corporal punishment waned and was replaced with a growing preference for the more humane system of reform that the penitentiary offered.

In order for the penitentiary system to work, there needed to be an equitable method of punishment that could be meted out by the sentencing judge, and in 1831, a new criminal code for the District of Columbia was established. Under the new code, the death penalty remained the punishment for crimes of murder, treason, and piracy.[16] Other crimes were punished as follows:

- Rape
  10-30 years for the 1st offense; Life for the 2nd
- Manslaughter or assault/battery with the intent to kill
  2-10 years for the 1st offense; Life for the 2nd
- Assault/battery with the intent to rape
  1-5 years for the 1st offense; 5-15 years for the 2nd
- Mayhem
  2-7 years for the 1st; 5-12 years for the 2nd
- Arson
  1-10 years for the 1st offense; 5-20 years for the 2nd
- Burglary/robbery
  3-7 years for the 1st offense; 5-15 years for the 2nd
- Forgery/counterfeiting
  1-7 years for the 1st offense; 3-10 years for the 2nd
- Stealing money or goods worth $5 or more (grand larceny)
  1-3 years for the 1st offense; 1-5 years for the 2nd
- Perjury
  2-10 years for the 1st offense; 5-15 years for the 2nd
- Bigamy
  2-7 years for the 1st offense; 5-12 years for the 2nd
- Seizing free blacks to sell as slaves
  up to 12 years and $5000 fine
- Non-specified felonies
  7-10 years
- Assault/battery
  6 months[17]

From 1802 to 1838, the U.S. District Court for the District of Columbia tried all cases, both civil and criminal, in the District. Those accused of committing a crime, as well as those who were witnesses, were held in the county jail at government expense, often for as long as six months awaiting trial. As well as infringing on the right to a speedy trial, the long delays were unjust for witnesses who often spent just as much time in jail as the accused did.

For example, "a person just landing on the wharf from an Eastern vessel, happened to witness some trifling assault and battery, was summoned before a magistrate, and being a stranger, and unable to give security, he was committed to gaol [jail] with the culprit, where they both remained more than four months; and although the defendant was convicted, yet the court, believing he had already suffered more than merited punishment, discharged him with the witness. So that both endured the same imprisonment, and were discharged at the same time."[18]

In 1838, a Criminal Court, specifically for handling crime, was established. Judge James Dunlop was appointed as its first judge. Dunlop presided over the Criminal Court until 1845 when Judge Thomas Hartley Crawford took over.

At the beginning of each term, a new set of jurors was chosen to serve for that term. The grand jury assessed accusations made against each prisoner and determined which cases warranted indictment. Those cases, listed by name and number on a docket, were presented before the court. After the petit jury heard the evidence and reached a verdict, the presiding judge passed sentence.

For many years, the Criminal Court shared the same courtroom with the District Court, resulting in delays and frustrations for both courts. To have a courtroom of its own was a request frequently made to Congress by the Criminal Court. Repeatedly, grand juries suggested that the East Wing of the county courthouse be extended for the purpose of housing the Criminal Court.

Criminal Court initially met four times a year--in March, June, October, and December. Temporarily reduced to meeting three times a year, the court became overwhelmed with cases and extended terms, and the four terms were reinstated. Court usually convened around ten o'clock in the morning, frequently adjourned for a few hours, and re-convened late in the afternoon. Many sessions lasted well into the evening, sometimes as late as 9 p.m., and it was not uncommon for the court to convene on Saturday.

An additional duty of each grand jury was to periodically inspect the county jail and the penitentiary and to report to the court on the condition of each. Conditions at the jail were usually reported to be adequate. The jail was clean and the prisoners content and well fed. However, the building itself was another story. It was in poor condition and "insecure for a county prison."[19]

Close contact and poor ventilation in the cramped quarters of the jail did little to enhance a healthy and environmentally friendly atmosphere, and in 1849, a suggestion was made that prison uniforms be distributed to prisoners to prevent "vermin" and ensure cleanliness. In 1850, the grand jury praised the recently-made arrangements for bathing and washing and reported the jail to be "free from any unpleasant smell."[20]

During the 1850s, an increasing number of juveniles, mostly teenage boys, roamed the streets of Washington, creating a ruckus and disturbing the peace of neighborhoods all over the city. These young boys were often guilty of committing minor crimes that landed them in the county jail for short periods of time. If the boys were to follow the straight and narrow, they needed to be sequestered away from hard-core criminals, so the grand jury recommended establishment of a house of corrections specifically for juveniles.

Numerous complaints and requests about the courthouse were made. In 1847, it was reported that the south steps were dangerous, that the vestibule leading to the courtroom was "very filthy," the whole building needed painting and many parts of the floor needed repairing.[21] Records, stored in halls and other exposed places, were vulnerable to mutilation, defacement, theft, and destruction due to a lack of proper storage facilities. Repeated reports affirmed the need for new court facilities.

On numerous occasions, the grand jury reported situations that it felt needed remedying. In 1846, recommendation was made not to reappoint Joseph N. Fearson as a justice in Georgetown. Fearson "has conducted himself with great impropriety as a citizen, and has moreover been presented by the said jury for sundry violations of law."[22]

In 1850, repeal of the 7 July 1838 law that prohibited any note, check, draft, bank bill or other paper currency worth less than $5 from being used as payment in the District of Columbia was recommended. The court was overwhelmed by several cases in which this law had been broken.[23]

The grand jury of 1852 requested the entire department of constables be dismissed and only "efficient and competent" ones re-appointed. Fifty-six constables acted little, if any, and of the other fifty-seven who did act, many acted under expired bonds.[24]

Congress was asked by the grand jury in 1853 to pass laws to prevent the "lawless idle and unprincipled"[25] from stealing crops to use for themselves or to sell in the City Market. These trespassers treated themselves to the bounty of Washingtonian gardens. When charged with an action of trespass, however, no good was accomplished because no compensation from fines or other means could be collected from those who hadn't any money to begin with.

A second appeal was made to Congress to pass laws to prevent the "lawless idle and unprincipled" from drunkenness, gambling, riots, etc. In one of its reports, the grand jury noted that many of these crimes were perpetrated by "persons of color" who were coming into Washington from Virginia and Maryland. "The municipal authority and the ordinances of the Corporation are found to be almost wholly inoperative and ineffective either to check the increase [of emigrants into the District] or to prevent the crimes and disorders consequent upon it; and for the security, peace and good order of the community, it has become most desirable and important that Congress should take the subject into consideration and pass some laws to prevent the evils complained of."[26]

"Frivolous" cases and "an unnecessary number of witnesses to establish proof" wasted the grand jury's time and government money in 1856 when 700 witnesses were examined, 291 cases investigated, and 172 of those cases dismissed. The total cases on the docket for the June 1856 term were 461. Many of these matters could have been handled by the magistrates rather than the court. Magistrates and constables who collected $36,196.33 over a six-year period between May 1848 and June 1854 and $28,325.58 in the eighteen months between July 1854 and the end of December 1855 were abusing the system. These figures prompted the grand jury suggestion that a "properly organized Magistrate or Police Court would greatly facilitate justice, and would result in a large saving in costs to the U.S."[27]

By the start of the Civil War, lawlessness abounded in the District. A huge influx of soldiers, fugitive slaves, free blacks, and others created chaos in the capital city. Numerous "disreputable persons" came taking advantage of those willing to spend money on liquor, prostitutes, or gambling.[28] In 1861, a metropolitan police force, headed by a chief and including ten sergeants and 150 patrolmen, was created to help maintain civil order in the District.[29]

In 1862, the penitentiary was closed and the property given to the War Department for munitions storage. On 3 March 1863 (12 Stat.762), the function of both the U.S. District Court and the U.S. Criminal Court was taken over by the Supreme Court of the District of Columbia.

Chapter Four

THE UNITED STATES PENITENTIARY

The United States Penitentiary was built on Greenleaf's Point at the northern end of the Washington Arsenal at 4½ Street SW, the present site of Fort Lesley J. McNair. It occupied about one to two acres on the arsenal grounds and was bordered on the west by the Potomac River and on the east by James Creek.

The main building consisted of four floors of 40 cells per floor. Each cell was 7' x 3½' x 7'. On one side of the main building were a chapel, a hospital, and a house for the warden and his family. On the other side was the female prison and living quarters for the deputy warden. Behind the main building, in the prison yard, were the workshop, the kitchen and the dining hall. There was a wharf on the Potomac for the intake of supplies. A wall, twenty-feet high and eighteen inches thick surrounded the entire complex.

Guidelines for running the prison were established in 1829. The President of the United States was required to appoint five inspectors to periodically inspect and report on the penitentiary. Prisoners were to be held one to a cell. No verbal exchange was allowed between them, and none was allowed visitors or mail without permission from the inspectors and later, the warden. The female prisoners had the same rules and were to be housed separately from the males.

Penitentiary philosophy, aptly expressed by Charles Bulfinch, architect for the penitentiary, was "that they will submit to the punishment which the laws may direct, with an assurance that it is not inflicted on them in revenge for their misdeeds, but with the hope of effecting their reform."[30]

Prisoners were to work, and work hard. All worked six days a week. The penitentiary was to be productive and aimed to be self-supporting. For most of its operational life, the U.S. Penitentiary actively engaged in shoemaking, though carpentering and broom making were also done. Male prisoners were taught a specific skill, and the products they made were sold to support the needs of the penitentiary. The female prisoners were engaged in "making, washing and mending for the male department."[31]

Upon entry into the penitentiary, each prisoner was examined by the doctor, bathed, given a short haircut, and dressed in a prison uniform. Each then had an introductory meeting with the warden and other officers during which each inmate was given the rules and assigned a job. The warden kept each prisoner's personal effects until time of discharge.

Upon discharge, personal effects were returned along with a new set of clothes and a small amount of money ($2 at first, and $10 by the 1860s). Each prisoner was required upon discharge to advise the warden of his address, and if the inspectors and the warden had been satisfied with his behavior while in the penitentiary, each was given a certificate.[32]

The prison day began at 7 a.m. between March 20th and September 20th, and at 8 a.m. between September 20th and March 20th. No prisoner was allowed to get up or go to bed until the sounding of the bell. Each had forty-five minutes for breakfast. One hour was allowed for dinner, which was served at 1 p.m. Initially, prisoners ate both daily meals in their cells until the dining hall was completed.[33]

Each prisoner was rationed 12 ounces of pork or 16 oz. of beef per day; 10 oz. wheat flour; 12 oz. Indian meal, and ½ gill of molasses.[34]

Each was also given a striped jacket, vest, and pantaloons; a matching cap; leather shoes; wool socks; and cotton or linen shirts. Inmates received a mattress, 2 wool blankets, and one sheet and were not permitted to sleep in their clothes.

Inmates were punished for using bad language, for disobeying orders, for being insolent, for fighting, for talking, for refusing to work or for ruining work materials.[35] Prisoner Samuel Peoples was given five days in solitary--only bread and water to eat and confinement in a solitary cell for up to twenty days--for whistling and singing. And, John Kelly was sent to solitary for mimicking a cat.[36] On occasion, some wardens were known to beat or flog the inmates who broke the rules.

The first warden, Benjamin Williams was appointed 24 March 1829 by President Andrew Jackson and moved himself and his family into the warden's house in May 1829. The first prisoner was not received, however, until 9 April 1831.

In 1842, instead of being called the U.S. Penitentiary, the pen became better known as the Penitentiary for the District of Columbia.

Occupying about one to two acres in the center of the Washington Arsenal, the U.S. Penitentiary operated for 33 years, from the appointment of Warden Williams in 1829 until Abraham Lincoln declared its closure in 1862.

For many years before its closure, the penitentiary took up space coveted by the War Department for storage of weapons/ammunitions. Throughout the 1850s, the War Department, repeatedly expressing a need for more storage space, wanted the penitentiary operations removed from arsenal grounds so that munitions could be stored in the space that then held prisoners, etc.

With the onset of the Civil War and increased production of weapons and ammunition, the War Department's request was finally heeded. On 19 September 1862, President Lincoln ordered the penitentiary closed, and the space was given to the War Department to use as a warehouse.

Many of the prisoners had already been pardoned and released by that time. On 4 August 1862, some forty soldiers who had been housed in the penitentiary for various crimes—desertion, subordination, etc.—and pardoned by President Lincoln were released and assigned to duty in the 19th Indiana Regiment. The 19th Indiana had recently lost most of its men in battle and needed reinforcements badly. Before the released penitentiary prisoners got to the 19th's camp; however, many ran away and had to be rounded up.

The approximate 130 prisoners who were left in the penitentiary were transported at government expense to the penitentiary at Albany, NY on 23 September 1862 aboard the steamer *Connecticut*. A gunboat was employed to accompany the steamer in the event that a problem arose en route.[37] Long-term felons from the District of Columbia continued to be incarcerated at Albany until 1916.[38]

By 1868, three years after the Civil War ended, all but two of the old penitentiary buildings were demolished. Those, too, were either demolished or renovated beyond recognition as part of the penitentiary. What remains today is not much more than a memory, if that.

Chapter Five

PRISON OPERATIONS

The penitentiary operated under the auspices of a Board of Inspectors whose initial membership was five but was reduced in 1833 to three. The first to serve on the Board were Henry Ashton, Thomas Carberry, William O'Neale, Thomson F. Mason, and James Dunlop.

Penitentiary personnel were to include a warden, a deputy warden, a clerk, a chaplain, a doctor, and assistant keepers/officers. It was not until the mid 1850s that a matron for the female prisoners was also added to the list of prison personnel. Until that time, the female department was overseen by one of the male officers.

Appointed by the President, the warden was initially paid an annual salary of $1200 and provided with a house on the prison grounds for himself and his family. He was to remain at the prison at night unless he had written permission from the inspectors to do otherwise. He was to keep a journal and record the reception, discharge, death, pardon, or escape of any prisoners as well as record any complaints or punishments. He was to visit each prisoner on a daily basis. In addition, he was to be in charge of the prison's inferior officers and to record the purchases and sales made by the prison.

The deputy warden was to be present at the daily open and close of the penitentiary, at religious services, and during all prison hours except for his personal meal times. He was to inspect the hospital, the kitchen, the cells, the yards and workhouse on a daily basis and keep tabs on officers employed at the penitentiary. He was also to see that each inmate received two clean shirts per week.

The clerk was to keep the books and keep articles bought for or made at the penitentiary safe and accounted for. He was responsible for bookkeeping tasks and kept track of, and issued, clothing.

It was the chaplain's duty to hold a daily morning and evening service, run a Sunday School, preach a sermon every Sunday, and to see that each cell had a Bible. Prison officers were present at each service to maintain order.

The doctor was to examine prisoners upon entry into the penitentiary. He was to use his discretion to prevent the spread of infection and disease among the prisoners and was to visit the hospital at least once each day. He was to care for the sick and keep records on each of his patients. In addition, he was to keep a record of medical supplies.

The assistant keepers/officers were to record the daily work of each prisoner; enforce the rules; avoid, as much as possible, conversing with the inmates; have no personal dealings with the inmates; abstain from drinking on duty; refrain from cursing and indecent language/conduct; and constantly attend to and supervise prison work from sunrise to sunset. Should any officer need to be absent from his job, he was to get the warden's permission to do so.

Chapter Six

THE WARDENS

Nine men, one of whom served two terms as warden, were appointed Warden of the U.S. Penitentiary during the 33 years the penitentiary served the citizens of Washington. Most of the wardens had been businessmen prior to becoming wardens at the U.S. Penitentiary.

Benjamin Williams (1829-1832)

The first warden, Benjamin Williams arrived in May 1829 and served until his disappearance in 1832, soon after President Jackson was presented with an accusation, alleging that Williams had abused his position, neglected his duty, and misappropriated penitentiary funds.

On 23 February 1832, "after a long and patient trial of nearly three years,"[39] the Board of Inspectors agreed that Williams was "incompetent and unfit to perform and execute the duties of warden or to have charge of the public money and property at the penitentiary."[40] During those three years, the Board had generously excused many of Williams' indiscrepancies by allowing him to return money or goods while promising never to break the rules again. After Williams continued to break the rules and renege on his promises, the Board resolved to write President Jackson, recommending Williams "be removed from the office of Warden of the Penitentiary."[41]

Reasoning behind the Board's recommendation to remove Williams from his position at the penitentiary included the following: personal use of public money (January 1830); presentation of false vouchers (October 1831); default of $1400 in a government audit in November 1831; storage of penitentiary supplies inside his own home; presentation of advances to contractors; falsification of unpaid bills marked "paid"; failure to enforce rules of the penitentiary as established by acts of Congress; employment of inmates outside the pen for his own personal use; failure to perform daily cell inspections; failure to properly discipline inmates; allowing his children and servants to mingle with and talk with the convicts; and mixing "private business" with penitentiary business.

Overall, the Board found Williams "deficient in common business habits"[42] and "deficient in ordinary intelligence and capacity to understand the rules."[43]

Facing this long list of charges, Williams chose to desert his post as warden, and he and his family disappeared.

Some one needed to be in charge at the penitentiary, and until a new warden could be appointed, Pierce Spratt, one of the keepers, became Acting Warden. Spratt, who at one time had served on the *U.S.S. North Carolina* was noted as being "honest, sober, industrious, and obliging."[44]

During the time he did serve as warden, Williams and his family lived in a home provided for them on the grounds of the Penitentiary. The home initially was deemed inappropriately situated to house a family because it opened onto the prison yard where prisoners would be in sight of the home and the warden's family. Consequently, by 1831, new and separate housing for the warden and his family was built at another site on the grounds. The basement of the new house flooded and sewers had to be built to alleviate the problem.[45]

In addition to his other problems, Williams' had two prisoners—Joshua Young and Wesley Hobbs—escape by scaling the walls of the U. S. Penitentiary on 12 January 1832. Both were apprehended and served out their terms at the Baltimore Penitentiary.

Isaac Clarke (1832-1841)

On 15 March 1832, President Andrew Jackson appointed Isaac Clarke as the new warden of the U.S. Penitentiary. Clarke's tenure as warden was overshadowed by numerous accusations of wrongdoing, too.

Clarke favored corporal punishment, and in his first annual report, he wrote, "It is my humble opinion, that the discipline of no prison can be perfect, unless corporal punishment be used."[46] The Board of Inspectors nixed that idea by noting that corporal punishment had been prohibited by an act of Congress and must be authorized by Congress before it could be used.

In the late 1830s, a letter from former-inmate William Nash to President Van Buren alleged "unmersifull punishment"[47] of convicts by Warden Clarke. In 1842, numerous charges were brought against Warden Clarke. For one, he was charged with employing prisoners, for his own purposes, outside the prison walls. Several of those who were so employed, escaped. Some of these prisoners also stole prison property and sold or disposed of it in the neighborhood and bought liquor.

Clarke kept some prisoners working until 10 or 11 p.m. shelling corn for him, and he allowed sale of the penitentiary's ice to an ice vender in Washington, making remuneration to prison funds only when ordered to do so.[48]

Accused of intimidating prison officers to capture prisoners who had escaped while doing Clarke's private jobs, Clarke allegedly also used public funds to pay rewards to his officers. He illegally disposed of public property—sold Venetian blinds and lumber to Thomas Carberry, a penitentiary inspector, and gave Carberry a workbench, window frames, tin water heads, tin waterspouts, and tin gutters which belonged to the penitentiary and were taken down from the penitentiary.[49]

Clarke was "overbearing, tyrannical and oppressive"[50] to the prisoners. He reportedly allowed prisoners to be beaten with wooden paddles.[51] According to Mason Piggott, a penitentiary guard employed since February 1836, Warden Clarke once ordered inmate Addison Brown be "cobbed." When Brown refused to submit because cobbing was illegal, John Young, a prison keeper since September 1831, hit Brown over the head with a cobbing board and a piece of oak flank, causing Brown to bleed. Pierce Spratt, also a keeper at the time, joined the foray, stabbing Brown through the arm with a sword.[52]

On 19 October 1832, shortly after Clarke became Warden, inmate Nancy Ashton, was discharged. She had been incarcerated at the penitentiary since October 1831, and upon release was apparently six to seven months pregnant. Word among the officers of the penitentiary was that John Young, keeper in charge of the female department of the penitentiary, was responsible. Clarke never checked into the matter. On 22 November 1832, a little over a month after she was discharged, Nancy Ashton had a baby. Records show she went to Richard Butt, attendant of the Washington Asylum, with an order from Mr. Harbaugh, guardian of the poor in Washington City, to bury her infant child. She told Butt that the child was born two to three weeks after she got out of the penitentiary. The child appeared to be about three to four weeks old.[53]

According to George B. Smith, a prison guard since August 1833, prisoner Harriet Smith was supposedly pregnant while incarcerated, and it was rumored that her child died and was buried in the prison yard.[54]

Judge James Dunlop, a former inspector of the penitentiary, felt that some of the allegations brought against Clarke in 1842 by William Wheatly, Clerk of the Penitentiary, were due to Wheatly's dislike of Clarke.[55] Due to insufficient evidence on the charges made against him, Warden Clarke suffered no consequence.

In 1832, under Isaac Clarke's administration, John Taylor and John Laurence escaped. Both were captured; however, while waiting in the jail in Fredericktown, MD, to be returned to the U.S. Penitentiary, Taylor died of cholera. After Laurence was caught, he served out his time in the penitentiary at Philadelphia where the President pardoned him on 4 July 1835.

By 1833, all the buildings at the penitentiary were complete and the business of shoemaking was in full operation. Dr. J. M. Thomas had all the convicts vaccinated for smallpox. From July to the first frost, a "bilious fever," which Dr. Thomas attributed to exposure to marsh effluvia, affected almost all of the inmates.[56] Chaplain William Kesley, who took office on 3 August 1833, started a Sunday School in September 1833 and began teaching the convicts to read.

In November 1834, Dr. Thomas C. Scott took over as prison doctor. In his yearly report, he asked that the marsh be drained. Autumn was the worst time of the year for fevers which Scott felt were marsh-related.

In 1835, five of the prisoners attacked a guard while they were working outside the penitentiary. According to the warden's annual report, a prisoner took his pistol and "snapped it at his [the guard] breast"[57] All five of them escaped and were later captured. Addressing the high rate of recidivism, Warden Clarke said he felt that high recidivism was due to the good food served by the prison and to the lenient rule. As he had requested once before, Clarke asked permission again in 1835 to use corporal punishment and "power to use" the lash.[58]

In 1836, John J. Ungerer took over as chaplain of the penitentiary.

Eighteen thirty-seven brought a new doctor and a new chaplain to the penitentiary. Dr. Scott died and was replaced with Dr. Benjamin S. Bohrer and C. B. Tippett replaced Chaplain Ungerer. The Board of Inspectors (James Dunlop, William A. Davis, and Thomas Carberry) noted in their annual report that the penitentiary was extremely clean. A note was also that addictions to tobacco and alcohol were on the decline.

As it had done in its first annual report, the Board of Inspectors petitioned Congress again in 1837 to establish a separate criminal court for the District. The District Circuit Court tried both civil and criminal cases. The establishment of a criminal circuit court would ensure speedy trials. In addition, money would be saved by getting the accused through the system and out of the jail where, at government expense, the accused, witnesses, etc. were held awaiting trial.

On 7 July 1838, the Criminal Court for the District of Columbia was established and presided over by Judge James Dunlop, appointed by President Martin Van Buren. The court met four times a year—October, December, March, and June—in a room in City Hall.

Clarke received a $300 salary increase in 1838, raising his pay to $1500 per year. Also in 1838, R. R. Gurley took over as the new chaplain, and William Wheatly was hired as clerk at a salary of $1000 per year. Three assistant keepers—John A. Young, Gabriel Bradley, and J. C. David—received salaries of $700 each per year, and five guards—Lewis Ratcliff, W. V. Reswick, George B. Smith, Mason Piggott, and John Fisher—were paid $500 each per year.

The cost of feeding each prisoner in 1838 was 11cents per day. An additional 16 cents per day covered each inmate's upkeep.

In 1839, "reform" was the primary concern of the penitentiary. Some of the prisoners were "old offenders," unable and unwilling to change. "They are, too, the most unprofitable subjects in the pen... These cannot enjoy liberty without indulging in crime."[59] While shoe and boot manufacture remained the primary industry of the penitentiary in 1839, the manufacture of corn brooms was undertaken to provide additional income for the penitentiary.

Two prisoners died during 1839—one from apoplexy and one of congestive fever.[60] A new Board of Inspectors—Bernard Hooe, Thomas Carberry, and William Minor—took over in 1839, and Walter Colton served as the chaplain.

In the spring of 1840, a portion of the wharf was carried away by ice, and "several hundred feet of coping and railing, with wooden platform attached to it,"[61] was ripped from the outer wall by a tornado in the summer of 1840. The estimated cost to repair it was $1500. John B. Ferguson took over as chaplain. One prisoner, Clement B. Weston, died from consumption on 24 February 1840.

Colonel John B. Dade (1841-1845)

John B. Dade, appointed by President John Tyler, became the new warden on 11 May 1841. Two new inspectors, Thomas Sewall and Thomas Donoho, joined Bernard Hooe on the Board, and became the new doctor.

The prison was still incapable of supporting itself in 1841. The Board reasoned that the U.S. Penitentiary held too few inmates to substantiate a profit-making endeavor and that most sentences were far too short for the inmates to have enough time to learn a skill well enough to contribute substantially to the support of the penitentiary. Consequently, the Board recommended that inmates from other states who had committed crimes that broke the laws of the United States be sent to the U.S. Penitentiary. This would increase the labor resource at the U.S. Penitentiary and, therefore, increase the income. The Board also argued that importing criminals from other penitentiaries would save the U.S. Treasury approximately twenty per cent in the costs of housing these criminals as they could be housed more cheaply at the U.S. Penitentiary.

New bedding was requested in the annual report for 1841[62] for prisoners still sleeping on the original bedding, put in place in 1829.

Doctor Young reported that during 1841, a female patient suffered from epilepsy but that the disease was under control. Cases of bilious fever were reported for 1841, as well as some cases of rheumatism, scrotal hernias, and slight derangement among the inmates due to the sedentary nature of their work.[63]

It was during 1842 that the penitentiary no longer was referred to as the U. S. Penitentiary. Instead, it was called the Penitentiary for the District of Columbia.

Dr. Young reported one death from pneumonia and one from haemopthyris in 1842. Bilious fever, epilepsy, hernia, hemorrhoids, indigestion and catarrhal infections afflicted several prisoners, and Dr. Young recommended that the prisoners be allowed to exercise to avert disease.[64] Shoemaking was too sedentary. He also requested wool undergarments for the inmates and suggested the installation of a better heating system. Men were getting sick after working all day by the warm stove and then sleeping in cold cells.

Clerk William Wheatly reported the salaries for 1842 as follows:

Warden	$1500/year
Clerk	$1000/year
Asst. Keeper (3)	$750 each/year
Guard (5)	$550 each/year
Inspector (3)	$250 each/year
Doctor (1)	$500/year
Chaplain (1)	$250/year
Messenger (1)	$180/year

In 1843, the Penitentiary for the District of Columbia was still operating in the red. After twelve years in operation, the shoemaking business still did not yield a profit for the penitentiary.

A major outbreak of scarlet fever was averted in 1843 when Dr. Young isolated the few who developed the disease, and several inmates suffered with the flu during the summer of 1843.

In 1844, the only major change in penitentiary operations was the replacement of Dr. Young with Dr. Harvey Lindsly. He served until 1845 when a major overhaul in prison personnel took place under President James K. Polk.

Robert Coltman (1845-1847)

Robert Coltman took over as warden on 1 September 1845, and two new inspectors—R. Jones and G. W. Phillips—joined William Minor on the Board. Dr. J. Webb Tyler became the new doctor on 21 November 1845, and Craven Ashford took over Wheatly's job as clerk.

It was during 1845 that the sessions for Criminal Court were reduced from meeting four times a year to meeting three times per year. This added extra stress to an already-overburdened court system trying to honor a prisoner's rights to a speedy trial. The number of cases, many trifling, increased, and the court felt overwhelmed.

In their report for 1846, the inspectors (Jones/Minor/Phillips) once again suggested receiving prisoners from other states. The Penitentiary for the District of Columbia continued to fail at being self-supporting. Dr. Tyler reported treating cases of rheumatism, pleurisy, syphilis, indigestion, bilious colic, fever, sarcocele, and stricture of the urethra. Prisoner William Stone died 30 January 1845 and prisoner William Gray (aka George McMannus) died 15 August 1845.

After serving a little over two years, Warden Coltman died in 1847.

Charles P. Sengstack (1847-1849)

Sengstack, a former businessman, was appointed by President Polk on 22 November 1847 to take over as warden of the Penitentiary for the District of Columbia. Inspectors R. Jones, Henry Haw, and G. W. Phillips reported once again that the penitentiary was not self-supporting due to the "small number of prisoners in confinement."[65]

Dr. Bohrer, the new doctor on staff, reported a high rate of dyspeptic problems among the prisoners, which was controlled by diet and medicine. The doctor suggested, however, that some outdoor activity, possibly horticultural in nature, be made available to the prisoners. The fresh air and exercise would do them good.

In 1848, there was "a high degree of cheerfulness" at the penitentiary, partly due to "the mild, gentle, and persuasive course pursued by the warden and his subordinates in enforcing the prison discipline."[66] Warden Sengstack preferred "gentle means" before the lash.[67] In his annual report, Sengstack suggested some type of "over-pay" as incentive for the prisoners to produce more. The "over-pay" would be added to a prisoner's account so that when discharged, the prisoner would receive the $2 due him by law plus the "over-pay" he had worked for and contributed to.[68]

Dorothea Dix, famed for her humanitarian efforts, visited the penitentiary in 1848 and furnished books to the prison library.

Also in 1848, new flooring was installed on the first floor of the workshops where rat infestation was a big problem. New pumps for the warden's house had to be installed. The basement of his home was dilapidated.

Legal problems occurred for the penitentiary in 1848 when the arrangements Robert Coltman made before he died to sell shoes to the Navy failed to meet contract deadlines. Before his death, Coltman had proposed to a certain Mr. Parsons to contract with the Navy by submitting the lowest bid to furnish 15,000 pair of shoes by a certain date. The penitentiary was to manufacture the shoes for Parsons who, in turn, would sell them to the Navy for the previously specified contract price. It was impossible, however, for the penitentiary to manufacture that many shoes by the determined deadline. Questions arose as to whom to hold responsible. The court decided Parsons was responsible for remedying the broken agreement.[69]

Dr. Bohrer reported two deaths in 1848—John Henry Butler, from tubercular phthisis and an old man, C.B., who was ill and "sunk under phthisis."[70]

In his report for 1848, Dr. Bohrer recommended the prison grounds be expanded so that the prisoners could grow some vegetables and work outdoors occasionally. "Under the arrangements existing, and those here recommended, the penitentiary may well be regarded . . . 'a model institution,' worthy of the capitol of our great empire."[71]

In 1849, in order to save money, the number of assistant keepers was reduced from three to two, and the guards were reduced in number from five to four. The porter took a cut in pay.

Personal troubles brewed in the Sengstack family in 1849 when on 25 June 1849, Charles P. Sengstack, Jr. was on tried for fathering an illegitimate child with Mary Kirby. He was ordered to pay $300 maintenance and $300 surety and "committed to the custody of the Marshal until the security is given," if he defaulted.[72]

Thomas Fitnam (1849-1850)

A new warden, Thomas Fitnam, was appointed on 5 April 1849, and began work on 14 April 1849. He complained in his first annual report that there were numerous small debts ignored by Warden Sengstack that probably never could be collected as those businesses were now insolvent or were no longer located in Washington. In addition, Fitnam reported the wharf to be dilapidated and in need of repair; the sewer and seawall in front of the penitentiary to be in bad shape; and the floor on top of the wall also in need of repair.[73]

All thirty-three inmates were vaccinated against smallpox in 1849, as there was smallpox in the family of one of the officers.[74] Dr. Young suggested that a diet of meat and vegetables would allay the numerous complaints of bowel problems.

In a report to Congress on 2 March 1849, Horace Mann, as a member of a committee to revise the penitentiary system, expressed concern about the high costs of the penitentiary. Captain Mordecai, commanding officer of the Washington Arsenal, added that the military could make better use of the site by using it for the munitions' storage it so desperately sought. The argument was made that when the penitentiary was established, President Adams was at his father's deathbed and had been unable to hear the arguments against building the penitentiary on Arsenal grounds. Captain Mordecai was in favor of moving the penitentiary and turning the property over to the military.[75]

In 1850, the Board of Inspectors, Thomas Donoho, John T. Towers, and William H. Edes, noted in their report that "one-half of prisoners are free blacks and many have probably come to Washington from nearby states by the milder character of the laws in respect to this species of the population."[76]

Census information for 1850 listed non-criminal residents of the penitentiary as Thomas Fitnam, Sr., (born Ireland, circa 1802), his unnamed wife, (born Ireland circa 1806) and unmarried children, Augustus (born PA circa 1833), Jerome (born PA circa 1841) and Mary (born DC circa 1844). Also listed were married son Thomas Fitnam, Jr. (born PA circa 1828) and his new unnamed bride (born DC circa 1830).[77]

Guard James Cosgrove (born Ireland circa 1806), his wife Mary (born PA circa 1815), and their two children, William (born PA circa 1842) and Mary (born PA circa 1844) also resided on penitentiary grounds in 1850.[78]

Jonas B. Ellis (1850-1853)

On 1 July 1850, President Millard Fillmore appointed Jonas B. Ellis, a former "mechanic," to the position of Warden. In his first annual report, Ellis suggested the women do additional work. They had too much idle time, and he felt a Matron was needed to take charge of the female department. Up until this time, one of the male officers had been in charge of overseeing the female prisoners.[79]

Ellis also suggested that the kitchen furnaces be adapted to use coal instead of wood, that heated air furnaces be used to warm the prison, and that lights be added to each cell and left on until 8 p.m. in the winter for reading.

Eighteen hundred fifty was a busy year at penitentiary's hospital. In his report for 1850, Dr. Young noted that prisoner Albert Mortimer suffered periodic episodes of epilepsy. "There is in this man a depression of the inner table of the frontal bone of the skull impinging upon the cerebral mass below. The outer table and the intermediate cancellous structure having been destroyed, there is fair reason to believe that his disease may be caused, or at least the predisposition excited, by this state of the parts; and I call your attention to it in order to receive your advice as to the propriety of an operation for his relief."[80]

Three births occurred in the penitentiary in 1850. All three babies were born to black female inmates who were pregnant upon arrival at the penitentiary. Two of the babies were full-term, and one was born at 7 months. All three died.[81]

Prisoner Madden suffered an "insane impulse"[82] as he attacked a fellow prisoner with a piece of iron taken off his bed and used to hit another prisoner on the head. Madden had a history of attacking prison officers and other prisoners.

A German prisoner named Dockhart, who served as a soldier in the Mexican War, died 9 February 1850 of diarrhea contracted in Mexico.

Chaplain Austin Gray agreed with his predecessor "that most of the crime that is committed is done by those whose moral and religious education has been entirely neglected."[83] In his report for 1850, Gray asked for more Bibles and a bookcase for the chapel.

Also in 1850, the grand jury of the Criminal Court visited the penitentiary and found it clean and neat. The "cells, including the bedding being in perfect order, the convicts clean, industriously employed, the men in making shoes, joiner work, brooms, etc., and the women in sewing by whom we are informed all the sewing for the penitentiary is performed."[84] Food was noted as being wholesome and abundant. Each prisoner was reported to have a Bible, Testament, and hymnal.

Dr. Young reported that prisoner John Hall had an abscess in his abdominal muscles and could not walk for a time. Prisoner Mortimer still suffered epileptic fits, and on 12 July 1851, Mary Butler, a black female inmate, died of consumption.

In his report for 1852, Warden Ellis requested a larger shop for carpentry/blacksmithing. Dr. Young asked for more suitable hospital room. Chaplain Gray reported that Miss Martha Lincoln and Charles Webster were volunteer reading teachers. James H. Shekell became Clerk, and inspector H. Lindsly replaced John T. Towers.

Still unable to support itself and relying on local markets to purchase its goods, penitentiary debt reached $12,175.66 in 1853.[85] Many locals would not buy products made by prisoners. Insufficient numbers of prisoners and terms too short to develop prisoner skills hampered every effort the penitentiary made at turning a profit. Many prisoners, unable to learn a particular skill, were used throughout the penitentiary in other than moneymaking capacities. For example, some were servants in the warden's house, some were bakers, cooks, washerwomen, prison gardeners, etc. Many of those who worked in one of the prison industries (primarily shoemaking) were careless and ruined materials, which also depleted profits as additional materials had to be bought to replace the damaged ones.

Thomas Thornley (1853-1859)

In his report for 1853, Thornley reported the end of the penitentiary broom-making industry. The shoemaking industry continued as the primary means of making money.

Thornley requested a new steamer for the kitchen and installation of a furnace system to heat the penitentiary rather than just stoves.

Shortly after Thornley took over as warden, financial problems arose at the penitentiary. When Thornley reviewed the financial records of the penitentiary, he came to the conclusion that many of the problems were a direct result of inflation. The price of supplies for the penitentiary soared. For example, in 1854, the price of flour doubled. Escalating prices forced Thornley to re-assess the return on all incoming and outgoing monies. The shoe shop continued to hold its own, but the carpentry and oakum shops proved too unprofitable to keep open, and in September 1854, both shops were closed.

At the water's edge, the penitentiary wharf was falling apart. Not only was it unfit, it was unsafe.[86] During 1854, the wharf had caught on fire. Steamboats traveling up the river would pass by, emitting sparks as they passed. The fiery sparks fell onto the wooden wharf, and little by little the wooden structure was being destroyed.

There was no fire equipment at the penitentiary, and Thornley worried about fire taking hold in one of the wooden hallways to the cells. The prison was lit with pine and etherial oils, which were explosive and presented a constant fire danger to the penitentiary. Thornley requested the Board to consider replacing the wood with iron. Additionally, the penitentiary was still heated with stoves, and Thornley also felt that the addition of a new furnace system would substantially decrease the chance of fire breaking out in the prison. In September 1855, the prison hospital had to be closed because it could not be properly manned at night.[87]

A "debtor and credit account" was suggested for the inmates in 1855. Under this system, each prisoner would be allowed a portion of his earnings on discharge if his behavior had been good and after money had been deducted for his food, clothing, etc.[88]

On 10 July 1855, Mrs. Elizabeth F. Marceron was appointed Matron. It was her responsibility to oversee the female prisoners who up until this time had been under the supervision of one of the male staff. She reported, "My endeavor has been to try and prevent quarrelling, and to encourage the prisoners to industry."[89] Most of the women in her charge washed, mended, and bound shoes.

Dr. Alexander Y. P. Garnett reported that inmate Stephen Lucas was confined to bed for more than 6 months with spine problems that required he remain laying down. Dr. Garnett knew of no cure for Lucas' problem and suspected "this man may have been melingering."[90]

In 1857, Inspectors Peter Force, George Parker, and Robert Ould reported that the penitentiary failed to support itself due to short prison terms that offered the convicts little incentive to exert any energy in learning a trade. There was not enough machinery and too few buildings to experiment with other trades. And, as always, the price of supplies continued to go up. Between 1852 and 1855, for example, the price of sole leather was 22 cents per pound. In 1857, it was 41 cents per pound, nearly double what it had been. Calfskins, $25 per dozen during 1852 through 1855, rose in 1857 to $37.50 per dozen.[91]

Dr. Garnett reported the death of inmate Joseph Brown who died after suffering for a year with heart disease. Brown "suffered repeatedly with paroxysms of severe pains across the anterior portion of his chest, inducing great dypuoa, and in some instances syncope; these were generally of short duration, lasting perhaps for an hour or two, leaving the patient somewhat exhausted, but able to attend to his daily vocation, that of shoemaking."[92] On 9 May 1857, Brown had a paroxysm and died within a few hours. An autopsy revealed a large quantity of "effused fluid in the pleural cavities, and a softened condition of the tissue of the heart." Cause of death was listed as adynamia, "a want of power in the heart's action."[93]

In 1858, inspectors Peter Force, George Parker, and Robert Ould reported a new system to eliminate cost to the government from the penitentiary was underway at the penitentiary so that no cost to the government would arise for the care of the convicts. The inspectors suggested taking $300 from the clerk's salary ($1200/yr) and adding that $300 to the chaplain's salary because the chaplain had to be at the penitentiary every day and thus had no opportunity to make other income.[94]

Warden Thornley reported that the penitentiary could have had more profit if it weren't for the "awkward squad"[95]--convicts totally unfit to learn shoemaking. Thornley listed incompetence as a major deterrent to making the penitentiary self-supporting.

Three inmates died during 1858: John Rowe died suddenly on 20 June 1858 from enlargement and valvular disease of the heart; George Handy died on 15 August 1858 of an enlarged heart and general dropsy; and on 1 September 1858, Vandora, a Mexican died of scrofula which had attacked both lungs.[96]

Requests came in every year from the chaplains for more books. Chaplain George W. Dorrance asked specifically for books that included Worcester's spelling books; Worcester's dictionaries; Davies' Arithmetics; Green's Grammars; Warren's Geographies; Definers; Malcom's Bible Dictionaries; and Kitto's Bible Illustrations.[97] It was Dorrance's responsibility to offer the convicts moral instruction as well as teach them to read and write.

The female department was responsible for doing the prison laundry. There was no piped-in water source, so water had to be carried into the washhouse and heated in two old boilers. The clothing and other laundry was then washed in one of the only three existing washtubs and hung on lines to dry. Matron Marceron repeatedly bemoaned the lack of space for washing and drying clothes. Many days, clothes were hung in the prison hallways to dry. The enormous amount of laundry, a small, ill-equipped washhouse, and insufficient drying space made it difficult to keep up with the large amount of wash the women were required to do.

Some of the females refused to work when they first arrived at the prison and gave Matron Marceron a hard time. Female prisoner Emily Bryant was one reported to have been quarrelsome and unruly upon entering the penitentiary. Her disorderliness created such a disturbance that some of the other females joined in and also misbehaved.

Charles P. Sengstack (1859-1861)
Second appointment as warden

Warden Charles P. Sengsack, Sr. became warden for the second time on 1 January 1859, eager to revamp a system that had become lackadaisical. First on his order of business was to reestablish discipline in the penitentiary which he quickly did with whipping and tricing.[98]

Secondly, he addressed the matter of cleanliness. The entire place was a vermin-infested mess. Every cell was cleaned from top to bottom. The totally infested wooden bedsteads were replaced with iron ones.

A dysentery epidemic in the summer of 1859 that was not occurring anywhere else in Washington prompted Dr. Garnett to suspect something at the penitentiary was making the prisoners sick. Upon checking out the sewer system, Garnett found the system to be blocked by sewage and emitting putrid odors. It took outside laborers eleven days to clean out the sewers, which yielded forty cartloads of sewage. Shortly after the cleanup, the number of cases of dysentery declined.

Next on Sengstack's list was the matter of clothing. Many of the inmates needed new clothing, and in 1859, many also began to request that underclothing be made part of their clothing allowance. Matron Marceron sent Warden Sengstack a letter dated 31 December 1860, asking for clothing for two of the female convicts who had just been received --Elizabeth Hamilton and Anna Boyle. Dresses for the women did not come readymade so Marceron's request was for bolts of fabric. She asked for nine yards of material for each woman so that each might have two dresses. Seventeen yards of cotton was also requested so that each might make themselves undergarments. Three yards of flannel and two baby dresses were also requested for Ann Boyle's baby, imprisoned with Boyle.[99] When prisoner Sarah Weems was received in January 1860, she desperately need clothes, and Marceron sent yet another letter to Sengstack requesting shoes, socks, sheets, and fabric for Weems.[100]

Four prisoners escaped in 1860, and the Board offered a total of $1100 reward for their capture and return. Five hundred dollars was offered for prisoner George W. Johnson; $250 for James Wilson; $250 for Major S. McDonald; and, $100 for John Small.

During 1859, prisoner Thomas (Henry) Croggins died of congestion of the brain. Prisoners William H. Douglass and Richard P. Jones were both moved to the lunatic asylum.

Several of the Sengstack family lived in penitentiary housing with Warden Sengstack, Sr. (born MD circa 1796) in 1860. Charles P. Sengstack, Jr., (born DC circa 1834) was Deputy Warden. Lewis K. Sengstack (born DC circa 1839) was a guard. Julia L. Sengstack (born DC circa 1830) and Sophia B. Sengstack (born DC circa 1838) were both music teachers. A child, Ellen M. Trailor (born DC circa 1848) also lived with the Sengstacks.[101]

Early in 1861, Dr. Alexander Y. P. Garnett resigned as prison doctor,[102] and in October 1861, six months after Garnett's resignation, Dr. John B. Keasbey took over.[103]

By this time, the Civil War had started. Every day, a new barrage of Union troops entered Washington, ready to fight the war. And when they came, crime came with them. Numerous "disreputable persons" flocked into the District of Columbia, ready to take advantage of any who were willing to spend money on liquor, prostitutes, or gambling.[104] Crime was rampant.

Hiram I. King (1861-1862)

Hiram I. King, the last of nine to serve as warden of the Penitentiary for the District of Columbia, was appointed on 12 April 1861 and took office that day at 6:30 p.m., a half-hour after the day watch left. Five of the six night watch resigned without notice that same day, leaving King and a few of his friends he temporarily assigned to help him, to control the inmates. He took charge of a penitentiary that, despite a growth in number of prisoners, was still not self-sufficient. King did not fail to express his opinion that one of the major pitfalls to the self-sufficiency of the penitentiary was the "stupid and inept" Negro convict with "predetermination to do as little as possible."[105]

In 1861-1862, over a hundred of the prisoners were ex-soldiers who had been court-martialed. Due to a lack of military prison facilities, these men had been sentenced to the penitentiary. Questions frequently arose over the legality of imprisoning those guilty of military crimes with those guilty of civilian crimes. Military crimes involved a whole separate set of criteria based primarily on punishment rather than on reform. The establishment of a military prison at the old Capitol building and the imminent closure of the penitentiary eventually resulted in removal of these soldiers from the penitentiary.

The whole time King was warden, the War Department sought to have the penitentiary closed so that it might have the space for weapons' storage. The War Department was actively engaged in making ammunition for the Union forces and the penitentiary buildings, sitting in the middle of the arsenal, were just what was needed.

Few records describe King's tenure as warden, but records exist that show King followed in the footsteps of some of the previous wardens as he frequently appeared before the court to answer criminal charges made against him:

> On 9 May 1861, King was arrested for harboring a slave and inciting that slave, the property of Mrs. Chew of Georgetown, to run away.[106]
>
> On 30 June 1861, King was charged with false vouchering when he submitted a receipt for $27.50 more than was actually paid to Guard Ezra K. Longley.[107]
>
> On 4 August 1861, King was charged with embezzlement in requiring false vouchers of employee Joseph L. Heise on 4 August 1861. King claimed more than he gave Heise.[108]
>
> On 18 November 1861, King was charged with assault on Lewis E. Walker[109] and found guilty on 24 June 1862.
>
> Again on 1 December 1861, King was charged with embezzlement of U.S. property. This time, he was accused of stealing ten barrels of potatoes ($20 value); twenty-two pieces of cotton ($66 value); three pair of boots ($13.50 value); forty pair of shoes ($40 value), ten cartloads of mortar ($20 value), and a table, sash, some doors, twenty window panes, etc.[110]
>
> Added to the embezzlement charge on 1 December 1861 was another charge of false vouchering. On 6 November 1861, King claimed $30 more than was paid to Joseph L. Heise for meat for

the penitentiary; $6.75 more than he paid Charles. M. Keyes; and $4 more than he paid William I. Murtaugh.[111]

On 19 September 1862, President Lincoln ordered the penitentiary closed, and the space was handed over to the War Department to use as a warehouse. Some of the prisoners who only had a small amount of time remaining to be served were pardoned and released. Some were released for good behavior, and others were pardoned and released to help in the war efforts. The rest were shipped aboard a steamer to the penitentiary at Albany, NY, where long-term felons from the District of Columbia continued to be incarcerated until 1916.[112]

Chapter Seven

STORIES ON THE PENITENTIARY

Occasionally, Washington's evening newspaper, *The Evening Star*, carried articles written about the penitentiary and those incarcerated there. What follows are a few brief synopses of some of those articles.

On 7 February 1856, the media visited the penitentiary. Members of the staff of *The Evening Star* went to the prison and met with Warden Thornley who gave them a tour of the facilities. A summary of the visit appeared in the *Star* on 8th, 9th, and 11th of February 1856.

The office at the penitentiary held an array of items, including a large book that listed all 680 prisoners who had been incarcerated in the prison since it opened on 9 April 1831. An office cabinet held "contraband" that had been found on the prisoners over the years. There were pipes; cords, that had been contrived by some of the prisoners to be used as escape aids; an iron wrench made to unscrew nuts on a prison lock; knives made years ago by convicts employed in a coach factory; and a pack of skillfully-drawn playing cards that an old black man had made one by one. The man couldn't read, so he spent his time secretly playing "dummy" with himself.

Letters, awaiting the warden's censorship, lay on the office desk, and the warden shared a particularly touching one of these letters with the reporters. It was from a woman who lived out West and had not seen her husband for five years when she heard he was incarcerated in the U.S. Penitentiary in Washington, D.C. Her letter to the warden asked, "Is he there?" Describing her husband as a tall man with fair skin and blue eyes, she asked the warden to give her husband the letter she had written just in case he was there. "God will bless you for your kindness to an almost heart broken woman." She continued by saying that she felt her husband was innocent of whatever he had been charged with because she knew him to be a noble gentleman. "I love him. He was ever kind and good to me." And in closing her letter to the warden, she added, "Will you not send me one little line that I may know if it is as I suspect."

The woman's letter to her husband was eight pages long, and in it she asked her husband's permission to come to Washington to speak to the President on his behalf—if she could raise the money to do so. She told her husband that since he had left home, she had changed. [I used to] "depend on you for everything; then I was incapable, because I had never been put to the trial of what I could do." She felt optimistic about getting in to see the President, saying his "heart is not marble."

She added that her health had been "giving way." She was thin due to anxiety. She offered to send her husband $5-- adding that she wished it could be $500-- so that he could buy paper, pen, ink, or whatever he wished, and asking him to write if he was allowed to and tell her when he could come home.

She desperately wanted to see her husband and to help him. "I love you—oh, how dearly, no tongue can tell. Oh, that would be too much happiness to feel your dear arms around me once more—may I come?" And then she added that since he left, her hair had grown long and beautiful, and that a woman had offered to buy her hair for $20. That same woman, she added, would probably be willing to give her additional money to make the trip.

The reporters were taken through the various workshops where the prisoners sat quietly engaged in making shoes. Though the prisoners were not allowed to talk among themselves, they communicated with body language, a "deaf and dumb alphabet," and with throat-scraping "hems." One convict had written a sign and posted it over his workstation—"I will positively loan no more tobacco." If they did their work well, prisoners were often given an extra bit of chewing tobacco as a reward. In the female department, the women, sitting around a large stove, were busy ironing and binding shoes.

The chapel was also included on the tour. Male and female prisoners were strictly forbidden to look at one another, so a piece of canvas separated the room into male and female sections. The canvas was full of little peepholes made by the women in order that they might catch a glimpse of one of the men. Should a female be caught peeping, she forfeited a meal. One female prisoner nearly starved because she was continuously caught peeking through the holes.

The "solitary cells," called the "dark cells" were for those who misbehaved. Confinement in these cells meant bread and water and total isolation for a period of up to twenty days at a time. It usually only took one night in solitary for the prisoner to straighten up and be returned to a regular cell. However, some required a longer stay. "The most obstinate and unmanageable cases are those of female convicts." One of the female prisoners remained confined in solitary for twenty days. Thinking one twenty-day stint was the limit, she began cursing any and all authoritative figures she could think of as soon as she was released from the "solitary cell." She was surprised when she landed right back in solitary for another twenty days, after which, she was very cooperative.

The penitentiary bakery was clean and well run, and the inmate in charge of bakery operations was very proud of his kitchen. The walls were covered with "engravings cut from pictorial papers."

The barbershop was the final indoor stop on the tour, and its white walls were beautifully decorated with "some remarkable fresco paintings."

Outside, the guards walked the walls in brutally cold conditions. Only seventeen prisoners had successfully managed to escape between 1831 and 1856, though many more had tried.

Dressed in their winter uniforms of black and white (blue and white in summer), the male prisoners were lined up a dinnertime and marched into the dining room where they ate in silence. When the allotted mealtime was over, they were lined up, checked for foreign objects, given a pail to fill with water, and taken back to their cells for the night. The female prisoners donned plaid "which just now happens to be the height of fashion, on both sides of the penitentiary wall!"

*****

"Attempted Revolt in the Penitentiary"
(*Star*, 10 April 1858)

On 9 April 1858, prisoner Joseph Cunningham attempted to break open a tool chest in the broom-making shop, supposedly to get tools to use as weapons. Officer Fry ordered Cunningham to his cell and Cunningham refused. Convict Henry F. Koss was sent by the officer to get the Deputy Warden, and Cunningham decided to obey the officer's orders.

Later that same day, prisoner Isaac Lambert, attacked Koss, hitting him repeatedly for going to the warden. Officer Fry interrupted and had to force Lambert to go to his cell. It was assumed that that was the end of the problem, until prisoner John Roe knocked down fellow prisoner Charles

Campbell. Warden Thornley was nearby, caught Roe, and hit him with shoe rubber. In the meantime, when someone hit the warden, several of the convicts headed over to join in the attack on Thornley but backed off when he drew his revolver. No one would say who had hit Thornley.

The plan of the convicts was to overtake the officers and escape, and it probably would have worked had Cunningham gotten the tools. The convicts were put under strong discipline as a result of the incident, which included no communication among them. Warden Thornley, however, told reporters that "the means they adopt to communicate with each other are, in some instances, however, so shrewd as to be almost beyond detection."

*****
"Insubordination in the Penitentiary"
(*Star*, 28 April 1859)

On Tuesday, 26 April 1859, about ten in the morning, convict William Lyons moved his bench to another part of the room without permission and refused to move it back. Deputy Warden C. P. Sengstack, Jr., grabbed Lyons and the two grappled with each other. Prisoner Joseph Cunningham tried to stop the fracas by coming between the two, and in the process, he was wounded when Sengstack fired his gun.

A stubborn and unruly prisoner, Lyons was 24 when sentenced to the pen for stealing a watch during a drunken spree. When he was arrested, Lyons was a midshipman in the Navy and had only been in the Navy for a short time.

*****
"Unique Celebration: The Fourth at the Penitentiary"
(*Star*, 5 July 1859)

In 1859, the inmates enthusiastically prepared for a Fourth of July celebration. Celebrations at the penitentiary were unusual, and this one, allowed "in such manner as would not conflict with the wholesome discipline of the prison," gave them more freedom than they were usually accustomed to getting. The celebration was to be held in the chapel, which they had decorated with flowers and evergreens. Across the front of the chapel hung a sign "We Still Love Our Country."

Amidst the preparations, Thomas Croggin, one of the prisoners, died suddenly. Spirits were dampened, but the prisoners sent a letter to the warden saying that Croggin had looked forward to the celebration and would have wanted it to go on. They asked that the celebration be allowed to go on as planned after Croggin's funeral.

The funeral was held on the morning of 4 July 1859, Rev. George W. Dorrance presiding. After the service, the body, in a "handsome walnut coffin," was given to Croggin's family who buried him in the Methodist Burying Ground. Croggin, one of the most daring of the Nailor gang of burglars, was about 24 years old when he died.

Just after 11 a.m., all the inmates gathered in the chapel. The male prisoners, dressed in their blue and white prison garb, sat behind the numerous guests who had come from town to participate in the event. The female convicts sat separated from the males by a cloth screen. Programs prepared by the prisoners were handed out, listing the events as follows:

1. National hymn (choir)
2. Prayer (chaplain)
3. Song, "The Invitation" (all)
4. Song, "My Native Land" (choir)
5. Reading the Declaration ([Inmate] C. H. Barrett)
6. Song, "Star Spangled Banner" (choir)
7. Oration (R. Smith)
8. Song, "Columbia the Gem of the Ocean" (choir)
9. Song, "Do They Miss Me At Home?" (choir)
10. Address of Thanks ([Inmate] J. P. Millard)
11. Song, "The Flag of the Free" (colored choir)
12. Song, "The Glorious Fourth of July" (all)
13. Prayer/benediction (chaplain)

Members of the choir were inmates John Day, John Smith, George Kreager, John Jones, and Benjamin Ogle.

Inmate Barrett impressed the audience with his clear reading of the Declaration of Independence. The *Star* reporter noted that it was hard to believe he was in the penitentiary for murder as he seemed so kindly a man.

Inmate R. Smith, a young and well-spoken man, delivered a cultivated speech. Smith asked that his full name not be printed in the paper as his aged mother did not know her only son was in prison. He said the convicts still felt patriotic in prison, and as for him, he sought to redeem his good name when he got out. He spoke of the "material progress" of the country, appealing in closing to his fellow inmates to aspire to better things.

Inmate Millard thanked all responsible for allowing the celebration to occur, including the ladies who brought desserts. He attributed his fall and the fall of his fellow inmates to "bad associations" brought about through drunkenness. He appealed to fellow inmates to aspire to "regain the regard of their fellowmen" upon release. Many convicts became teary eyed at the singing of "Do they miss me at home?" (See words below under "Letters to Newton G. Shreeve," 9 December 1854)

*****

"Thanksgiving at the Penitentiary"
(*Star*, 26 November 1859)

The inmates met in the chapel around 10 a.m. The warden, his family, and several citizens came in soon afterward for a service by Chaplain Samson of Columbian College. The message was on the customs and history of the Holy Land. The warden saw to it that the inmates received something extra in their Thanksgiving dinner.

*****

When letters to the prisoners arrived at the penitentiary, they were read by the warden who decided which, if any, of the letters would be passed along to the inmate. The following letters were found in a file kept by the warden. No indication was given as to whether the warden ever passed these letters along to each inmate.

Letters to inmate Newton G. Shreeve [113]

9 May 1854—Unaware of his brother's imprisonment, John A. Shreeve writes from Marysville, CA that he plans to go to Oregon to live. He recommends his brother stay home and get "all the education you can" rather than go to California. He suggests bookkeeping as a good profession. He tells Newton to tell the ladies at home "I am coming back for one of them."

10 September 1854—John B. Shreeve to son about the drought.

10 December 1854—John B. Shreeve to son of his distress over his son's imprisonment.

25 June1854—John Shreeve to son, writes that he hopes Newton will read his Bible and "be come a good boy and repent of all the evils you have bin led into." He hopes he will "never tast spirits of any kind again...I have shed more tears for you that I ever shed in my life." He says that he is not telling Allen (brother in California) of Newton's imprisonment as he wants Allen to come home and go the University of VA or to Philadelphia to finish his studies. He reports that Newton's mother "frets and crys every time any one talks about you."

12 August 1855—John B. Shreeve to son that "you don't know the tears that I have shed, the sleep that I have lost, the grief that I have underwent. Tongue can't express...My wheat, corn and oats is good. I have some cattle on hand and they look well. I have a fine lot of hogs on hand. We are improving our land. Still are clearing...I hope to see you one more before I die. I am (braking)? fast. I am getting gray fast. My head will soon be white. As I have said before, be a good boy. Don't keep bad company at any time."

28 January 1855—John Shreeve to son. "Our house is nearly finished." It hasn't rained in California from last April up to the 2nd of December. Allen (Newton's brother) says that there was a lump of gold dug up close to where he is that brought 150 pounds. Allen says "the Indians is gitting to be troublesome more so than formerly." John expresses fear that he will die before his son gets out of the pen.

8 December 1854—poem in a letter from Allen Shreeve in California in response to not having received any mail from home in awhile

        Do They Miss Me At Home?

    Do they miss me at home, do they miss me,
    Twould be an assurance moste dear
    To know that this moment some loved one
    Was saying I wish he were here
    To feel that the group at the fireside
    Were thinking of me as I [serve]

Oh yes twould be joy beyond measure
To know that they missed me at home.

When twilight approaches the season
That ever is sacred to song
Does some loved one repeat my name over
And sign that I tarry so long
And is there a chord in the music
That's missed when my voice is away
And a chord in each heart awaketh
Regret at my wearisome stay.

Do they set me a chair near the table
When evenings pleasure are nigh
When the candles are lit in the parlor
And the stars in the calm azure sky
And when the good nights are repeated
And all lay them down to their sleep
Do they think of the absent and [wish] me
A whisper good night o'er the [deep]

Do they miss me at home, do they miss me?
At morn at noon or at night
And lingers one gloomy shade around them
That only my presence can light
Are joys less invitingly welcome
And pleasures less hole than before
Because one is missed from the circle
Because I am with them no more.*

*These are the words as Allen Shreeve wrote them in his letter. The words as sung by the musical group, The Amphions, were published several years later (ca. 186_) by Blackmar and Brother in Augusta, GA.

16 June 1855—letter from Allen Shreeve to his father suggesting his father move to California. Allen doubts he will ever move home.

22 June 1855—J. B. Shreeve writes his son that brother Allen works at a livery stable in Mariposa, CA. The elder Shreeve is being charged by Samuel

Spitler for some purchases made by Newton and asks his son to verify amounts.

28 October 1855—J. B. Shreeve to his son that he has just returned from Augusta where Martin lives. Martin [a brother?] is moving back in the spring. "The Irish is buying land here...Try and become pious. Remember you had a pious mother and have a praying father."

9 March 1855—Upon learning of his brother's imprisonment, Allen Shreeve writes from Mariposa, CA, "Why didn't you obey your parents?" Allen had been very sick since he left home but said his condition was nothing when compared to his brother's situation.

*****
Letters to inmate Penuel Hendricks [114]

26 August 1855—George Hendricks (from Randolph Co, NC) writes his brother Penuel that they are working on getting him released. He adds that the "corn crops looks remarkable well we had the best season here this year...wheat was tolerable good." George said that he had been going to school and had begun teaching school

15 August 1855—Tobias Hendricks writes his nephew Penuel a letter of encouragement. "Gives me great satisfaction to hear that you are in possession of that hope which will make you happy in the world to come."

4 March 1855—George Hendricks to brother that "you do not know how bad I want to see you." George tells Penuel they are working on a petition to get him out. Penuel's sister (M. Hendricks) and father (Reuben Hendricks) added a note, too.

23 April 1855—Willie Tinnin to friend Penuel Hendricks that he has been sick for five months; everybody is working on the petition for Penuel's release. Penuel's wife and daughter have not been well recently. There has been a lot of sickness and many deaths in Raleigh as of late. It has been very dry and hot.

Also with this letter, is a letter from Penuel's friend George E. Keith telling Penuel that he [Keith] had had his trial and was convicted of manslaughter. He was branded and put in jail for 12 months. Keith adds that he wants to have fun "like ole times...I am as fat as a pig...you know it [Randolph Co.]is a dull place for fun."

5 September 1856—George Hendricks writes his brother that all is well after a heavy rain and windstorm Sunday last. Much of the corn and timber was blown down or damaged. Alexander Hooker shot John Chavos through the head with a rifle a few days before George wrote this letter. Hooker went right home and put up his rifle and turned himself in at Asheborough. Hooker's trial comes up in two weeks.

23 October 1856—Having just returned from Washington, George Hendricks writes his brother of an impending trip to Raleigh to get the petition signed for Penuel's release.

15 August 1857—Reuben Hendricks writes his son, "I have not forgotten my son...I have been doing [all] I could do for you and has shed many a tear for the directions you met with in passing $4 of gold." He promises to do all he can for his son.

25 October 1857—Having returned the day before from Montgomery where he was teaching school and visiting Uncle William Simmons, George Hendricks reassures his brother of continued work on his pardon.

****
Letter to inmate Robert Biddle[115]

1 May 1854—Friend John Bartow writes Dick Biddle from on board the *U.S. Ontario* at Baltimore, telling Biddle that his duty on the Pennsylvania was over after he finished serving time for "hiting a Marine in the head with an iron bolt." Bartow had been in Baltimore about six months when he wrote Biddle the letter. "Everyone knows that you are there for your sentence was read on bord of every ship in the navy...Frank Thorn has been sentence to the peneitenchary for ten years for stabbing a mate of a merchant vessel in New York."

*****
Letters to inmate Charles Carr [116]

23 August 1854—Mary Carr of Philadelphia writes son Charles Carr, saying, "God only knows the misery I have suffered since your incarceration for a crime that none of your acquaintances think you capable of committing..."

19 September 1855—Mary Carr to son Charles, "I am very sorry to here that you are so discontented whare you are." She tells him that Uncle Samuel and Uncle Charles are doing what they can to get Carr released. "I have done all that I can do for you." His mother hopes if he gets out of the pen he will be a "better man and keep different kind of company seing that bad company has brought you whare you are. I hope that you will lerne you a lesson that you will never forget as long as you live and that you may live a different life from what you have been living...[signed] your afflicted mother."

*****
Letters to inmate George Montgomery [117]

3 February 1856—Sarah A. Donnelly, sister of George Montgomery writes from Baltimore that she is trying to get his release. Montgomery's mother is too old and feeble to do it. Upon release, Donnelly hopes "you will look back on this and never be persuaded by eny one to do eny unlawful thing." She sends him a religious tract saying "I would not give the piece of mind I have enjoyed since I joined the Church of Christ for all the world if I could have the world...."

10 April 1856—Sarah A. Donnelly writes brother George Montgomery after she had been up to see him that she had gotten home safe. "I must have walked twelve miles that day besides riding in a hack between Washington and Baltimore." If he is pardoned, she hopes her brother will prove worthy of it.

*****
Envelope titled "Improper letters to and from convicts" [118]

8 September 1858—John Johnson writes wife Frances Penny, hoping that she feels better soon. The letter was smuggled in and intercepted by the warden.

December 1857—a letter from inmate Robert Cross to his friend Dan. Cross reminds Dan to "be true to the American Party." Cross adds that he has tried several ways to get out of the penitentiary, but nothing has worked so far. He says "I made up a song about trying to get over the wall." Cross included the poem, which follows, in his letter, which was intercepted by the warden and retained in the prison files.

"Bob Cross' Attempt to escape prison"

Twas an eirly day as poets say
Just as the sun was rising.
A prisoner stood on a peace wood,
And saw a sight surprising.
Old Riley too, in his jacket blue
Stood there upon a viewing
First [deemed] his eyes in great surprise
Says there is mischief brewing.

That blanket hide, a rope to guide
A prisoner over the wall
And if he don't heed, he'll surely bleed.
If he should chance to fall
Twas at the pump poor Bob did thump
Pretending to wash his face.
Though that very well, he wished in hell
And Riley in some such place.

The rope was stretched, and the weaked wretch
Was just about to throw it
When old Riley stood in a pleasant mood
Says "that won't do if I know it"
Poor Bob so bold saw he was sold.
But did not lose his spirits.
Though he was duped, he damed his soup
Says, "I try another merit."

Bill Waugh he come, all in a run,
And with excited fears,
The rope game blown, and it was shown
And Bob was shown upstairs.
He had no fears, likewise no cares,
He says "heave a head my [hardies]
But it was in a maize he stops to gaize
On a thundering pair of derbies.

Poor Bob sat down upon the ground
The derbies was nailed on.
Twas in a cell as strong as hell
Where poor Bob then was thrown.
Bill Waugh did rage to see his cage,
For Bob did not stay, a half a day
Before he <u>tore it</u> down

Moral

Now Bob must go as you all know
To leirn how to make shoes
But when he come, out he'l strut about.
And tell you all some news.
He'l dam the gate, and sleep with Kate
For he loves her to distraction
He will grasp his knife and risk his life
For revenge and satisfaction.

Signed: Robert R. Cross

9 August 1858—Inmate H. O. Croggin, who couldn't write, had convict Bailey write a letter for him at night in the dark. The letter was found in Bailey's cell in an old boot. The letter to Croggin's uncle asked the uncle to go to the Secretary of the Navy and get him on a ship, with or without pay, just to get him out of the pen. Croggin also requested a neck and pocket-handkerchief and some tobacco.

Chapter Eight

INTAKE 1831

The initial lists of inmates contained only a prisoner's initials. Many sources were consulted to come up with the correct names to match the initials. Due to missing information in the various records, some prisoners remain identified by initials only. Endnotes list sources in which the prisoner's name appears. Each prisoner is listed by name, birthplace and year, reception date, color/gender, crime committed, and sentence.

Thomas Williams, born NY circa 1790, received 9 April 1831, w/m, stealing, 1y. Williams worked in the blacksmith shop of thepenitentiary.[119]
James MacDaniel, received 21 May 1831, theft, 1y.[120] Pardoned.
Robert Mitchell, born MD circa 1806, received 21 June 1831, w/m,stealing, 1y.[121]
Jane Byers, born Georgetown circa 1808, received 21 June 1831, b/f, stealing, 1y.[122]
Kitty Gill (aka Catherine Clarke), born Georgetown circa 1804, received 21 June 1831, b/f, stealing $10, 1y.[123]
Henry Cartwright, received 21 June 1831, b/m, stealing, 1y.[124]
Joshua Young, born MD, received 19 October 1831, w/m, stealing, 3y. Young escaped 12 January 1832 by scaling the prison walls and finished his sentence at the Baltimore Penitentiary.[125]
Wesley Hobbs, received 19 October 1831, w/m, stealing, 3y. Hobbs escaped 12 January 1832 by scaling the prison walls and finished his sentence at the Baltimore Penitentiary.[126]
Nelson Sims, received 19 October 1831, b/m, stealing, 3y.[127]
Nancy Ashton, received 19 October 1831, mu/f, stealing, 1y. When released on 19 October 1832,Ashton was 6-7 months pregnant. Word among the officers of the penitentiary was thatJohn Young, keeper in charge of the female department of the penitentiary, was responsible. On 22 November 1832, Ashton went to Richard Butt, attendant of the Washington Asylum, with an order from a Mr. Harbaugh, guardian of the poor in Washington City, to bury her infant child. She told Butt that the child was born two to three weeks after she got out of the penitentiary. The child appeared to be about three to four weeks old.[128]
Harriet Smith, received 19 October 1831, b/f, stealing, 1y.[129]
Isaac Brogden, received 26 October 1831, b/m, stealing, 1y.[130]

John Taylor, received 26 October 1831, horse theft, b/m, 3y. Taylor escaped 25 September 1832 by scaling the prison walls. Held in jail in Frederick Town, MD, awaiting return to the U.S. Penitentiary, Taylor died of cholera.[131]

John Smith, born circa 1806, received 27 October 1831, w/m, stealing, 1y. He was a penitentiary cook.[132]

John Owens, born Baltimore, MD circa 1803, received 5 November 1831, w/m, horse theft, 2y. Pardoned 28 July 1832.[133]

Alfred Rounds, received 5 November 1831, mu/m, stealing, 2y.[134]

Benjamin Bell, received 5 November 1831, b/m, stealing/counterfeiting, 2y.[135]

Fontain H. Pettis, received 12 November 1831, perjury, 5y. Pardoned.[136]

William Brooke, received 19 November 1831, mu/m, stealing/ counterfeiting, 2y.[137]

John Ryder, received 19 November 1831, w/m, stealing, 2y.[138]

Thomas Hunter, received 13 December 1831, w/m, stealing, 3y.[139]

William McLauglin, received 15 December 1831, w/m, horse theft, 3y.[140]

Samuel Peoples, received 22 December 1831, w/m, stealing, 2y. Peoples was given 5 days in solitary for whistling/singing.[141]

Chapter Nine

INTAKE 1832

William VanBrune, received 7 January 1832, w/m, stealing, 3y.[142]
John H. Laurence, received 7 January 1832, w/m, stealing, 3y. Laurence escaped 25 May 1832 by scaling the walls of the Penitentiary and finished his sentence at the penitentiary in Philadelphia where he was pardoned 4 July 1835.[143]
John Kelly, received 19 May 1832, w/m, stealing, 4y.[144]
Lewis Waggoner, received 19 May 1832, w/m, stealing, 2y. Waggoner worked in the carpentry shop at the pen.[145]
Abraham Spellman, received 19 May 1832, b/m, stealing, 2y6m.[146]
John Carter, received 19 May 1832, w/m, stealing, 5y.[147]
Joseph Blanford, received 19 May 1832, w/m, stealing, 6y.[148]
Rezin Barker, received 19 May 1832, mu/m, stealing, 2y6m. He did lathing/plastering.[149]
Henry Barker, received 19 May 1832, mu/boy, stealing, 3y. He was a tailor in the pen.[150]
Henry Whaley, received 19 May 1832, w/m, stealing, 2y. Whaley was a cook in the pen. He died 19 March 1833 of bowel disease.[151]
William Young, received 21 May 1832, w/m, stealing, 2y6m. Young worked in the carpentry shop at the pen.[152]
Nelson Harper, received 21 May 1832, dark mu/boy, manslaughter, 6y.[153]
Thomas Mace, received 30 June 1832, w/m, stealing, 2y.[154]
Edward Hall, received 30 June 1832, w/m, passing counterfeit money, 2y.[155]
John Harris, received 4 July 1832, w/m, passing counterfeit money/forgery, 3y. Harris was pardoned 3 July 1832 and released 13 July 1832.[156]
William B. Devaughn, received 8 Nov 1832, w/m, stealing, 4y.[157]
John Davis, received 8 Nov 1832, w/m, larceny, 2y. Davis was a tailor at the pen.[158]
Henry Mump(?), received 8 November 1832, b/m, larceny, 3y.[159]
Thomas H. Hines, received 7 December 1832, w/m larceny, 3y.[160]
Henry White, received 15 December 1832, w/m, felony, 2y.[161]
William Hodges, received 18 December 1832, b/m, larceny, 3y.[162]

Chapter Ten

INTAKE 1833

John Burnes, received 17 January 1833, w/m, larceny, 3y.[163]
Isaac Brogden, received 18 January 1833, b/m, larceny, 5y.[164]
Henry Berry, received 19 January 1833, mu/m, manslaughter, 5y.[165]
William Ward, received 19 January 1833, w/boy, larceny, 3y.[166]
Washington Barker, received 19 January 1833, mu/boy, larceny, 3y.[167]
Joseph Douglas, received 21 January 1833, b/m, larceny, 1y.[168]
John Hutton, received 25 January 1833, mu/boy, larceny, 2y from 23 January 1833).[169]
Bernard Finnigan, received 28 January 1833, w/boy, assault with intent to kill, 4y.[170]
Washington Causine, received 9 April 1833, w/boy, theft, 3y.[171]
Dennis Larkin, received 4 May 1833, w/boy, theft, 2y.[172]
Charley Brown, received 4 May 1833, b/m, theft 2y.[173]
John Bush, received 4 May 1833, b/m, theft, 2y.[174]
Betsy Grant, received 4 May 1833, b/woman, theft, 2y.[175]
Harriet Smith (aka Harriet Jones), received 4 May 1833, b/f, theft, 2y.[176]
George Holly, received 11 June 1833, b/m, theft, 2y. Pardoned 6 Sep 1833.[177]
James McDowell, received 4 July 1833, w/boy, theft, 3y. McDowell was sentenced to serve two months in jail plus pay a $1 fine before serving 3y in the pen.[178]
Benjamin Morgan, received 16 September 1833, w/m, theft 1y6m.[179]
Thomas Morgan, received 16 September 1833, w/m, theft, 1y6m.[180]
John Reynolds, received 16 September 1833, w/m, theft, 2y. Reynolds was a cook in the pen.[181]
Sandy Spriggs, received 16 September 1833, b/m, theft, 2y.[182]
John Brown, received 16 September 1833, mu/m, theft, 2y.[183]
William Thomas, received 16 September 1833, w/m, theft 2y.[184]
John Weston, (aka John White), born DC circa 1786, received 16 October 1833, w/m, theft, 2y.[185]
John Owens, received 1 November 1833, w/boy, horse stealing, 6y. Owens was a prison baker.[186]
Christian (Christopher) Clopher, received 1 November 1833, w/boy, theft, 5y. Pardoned 17 January 1834.[187]
Joseph Larned, received 16 November 1833, w/boy, forging free papers for absconding slaves, 7y from 15 November 1833. Pardoned 29 January 1836.[188]

Addison Brown, received 18 November 1833, mu/boy, larceny, 7y from 16 Nov 1833.[189]

Albert Taylor (aka George A. Rose), received 18 November 1833, mu/boy, stealing, 5y from 16 Nov 1833.[190]

William B. Nash, received 6 December 1833, w/m, forgery, 4y. Nash worked in the carpentry shop at the pen.[191]

William Franks, received 7 December 1833, w/m, theft, 2y.[192]

Charles Morsell, received 7 December 1833, b/m, theft, 2y.[193]

Chapter Eleven

INTAKE 1834

John H. Rigart, received 9 January 1834, w/m, theft, 2y.[194]
William Collins, received 8 April 1834, w/m, stealing, 2y. Pardoned 9 July 1834.[195]
Washington Williams, received 2 May 1834, mu/m, stealing, 2y.[196]
Calvin Jones, received 2 May 1834, b/m, stealing/breaking into house, 4y.[197]
Susan Lowe, received 5 May 1834, b/f, stealing, 1y. Lowe was sentenced to serve 4 days in jail and pay a 50-cent fine before serving 1y in the pen.[198]
James Goddards, received 5 May 1834, w/m, cow stealing, 5y.[199]
William Weaver, received 16 May 1834, mu/m, stealing, 2y.[200]
Thomas Albritton, received 16 May 1834, w/m, horse theft, 2y.[201]
Negro Jane, received 16 May 1834, b/f, stealing, 1y.[202]
Rilan Ballard, received 16 October 1834, w/m, counterfeiting, 20y. Ballard was a tailor in the pen and was pardoned 29 December 1837.[203]
David Baker, received 16 October 1834, w/m, counterfeiting, 10y. Baker was a cook in the pen and was pardoned 29 December 1837.[204]
Henry Thompson, received 7 November 1834, b/m, stealing, 2y.[205]
George Daniel, received 30 December 1834, w/m, stealing, 2y. Daniel was a tailor in the pen.[206]
Reubin Boss, received 30 December 1834, b/m, stealing, 2y.[207]

Chapter Twelve

INTAKE 1835

William Woods, received 3 January 1835, w/m, stealing, 2y.[208]
William Young, received 15 January 1835, w/m, stealing, 3y.[209]
Henry Effords, received 15 January 1835, b/m, stealing, 2y6m.[210]
Niel Gray, received 15 January 1835, w/m, stealing, 2y6m.[211]
Jim Diggs, received 15 January 1835, b/m, stealing, 2y6m.[212]
Nelson Simms, received 15 January 1835, b/m, stealing 2y6m.[213]
Joseph Hornsberry, received 15 January 1835, b/m, stealing, 1y9m.[214]
Richard Thornton, received 15 January 1835, b/m, stealing, 1y9m. Thornton was a cook in the pen.[215]
Samuel Coleman, received 15 January 1835, w/m, stealing, 1y6m. Coleman worked in the carpentry shop in the pen.[216]
Abraham Spellman, received 8 April 1835, b/m, stealing, 3y.[217]
Richard Eagan, received 15 April 1835, w/m, manslaughter, 3y.[218]
Nicholas Lomman, received 15 April 1835, w/m, stealing, 2y.[219]
Rezin Barker, received 15 April 1835, mu/m, stealing, 2y. He made sacks in the pen.[220]
Samuel Hoot, received 18 May 1835, w/m, stealing, 2y.[221]
Ezekial D. Withers, received 18 May 1835, b/m, manslaughter, 2y.[222]
Harriet Smith (aka Harriet Jones), received 6 June 1835, b/f stealing, 4y.[223]
Alfred Keene, received 6 June 1835, w/m, stealing, 2y.[224]
Henry Owen, received 6 June 1835, w/m, stealing, 2y.[225]
William H. Jones, received 6 June 1835, b/m, stealing, 2y.[226]
Owen McMahon, received 6 June 1835, w/m, manslaughter, 8y.[227]
Alfred Rounds, received 6 June 1835, mu/m, stealing, 5y.[228]
Nathan Cole, received 6 June 1835, b/m, manslaughter, 4y. He was a cook in the pen.[229]
Allen Cole, received 6 June 1835, b/m, manslaughter, 5y. Cole made sacks in the pen.[230]
George Davis, received 6 June 1835, mu/m, manslaughter, 5y.[231]
John Brown, received 2 November 1835, w/m, larceny, 3y.[232]
HB, received 2 November 1835, mu/boy, 2y.[233]
Richard Jones, received 14 December 1835, mu/m, highway robbery, 4y.[234]
William Evans, received 14 December 1835, b/m, larceny, 1y. He picked oakum in the pen.[235]
Nehemiah Brown, received 14 December 1835, w/m, larceny, 2y. He made sacks in the pen.[236]

Benjamin Thompson, Jr., received 15 December 1835, w/m, larceny, 1y6m.[237]
Andrew Scrivener, received 15 December 1835, w/m, larceny, 2y.[238]
John Brown, received 19 December 1835, mu/m.[239]
Thomas Hunter, received 19 December 1835, w/m, larceny, 5y.[240]
JP, received 19 December 1835, mu/boy. JP picked oakum in the pen.[241]
Sandy Spriggs, received 19 December 1835, mu/m, robbery, 4y.[242]

Chapter Thirteen

INTAKE 1836

Richard Barry, received 21 January 1836, w/m, stealing, 3y.[243]
Dennis Larkin, received 21 January 1836, w/m, assault with intent to kill and robbery, 6y. Larkin died 24 August 1841.[244]
W. Henning, received 21 January 1836, w/m, attempt to sell a free Negro, 1y. He was a baker at the pen.[245]
James Layland, received 22 January 1836, w/m, stealing, 3y.[246]
Frank Neale, received 30 April 1836, b/m, stealing, 2y.[247]
Frank Hays, received 30 April 1836, b/m, stealing, 2y.[248]
Samuel C. Fox, received 30 April 1836, b/m, stealing, 3y.[249]
Priscilla Brown, received 30 April 1836, b/f, stealing, 1y.[250]
John Callahan, larceny, 3y.[251]
George McDaniel, larceny, 3y.[252]
Ignatius Spalding, larceny, 2y.[253]
Lewis Waggoner, received 30 April 1836, w/m, larceny, 3y.[254]
SL, received 16 May 36, b/f, stealing, 2y.[255]
EG, received 16 May 36, mu/f, stealing, 2y.[256]
William Lodge, received 6 July 1836, b/m, stealing, 2y.[257]
Tom Bonds, received 6 July 1836, b/m, stealing, 3y.[258]
Hanna Butler, received 6 July 1836, b/f, stealing, 3y.[259]
Ellen Dowling, received 6 July 1836, b/f, stealing, 1y.[260]
Joseph Parsons, received 11 July 1836, w/m, stealing, 3y. Parsons was pardoned 26 January 1837.[261]
John Johnson, received 11 July 1836, w/m, forgery, 4y.[262]
William Smitson, received 11 July 1836, w/m, larceny, 3y.[263]
Lewis Tarlton, larceny, 2y.[264]
WB, received 22 October 1836, mu/m, stealing, 3y.[265]
George McDaniel, received 22 October 1836, b/m, stealing, 3y.[266]
John Callahan, received 22 October 1836, b/m, stealing, 3y.[267]
Henry Simms, received 12 December 1836, b/m, robbery, 7y.[268]
Washington Williams, received 12 December 1836, mu/m, assault and highway robbery, 7y. Williams died 11 October 1842.[269]
Henry Butler, received 12 December 1836, b/m, receipt of stolen goods, 3y.[270]
Priscilla West, received 12 December 1836, b/f, larceny, 3y.[271]
Henry Savoy, received 17 December 1836, b/m, larceny 3y.[272]
William Posey, received 17 December 1836, mu/boy, larceny, 3y.[273]

TM, received 17 December 1836, b/m, larceny, 2y.[274]
Richard Plummer, received 17 December 1836, b/m, larceny, 5y.[275]
H. Thomas, larceny, 3y.[276]

Chapter Fourteen

INTAKE 1837

William Kurtz, received 2 January 1837, stealing, 2y6m.[277]
John Collins, received 18 January 1837, yellow man, burglary/larceny, 2y6m.[278]
Allen Banter, received 18 January 1837, b/m, stealing, 2y6m.[279]
John Weston, received 18 January 1837, born DC circa 1786, w/m, stealing. Weston made sacks at the pen.[280]
Henry H. White, received 27 January 1837, w/m, burning U.S. Treasury office, 10y. Pardoned 2 August 1841.[281]
Madison Carter, received 27 January 1837, b/m, stealing, 2y6m. Pardoned 18 March 1837.[282]
Harry Howards, received 27 January 1837, mu/m, stealing 2y6m.[283]
James Herbert, received 2 February 1837, b/m, assault with intent to kill, 2y6m. Herbert was a cooper. Pardoned on 13 April 1837.[284]
William Bradley, received 2 February 1837, b/m, assault with intent to kill, 2y6m. Bradley was a cooper. Pardoned 13 April 1837.[285]
William Williams, received 10 April 1837, b/m, larceny, 3y.[286]
Nace Cole, Jr., received 15 April 1837, b/m, larceny, 3y.[287]
LP, received 13 May 1837, w/m, manslaughter, 5y.[288]
JF, received 13 May 1837, b/m. forgery, 7y.[289]
CR, received 13 May 1837, b/m, burglary, 3y.[290]
WR, received 13 May 1837, b/m, stealing, 2y.[291]
Nicholas Lomman, received 24 June 1837, w/m, stealing, 6y.[292]
Henry Brown, received 24 June 1837, mu/m, stealing, 2y. Brown was a barber.[293]
Ann Mason, received 24 June 1837, b/f, stealing, 1y.[294]
WHW, received 14 July 1837, w/m, assault with intent to kill, 2y.[295]
BM, received 14 October 1837, w/m, larceny, 2y.[296]
Thomas Miles, received 14 October 1837, mu/m, larceny, 2y.[297]
William William (aka William Williams aka William Spargs), received 7 December 1837, w/m, stealing, 2y.[298]
Joseph Hornsberry, received 21 December 1837, mu/m, stealing, 2y6m.[299]
James Conner, received 21 December 1837, b/m, stealing, 1y.[300]
Jeremiah Morris, received 21 December 1837, b/m, stealing, 2y.[301]
William Johnson, received 21 December 1837, b/m, stealing, 2y.[302]
William Carpenter (aka Bill Jett), received 23 December 1837, b/m, stealing, 3y.[303]

Teresa Granderson, received 23 December 1837, b/f, stealing, 1y.[304]
William Peters, larceny, 2y.[305]
Mary Robbisin, received 23 December 1837, w/f, stealing, 1y.[306]
Sarah Young, received 27 December 1837, w/f, stealing, 1y.[307]
Elizabeth Wise, larceny, 3y. Pardoned.[308]

Chapter Fifteen

INTAKE 1838

John Leland, received 9 January 1838, w/m, stealing, 4y.[309]
David Michael, larceny, 1y.[310]
Rezin Barker, received 9 January 1838, mu/m, stealing, 3y. He was a broom maker in the pen.[311]
Jane Brown, received 9 January 1838, b/f, stealing, 1y.[312]
Robert Cole, received 9 January 1838, b/m, stealing, 1y.[313]
Nancy Ashton, received 18 January 1838, mu/f, stealing, 1y.[314]
Mary Jenifer, received 18 January 1838, b/f, stealing, 1y.[315]
David Graby, received 18 January 1838, w/m, stealing, 1y.[316]
WL, received 22 January 1838, w/m, stealing, 1y6m.[317]
Nathaniel G. Noble, received 24 January 1838, w/m, forgery, 7y. Noble died 22 November 1841.[318]
Charley B. Stewart, received 23 April 1838, w/m, stealing, 1y. He was a tailor at the pen.[319]
Henry Beerman, received 23 April 1838, w/m, stealing, 5y. He made brooms at the pen.[320]
WG, received 5 June 1838, w/m, stealing, 1y.[321]
Julia Jackson, received 29 June 1838, b/f, stealing, 2y.[322]
Nelson Sims, received 29 June 1838, b/m, stealing, 3y.[323]
Joseph Lafontaine, received 2 July 1838, w/m, forgery, 1y.[324]
Isaac Bedds, received 2 July 1838, mu/m, stealing, 2y.[325]
John B. Henderson, received 27 September 1838, w/m, forgery, 10y. Pardoned 12 July 1843. On 20 June 1838, while awaiting trial, Henderson escaped from the local jail, was caught and returned. The jury found him guilty of counterfeiting and forging Treasury notes in the amounts of $874, $782, $100, two $50 notes, and $4000. Henderson then lied under oath, saying someone else passed the notes on him, knowing them to be counterfeit. He was pardoned on 12 July 1843.[326]
Mary Scott (aka Mary Armstrong), received 28 September 1838, w/f, stealing, 3y. On 25 May 1838, Scott stole one $7 chintz frock and a $3 calico wrapper for which she was sentenced to 1y in the pen. Also on 25 May 1838, she stole a $15 silver watch, an $8 straw bonnet, a $3.25 silk shawl, a $1.37 pair of Morocco shoes, a $1.25 silk handkerchief, a 75-cent corded skirt, a $1.50 flannel skirt, a $1.25 night wrapper, a 37-cent pair of hose, a $1 undergarment, a 37-cent

night cap, a 25-cent pair of hose, and a 50-cent bead purse, all property of James Brown.[327]

Michael McCarty, received 28 September 1838, w/m, stealing, 2y.[328]

James Alexander, received 28 September 1838, w/m, stealing, 2y. On 14 August 1838, Alexander stole one $20 bank note and one 50-cent note, goods of George Oyster.[329]

Jim Diggs, received 28 September 1838, b/m, stealing, 1y. On 27 August 1838, Diggs stole a $1 net covering for a horse, property of Lewis Vevan (?).[330]

William Herbert (aka William Diggs), received 28 September 1838, b/m, stealing, 2y. On 14 August 1838, Herbert stole one $4 pair of pantaloons, three pair summer pantaloons ($2 each), three waistcoats ($2 each); 1 $10 cloth coat, goods of Reverend John Johns. Herbert died 16 March 1839 in the penitentiary.[331]

John Butler, received 28 September 1838, b/m, stealing, 1y. On 1 August 1838, Butler stole three pounds of butter (25 cents/lb.), goods of James Hillard. Butler died 11 June 1839 in the penitentiary.[332]

William Mackinamer, received 28 September 1838, w/m, stealing, 2y. On 20 September 1838, Mackinamer stole a $1.75 bridle, a $3.50 bridle, a $3 whip, one 37½ cent martingale, one $10 servant's livery coat, all goods of Levi Woodbury. Mackinamer made sacks in the penitentiary.[333]

Lydia Green, received 28 September 1838, b/f, stealing, 2y. On 1 August 1838, Green stole three half-eagles ($5 each), four Mexican dollars ($1 each), one Spanish dollar ($1.00), five Francs (about 93 cents), and a pair of gold earrings ($1.50), goods of Elizabeth Brown.[334]

George Landvoight, received 3 October 1838, w/m, stealing, 2y. On 8 August 1838, Landvoight stole $18 in American gold coins, one English sovereign, one $20 bank note, one $10 bank note, one $12 watch-making vice, three $2 files, two hammers ($1 each); one $2 French foot measure, and one $3 bevel, goods of Conrad Swartz. Landvoight was pardoned 28 March 1840.[335]

James Dean, received 20 October 1838, w/m, mail robbery, 10y. Dean was sentenced by the District Court Western Virginia in September 1838 to 10y at hard labor. He worked as a baker in the penitentiary. On 5 December 1844, Dean was pardoned.[336]

WC, received 12 November 1838, w/m, stealing, 3y.[337]

WW, received 12 November 1838, w/m, stealing, 3y.[338]

HB, received 12 November 1838, w/m, stealing, 2y.[339]
JD, received 12 November 1838, b/f, stealing, 1y.[340]
TC, received 10 December 1838, w/m, stealing, 2y.[341]

Chapter Sixteen

INTAKE 1839

William Taylor, received 27 March 1839, w/m, stealing, 2y. On 11 November 38, Taylor stole six hogs ($30) from Nace Adams. Taylor was a baker in the penitentiary.[342]

Samuel Cissell, received 27 March 1839, w/m, forgery, 3y. On 11 July 1838, Cissell forged a $2 due bill with intent to defraud George A. W. Randall. Cissell was sentenced to 1y for this offense. On 7 November 1838, Cissell forged a $10 due bill and was sentenced to 2y for this offense. Cissell worked in the broom making department in the penitentiary.[343]

Lewis A.Tarlton, received 27 March 1839, w/m, stealing, 3y. On 1 September 1838, Tarlton stole 3 silver salt spoons ($3), a silver mustard spoon ($1), 12 silver tablespoons ($24), and 18 silver teaspoons ($18), all goods of Eliza Queen.[344]

John W. Webb, received 27 March 1839, w/m, stealing, 2y. On 19 October 1838, Webb stole a $130 gold watch and a six-cent paper box from Ward Taylor.[345]

Thomas Davis, received 28 March 1839, w/m, assault with intent to kill, 2y. On 4 August 1838, James King got off his horse to strike Thomas Davis but was prevented from doing so by Davis' brother. Thomas Davis had an open knife and, without warning, came at King, struck him, and with his right hand stabbed King three times in the side and chest. His fourth attempt to stab King was thwarted, and he threw the knife away and ran. Davis denied the stabbings. Davis worked in the carpentry shop at the penitentiary. He was pardoned 31 October 1839.[346]

Frederick Strother, received 28 March 1839, b/m, stealing, 2y. Strother stole 3 barrels of flour ($7 each) from Walter Smoot.[347]

Isaac Brogden, received 28 March 1839, b/m, stealing, 5y. For stealing 4½ yards of cloth ($12.37½) of Michael McCarty on 27 September 1838, Brogden was sentenced to 3y in the penitentiary. For stealing one $6 mahogany work stand on 20 September 1838 from Samuel Drury, Brogden was sentenced to 2y in the penitentiary. Brogden was a cook in the penitentiary and died in the pen on 29 November 1842.[348]

James Collins, received 28 March 1839, b/m, stealing, 2y. On 26 December 1838, Collins stole one silver ladle ($12) and four silver spoons ($8), goods of S. R. Hobbey.[349]

Clement B. Weston, received 1 April 1839, w/m, stealing, 1y. In August 1838, Weston obtained money under false pretenses. When Weston entered Sophia Brasey's house and saw her counting money, he told her he was Mr. Wilson, a postal clerk, and he would change the money into gold for her. She believed him and let him take the money from the table with his promise to return and bring her the gold. Weston stole twenty-six silver coins (50 cents ea.), sixteen silver coins (25 cents ea.), and nine silver coins ($1 ea.), goods of Ms. Brasey. Weston picked oakum while in the penitentiary and died there on 24 February 1840.[350]

AH, received 4 April 1839, b/m, stealing, 2y. AH was a broom maker in the pen.[351]

AO, received 4 April 1839, b/m, stealing, 2y.[352]

GE, received 4 April 1839, b/m, stealing, 2y.[353]

William Nash, received 15 June 1839, mu/m, forgery, 5y. Pardoned 2 November 1843.[354]

William Kurtz, received 17 June 1839, w/m, stealing, 5y. For stealing four silver tablespoons ($8), three silver dessert spoons ($4.50), one pair silver sugar tongs ($3), and one salt spoon (37 cents) on 1 September 1838 from Roswell Woodward, Kurtz was sentenced to 2y in the penitentiary. And, for stealing three silver salt spoons ($3), one silver mustard spoon ($1), twelve silver tablespoons ($24), and eighteen teaspoons ($18) from Eliza Queen on 1 September 1838, he was sentenced to 3y in the pen.[355]

Francis Fenwick, received 19 November 1839, w/m, perjury, 2y. Fenwick was a broom maker in the penitentiary and was pardoned 17 April 1840.[356]

WW, received 19 November 1839, w/m, stealing, 4y. He was a broom maker at the pen.[357]

BF, received 19 November 1839, w/m, stealing, 2y.[358]

MF, received 19 November 1839, w/f, stealing, 2y.[359]

Moses E. Harte, received 25 November 1839, w/m, stealing, 1y. Harte worked as a broom maker in the pen.[360]

Mary Ann Conn, received 25 November 1839, mu/f, stealing, 2y.[361]

Henry Smith, received 25 November 1839, w/m, stealing, 2y. Smith was a baker at the penitentiary.[362]

Joseph Goddard, received 25 November 1839, w/m, horse theft, 5y. Goddard was a broom maker at the pen.[363]

J. Culp (aka J. J. Kobb), received 25 November 1839, w/m, forgery, 2y. Culp picked oakum at the pen.[364]

Lucretia Clark, false pretense, 2y. On 26 October 1839, Clark conspired with Harriet Jones to sell herself as a slave to Thomas Williams for $300, under the pretense that she was a slave and could be sold.[365]

Harriet Jones (aka Harriet Smith), received December 1839 false pretense, 2y. Jones conspired to sell Lucretia Clark, a free black, as a slave and thereby defraud Thomas Williams of the $300 sale price.[366]

Chapter Seventeen

INTAKE 1840

Joseph Hardy, received 19 March 1840, copper colored/m, stealing, 6y. For stealing one coat ($15) from Philip Riley on 22 December 1839, Hardy was sentenced to 3y in the pen and for stealing one pair of $2.50 pair of pantaloons from the Howard Institution on 18 January 1840, he was sentenced to another 3y in the pen.[367]

Sandy Spriggs (aka Amos Queen), born Washington, DC, received 19 March 1840, b/m, stealing, 9y. For stealing one coat ($20) property of James Rodgers on 17 February 40, Spriggs was sentenced to 3y in the pen. And, for stealing one coat ($40), property of Philip F. Thomas, on 19 February 40, he was sentenced to an additional 6 years.[368]

James Herbert, received 19 March 1840, b/m, stealing, 2y. On 12 February 1840, Herbert stole a $10 saddle, a $2 bridle, and one 50-cent martingale, goods of Samuel Smoot.[369]

William H. Martin, received 21 March 1840, w/m, stealing 4y. For stealing one coat ($20) and one pair of $5 pantaloons from William Ogdon on 15 January 1840, Martin was sentenced to 3y in the pen. For stealing one silk waistcoat ($4), $2 in silver, one linen shirt bosom (50 cents), and one silver pencil case (50 cents) on 15 January 1840 from Harman Korff, Martin was sentenced to an additional year in the pen.[370]

JC, received 9 April 1840, w/m, stealing, 3y.[371]

JE, received 9 April 1840, stealing, 2y. JE worked in the carpentry shop.[372]

RH, received 9 April 1840, b/m, stealing, 2y.[373]

James Diggs, received 13 June 1840, b/m. stealing, 2y.[374]

Charles Green, received 13 June 1840, b/m, stealing, 4y. Green was pardoned 25 July 1840.[375]

Addison Brown, received 13 June 1840, w/m, stealing, 2y.[376]

John Collins (aka John Path, aka Patrick Collins), received 4 November 1840, mu/m, stealing, 1y6m. On 14 August 1840, Collins stole one cloth coat ($5) from Walter DeVaughn.[377]

GP, received 6 November 1840, b/m, stealing, 2y.[378]

James Simms, received 27 November 1840, w/m, stealing, 2y. Simms was charged with stealing a $200 gold watch and a $70 gold chain from Julia Sims. He was acquitted for stealing the watch, even though it was in his possession and he knew it was stolen. Simms was pardoned 24 November 1842.[379]

Henry Wootten, received 27 November 1840, b/m, stealing, 2y. Wootten was seen between 5-6p.m. on Friday, 14 October 1840, passing through the stable yard where the calf was tied and then standing under a nearby apple tree, knocking apples off the tree. The calf, which belonged to John Mason, Jr., and was worth $5, was stolen between 7-8 p.m. that same night.[380]

Julia (aka Judy Jasper), received 27 November 1840, b/f, stealing, 2y. On 27 September 1840, Jasper stole two silver half dollars, one silver quarter dollar, one silk frock ($3), one plaid shawl ($3), one tablecloth (12½ cents), 1 pair white stockings (25 cents), one silk bag (12½ cents), three yards of crepe and one lace veil (18¾ cents), all the property of Patrick Robbins. She was found guilty on 24 November 1840 and sentenced to 2y in the pen.[381]

Isaac Beddo, received 27 November 1840, mu/m, stealing, 3y. For stealing one $25 cloth coat, one $5 pair of pantaloons, and one $5 vest, goods of Dr. P. A. Lacey on 11 August 1840, Beddo was sentenced to 2y in the pen. And, for stealing one $10 cloth coat, one pair of pantaloons ($1), and one pair of gloves (25 cents) of Peter H. Brown on that same day, Beddo was sentenced to an additional year in the pen. He died in the pen on 24 November 1841.[382]

John Allinger, received 27 November 1840, w/m, stealing, 2y. On 19 September 1840, Allinger stole two foreign gold coins ($8 ea.) and one foreign silver coin (6 cents), goods of Michael Folhouse.[383]

John Smith, received 27 November 1840, arson, 3y. Smith set fire to Samuel W. Handy's store, workshop, and out house. The buildings were full of wool, furs, hats, and tools.[384]

Chapter Eighteen

INTAKE 1841

James H. Sims, received 7 January 1841, b/m, forgery, 4y. On 8 November 1840, Sims falsely pretended to Anthony McCready, a barkeeper, that he [Sims] was the servant of Charles Downing sent to get $5 from McCready. McCready did know Downing and gave Sims a $5 bank note. Truth is, Sims was NOT a servant of Downing and was not sent by Downing. Sims was sentenced to 2y years in the penitentiary for this offense. On 28 December 1840, Sims forged a note from John Suder to William Graham for one pair of shoes ($3.50) and was sentenced to an additional 2y in the pen.[385]

William McManus (aka William Gray), received 7 January 1841,w/m, stealing, 2y. On 25 November 1840, McManus stole one vest ($1.50) and a hand saw ($2), goods of John Wilson. McManus died in the pen on 15 August 1842.[386]

John Brown, received 16 January 1841, mu/m, stealing, 2y. On 14 December 1840, Brown stole two pair of boots ($5.50), one pair of shoes ($1.50), and one pair of pantaloons ($4), goods of Job Carson. Brown was a tailor in the pen.[387]

Nehemiah Brown, received 18 March 1841, w/m, stealing 2y. Brown stole a $5 cloth coat from Michael Ferrell on 20 Jan 1841. He was sentenced on 13 March 1841 to 2y in the pen.[388]

Samuel Chase, received 18 March 1841, b/m, stealing/burglary, 3y. On 27 February 1841, Chase was arrested for breaking and entering the house of Thomas J. Fletcher between 12 a.m. and 4 a.m. Chase forced the door lock leading from the barroom to the rooms upstairs.[389]

William Carpenter, received 18 March 1841,mu/m, stealing, 5y. For stealing a $30 cloth cloak, property of Ann McDaniel, on 4 March 1841, Carpenter was sentenced to 1y in the pen. For stealing a cloak from Mary McDaniel that same day, he was sentenced to another year. For stealing a $35 cloth coat of William McDaniel, also on 4 March 1841, Carpenter was sentenced to another year, and for stealing a $25 cloth coat of Osborn M. McDaniel on 4 March 1841, he was sentenced to an additional 2y in the pen, a total of 5y in the pen.[390]

John Andrews, received 18 March 1841, w/m, stealing, 2y. On 4 March 1841, Andrews stole a 50-cent pocketbook; four promissory notes ($50); one promissory note ($47.60) drawn by James Hansbroagh to John T. Ashby; and one promissory note ($20), goods of John T. Ashby.[391]

Lucretia ("Letty") Clark, received 18 March 1841, b/f, stealing,1y6m. On 1 February 1841, Clark stole six pair of silk hose ($12), goods of Elizabeth Hall.[392]

Edward Brown, received 18 March 1841, w/m, stealing, 1y. On 20 January 1841, Brown stole one cloth coat ($5), property of Michael Ferell.[393]

Frank Tolson, received 18 March 1841, b/boy, stealing, 2y. On 29 January 1841, Tolson broke into the storehouse of Walter Smoot in the night and stole one foreign coin (50 cents); one $5 bank note, and $3 in coins.[394]

Joseph Johnson, received 27 March 1841, mu/m, stealing, 1y6m. On 5 February 1841, Johnson stole a $5 quilt and a 50-cent tablecloth, goods of Betsy Wood.[395]

JB, received 10 April 1841, w/m, stealing, 3y.[396]

James P. Smith, received 20 May 1841, w/m, stealing, 2y. On 16 Jan 1841, Smith stole a $30 cloth coat, property of Enoch Tucker and a $5 cloth coat and 75-cent silk handkerchief of William M. Tucker, son of Enoch Tucker. Smith was pardoned 24 November 1842.[397]

MJL, received 9 June 1841, b/f, stealing, 1y6m.[398]

Charles Morgan, received 19 June 1841, w/m, horse stealing, 3y. On 16 May 1841, Morgan stole a bay horse ($100), property of Jacob Kingla.[399]

Thomas Morris (aka Thomas Barker), received 19 June 1841, b/m, horse theft, 3y. On 16 May 1841, Morris stole a bay horse ($100), property of Jacob Kingla.[400]

Tom Johnson, received 19 June 1841, b/m, stealing, 2y. On 22 May 1841, Johnson stole a $5.50 barrel of herring, property of William Bird.[401]

Alex Wilson (aka Alex Whistler aka Alexander Johnson, aka Thomas Morris), received 19 June 1841, b/m, stealing, 2y. On 30 May 1841, Wilson stole a $10 silver watch, property of Mr. Perry.[402]

James McKane, received 19 June 1841,w/m, stealing, 2y. On 7 June 1841, McKane stole three German silver spoons ($1.12), a $3 pair of silver sugar tongs, and a $3 silver cream ladle, goods of Deidrich J. Visser (?).[403]

Charles B. Bentley (aka Lemuel I. Bliss), received 19 June 1841, w/m, forgery, 3y. On 18 March 1841, Bentley forged the name of Isaac C.

Bates to a $100 note and used the forged note to pay Francis Masi for a gold watch.[404]

Perry Biggs, received 19 June 1841, w/m, hog stealing, 2y. On 1 March 1841, Biggs stole two hogs and the grindstone ($6.50 total), goods of John Hoover, near Georgetown.[405]

James Greaves, larceny, 2y. On 14 June 41, Greaves stole an $8 gun, a $10 clarinet, a $4 cloth overcoat, and a $2 pair of pantaloons from Robert Taylor.[406]

William H. Thornberry, received 6 November 1841, w/m, obtaining goods under false pretenses. Pardoned 15 May 1842.[407]

Henrietta Magruder, received 20 November 1841, b/f, 1y6m.[408]

Henry Smith, received 20 November 1841, mu/m, larceny, 2y. On 28 June 1841, Smith stole a $15 cloth coat and one pair of shoes ($1.50), goods of Robert Hodge.[409]

Thomas Smith, received 20 November 1841, w/m, larceny, 2y. On 3 September 1841, Smith stole a $1 pocketbook, a $20 bank note, and nine Baltimore and Ohio Railroad stock orders ($9 ea.), goods of William Hardy.[410]

William Miller, received 20 November 1841, w/m, larceny, 2y. On 3 September 1841, Miller stole a $1 pocketbook, a $20 bank note, and nine Baltimore and Ohio Railroad stock orders ($1 ea.), goods of William Hardy.[411]

Henry Dunlop (aka Lewis Conner), received 24 November 1841, mu/m, passing counterfeit money, 2y. On 18 October 1837, Dunlop passed a $10 counterfeit note on Benjamin Thompson.[412]

Andrew Sloat, received 27 November 1841, w/m, larceny, 2y.[413]

Chapter Nineteen

INTAKE 1842

Thomas Taylor, received 12 March 1842, b/m, stealing, 2y. On 3 November 1841, Taylor stole one barrel of flour ($5.87½), property of B. F. Middleton.[414]

Vincent Garner, received 12 March 1842, b/m, stealing, 1y6m. On 1 January 1842, Garner stole four turkeys ($4.44), a bag (50 cents), and four cotton cloths (25 cents), goods of James. F. Brown.[415]

Jacob Fisher (aka Aaron Lenox aka Jacob Lenox), received 12 March 1842, w/m, stealing, 2y. On 26 January 1842, Fisher stole a $10 cloth coat, property of Frederick Charles Erb.[416]

Christopher Sewalls, received 12 March 1842, b/m, stealing, 1y6m. On 1 February 1842, Sewalls stole a chest ($1), a $5 silver watch, two gold pieces ($10 ea.), one $5 gold piece, $2.50 in notes and silver, 3 pair of pantaloons ($5), 5 white linen handkerchiefs ($1.75), a black velvet cap (50 cents), a black silk handkerchief (50 cents), a $16 cloth coat, a $2 cloth coat, a $1 hairbrush, and one gold breast pin ($1), goods of Albert Parker.[417]

Basil Brooks, received 19 March 1842, b/m, stealing, 1y6m. On 12 December 1841, Brooks stole 1,845 shingles ($10), property of John Queen and William Gunnell, joint merchants of Queen & Gunnell. Brooks was a cook in the pen.[418]

George McDaniel, received 26 March 1842, w/m, stealing, 4y. On 27 January 1842, McDaniel broke into the house of Aquilla Rickets about 11 p.m. and took two bank notes ($20 ea.), six certificates of deposit ($5 ea.), one $1 promissory note; three $1 bank notes, a $15 bank note, nine $10 bank notes, two $8 bank notes, a $7 bank note, two $6 bank notes, eight $5 bank notes, a $1 promissory note, two 50-cent notes, five 25-cent notes, ten 12½ cent notes, and 100 miscellaneous other bank notes, promissory notes, orders, and drafts totaling $164.[419]

John Tobin, received 26 March 1842, w/m, violent assault, 2y. Tobin struck Catharine Hughes, wife of William Hughes in the left eye and elsewhere with a glass bottle. She lost the use of the eye and was "sick, weak, languid, and distempered" after the day of the blow on 19 December 1841.[420]

Thomas Jones, received 26 March 1842, w/m, manslaughter, 4y. On 5 March 1842, Jones violently beat John Collins over the head with a gun, causing Collins' death on 6 March 1842.[421]

Malone Jones, received 26 March 1842, w/m, stealing, 2y. Jones worked in the carpentry shop at the pen.[422]

Arton Savoy, born MD circa 1799, received 26 March 1842, b/m, stealing, 2y.[423]

Wesley Scott, received March 1842, false pretense, 2y. Scott forged a note to obtain a pair of shoes from Charles Good on 28 November 1841, by signing the note "William Van Skiver."[424]

Alfred F. Butler, received 9 April 1842, w/m, stealing/burglary, 13y. Butler was pardoned 15 January 1847.[425]

JM, received 9 April 1842, b/boy, stealing, 2y.[426]

WR, received 9 April 1842, yellow boy, burglary, 3y.[427]

JB, received 13 June 1842, mu/m, stealing, 2y6m.[428]

Washington Clark, received 25 June 1842, b/m, stealing/burglary, 3y.[429]

Joseph Parsons, received 25 June 1842, w/m, 4y. On 13 November 1841, Parsons was found guilty of rioting.[430]

George Thompson (aka John Thomas), received 25 June 1842, b/m, stealing, 2y.[431]

John Thomas (aka William Thomas), received 27 June 1842, b/m, stealing, 1y6m.[432]

Thomas Bell, received 2 July 1842, w/m, stealing, 4y. Bell worked in the carpentry shop at the pen and was pardoned 13 June 1844.[433]

R. Barker, received 25 November 1842, mu/m, larceny, 2y.[434]

John Weston, received 25 November 1842, born DC circa 1786, w/m, larceny, 2y. Weston was a cook in the pen.[435]

Amelia Ellis, received 25 November 1842, b/f, larceny, 2y.[436]

WM, received 30 November 1842, w/boy, stealing, 2y.[437]

FR, received 30 November 1842, w/boy, stealing, 1y6m.[438]

Chapter Twenty

INTAKE 1843

George C. Weigley, received 15 February 1843, w/m, stealing, 1y. Weigley was a baker in the penitentiary.[439]
Samuel White, received 15 February 1843, b/m, stealing, 1y6m.[440]
Erastus Stimpson, received 9 March 1843, w/m, stealing, 2y.[441]
James Diggs, received 9 March 1843, b/m, stealing, 3y.[442]
William Noland, received 21 March 1843, w/m, stealing/robbery, 4y.[443]
David Jenkins, received 21 March 1843, b/m, stealing, 3y. Owner Joseph D. Evans of Lynchburg, VA called Jenkins "Negro Pleasant"--"our Boy Pleasant." Upon Evans' identification of Jenkins, Jenkins was pardoned and released on 26 August 1843.[444]
Washington Causine, received 21 March 1843, w/m, stealing, 2y.[445]
Betsy Brown, received 21 March 1843, b/f, stealing, 2y.[446]
William Gibbs, received 21 March 1843, b/m, stealing, 3y.[447]
Dominic Borg or Burke, received 21 March 1843, w/m, stealing, 2y.[448]
Frederick Rothpitz (?), received 28 March 1843, w/m, stealing, 3y.[449]
HM received 10 April 1843, b/m, stealing, 3y.[450]
EB, received 10 April 1843, w/m, stealing, 3y.[451]
WD, received 10 April 1843, mu/boy, stealing, 2y.[452]
JT, received 14 April 1843, w/m, stealing, 3y.[453]
JWC, received 29 June 1843, w/m, false pretense, 2y. The prisoner was released 23 August 1844.[454]
George Butler, received 20 July 1843, b/m, stealing, 2y. Butler stole twenty pieces of gold coin ($97 value), property of William M. King.[455]
Robert Black, received 14 August 1843, b/boy, arson, 2y. On July 1843, Black set fire to James Turton and Henry Barron's carpenter shop at the corner of E and 10th St. in Washington.[456]
James Shorter, received 5 September 1843, b/m, stealing, 3y.[457]
James Curtis, received 11 November 1843, b/m, stealing, 1y6m. Curtis stole a $5 bank note, property of George Knott on 21 April 1843.[458]
Henrietta Butler, received 11 November 1843, b/f, stealing, 1y6m.[459]
Aloiseus Cole, received 11 November 1843, b/m, stealing, 2y.[460]
William Gray, received 11 November 1843, w/m, burglary, 3y. Gray was a tailor in the penitentiary and died there on 15 August 1845.[461]
William Fords (Samuel C. Fords), received 11 November 1843, b/m, false pretences, 1y6m.[462]
Charley Brown, received 11 November 1843, b/m, stealing, 2y.[463]

George (or McKendree) Dean, received 18 November 1843, w/m, stealing, 1y6m. Dean was pardoned 7 December 1843.[464]
CB, received 29 November 1843, w/m, burglary, 14y. The prisoner died 16 July 1848 when he "sunk under phthisis."[465]
JT, received 29 November 1843, w/m, stealing, 3y.[466]
GB, received 29 November 1843, b/m, stealing, 2y.[467]
JT, received 29 November 1843, b/m, stealing, 2y.[468]
SM, received 29 November 1843, w/f, stealing 1y6m.[469]

Chapter Twenty-one

INTAKE 1844

William Stone, received 9 March 1844, w/m, stealing, 2y. Stone died in the penitentiary on 30 January 1845.[470]

James H.Winfrey, received 9 March 1844, w/m, stealing, 2y.[471]

William Garner, received 13 March 1844, w/m, stealing, 2y.[472]

GO, received 13 March 1844, w/m, assault with intent to kill, 2y.[473]

George (or McKendree) Dean, received 15 March 1844, w/m, stealing, 4y. Dean, released in December 1843, was tried for stealing 3 pieces of sails ($2), one bed (75 cents), one blanket ($1.50), and one bolster (25 cents), all property of John Coburn and was accused of stealing one shirt ($1) of James Cisil.[474]

John Collins, received 15 March 1844, mu/m, stealing, 3y. Collins stood trial for stealing the following property of George W. Rowles: pocketbook (12½ cents), a half dollar, 4 quarters, 15 pieces of silver coin (10 cents each), several smaller silver coins, 9 silver Mexican dollars, and 1 other silver dollar, not in the pocketbook. Collins was a baker in the penitentiary.[475]

John Brown, born MD, received 2 April 1844, b/m, stealing, 8y.[476]

GR, received 15 April 1844, b/m, stealing, 4y.[477]

Albert Mortimer, born VA circa 1800, received 4 June 1844, mu/m, burglary, 14y. In 1853, Mortimer suffered increasingly from epileptic seizures. Mortimer had a wife and seven children, one of whom was sentenced for stealing and died pleading his father's innocence. The grand jury recommended Mortimer be pardoned, and on 25 June 1853, he was.[478]

JS received 4 June 1844, w/m, burglary, 4y.[479]

Robert Scott, received 4 June 1844, w/m, burglary, 4y. The prisoner worked in the penitentiary carpentry shop and was pardoned 2 June 1848.[480]

GC, received 20 June 1844, yellow/man, assault with intent to kill, 2y.[481]

Nick Clark (aka Meeker?), received 20 June 1844, w/m, stealing, 3y.[482]

Thomas Stewart, received 20 September 1844, w/m, stealing, 1y.[483]

JS, received 19 October 1844, w/m, counterfeiting, 2y.[484]

SY, received 11 November 1844, w/f, stealing, 1y6m.[485]

JB, received 11 November 1844, b/m, assault/battery with intent to kill, 2y.[486]

Thomas Bond, born MD, received 18 November 1844, b/m, burglary, 5y.[487]

Robert J. H. Davis, received 18 November 1844, b/m, stealing 1y6m.[488]

Henry Ware (aka William Beckley), received 18 November 1844, yellow/m, stealing, 3y.[489]

James McKane, born MD, received 18 November 1844,w/m, stealing, 3y. McKane stole one bar of iron (12½ cents) and various other items.[490]

Richard Morgan, received 18 November 1844, w/m, stealing, 3y. Morgan stole one bar of iron (12½ cents) and various other items.[491]

Capa A. Doras, received 18 November 1844, b/f, stealing, 1y6m.[492]

Arthur Bradley, received 26 November 1844, b/m, stealing, 3y. Bradley's first conviction was for stealing an item valued at $1, and this conviction was for stealing a $6 saw.[493]

AH, received 14 December 1844, b/boy, manslaughter, 3y.[494]

Chapter Twenty-two

INTAKE 1845

William S. Wright, received 6 January 1845, w/m, false pretenses, 2y. Wright, pretending to be the brother of Senator Silas Wright, falsely got a note for $250 from Edward Dyer. All totaled, Wright was accused of falsely receiving (about 29 May 1843) one $250 note, one $100 note, one $50 note, one $20 note, one $10 note, one $5 note, one US gold eagle coin ($10), one U.S. half eagle ($5), $4.85 in UK/Irish money, three U.S. silver dollars, two silver Mexican dollars, 56 U.S. half dollars, 10 Spanish half dollars, 6 U.S. quarters, 2 Spanish quarters, 7 U.S. dimes, 10 U.S. ½ dimes, 3 U.S. cents, and on 5 September 1842, a bank note for $251.75.[495]

George A. Moody, received 6 January 1845, w/m, assault with intent to kill, 2y. Moody was pardoned 4 August 1845.[496]

Alfred Rounds, received 22 March 1845, b/m, stealing, 3y. Rounds stole one beef hide ($3) from the slaughter house of William P. Shed and James J. Shed, the hide being the property of William Spelman.[497]

John Thomas (aka William Thomas), received 22 March 1845, b/m, stealing, 5y. Thomas was a broom maker in the pen.[498]

Henry Cole, received 22 March 1845, b/m, stealing, 1y6m.[499]

Thomas Tanner, Jr., received 22 March 1845, w/m, grand larceny, 3y. Tanner was pardoned 20 March 1848.[500]

Ellen Lindsley, received 22 March 1845, b/f, stealing, 1y6m.[501]

John Thomas, born MD, received 22 March 1845, w/m, stealing, 1y6m. Thomas was a broom maker in the pen.[502]

John W. Weston (aka John Weston), born VA circa 1786, received 24 March 1845, w/m, stealing, 6y.[503]

John B. Frizzell, received 27 March 1845, w/m, receipt of stolen goods, 2y.[504]

Edward Williams, received 29 March 1845, yellow/m, stealing, 1y6m.[505]

John Brown (aka John Black), received 29 March 1845, w/m, forgery, 1y6m.[506]

John Davis, received 1 July 1845, mu/m, manslaughter, 6y.[507]

SS, received 1 July 1845, b/m, assault with intent to kill, 3y.[508]

Lewis Lee, received 1 July 1845, b/m, stealing, 2y.[509]

Silas Kelly, received 3 September 1845, b/m, stealing, 2y.[510]

William Barker (aka Wm. Barton), received 10 December 1845, mu/boy, larceny, 14m. Barker stole pantaloons, drawers, and a shirt.[511]

Washington Barker, received 11 December 1845, mu/m, larceny, 18m.[512]
Ashbury Tyler (aka Burk Brooks), received 11 December 1845, b/m, larceny, 1y6m.[513]
John Suter, received 11 December 1845, mu/boy, larceny, 1y3m.[514]
James Baker, born NC c. 1819, received 12 December 1845, w/m, burglary, 5y6m.[515]
James Herbert, received 17 December 1845, b/m, horse stealing, 2y.[516]
Elizabeth West (aka Sarah and Ann Price), received 17 December 1845, mu/f, larceny, 2y.[517]
Moses Butler, received 19 December 1845, b/m, larceny, 1y5m.[518]
Benedict Howard, received 22 December 1845, w/m, larceny, 1y.[519]
Thomas Mailing, received 22 December 1845, w/m, larceny, 1y.[520]
John Black, received 27 December 1845, w/m, larceny, 1y.[521]
William Dowling (aka William C. Brown), born VA circa 1805, received 27 December 1845, w/m, larceny/burglary, 8y6m.[522]
Thomas Cook, born VA, received 31 December 1845, w/m, manslaughter, 7y. Cook was pardoned 1 March 1849.[523]

Chapter Twenty-three

INTAKE 1846

John Carroll, born MD c. 1798, received 7 January 1846, b/m, manslaughter, 6y.[524]

Thomas Gardner, received 13 January 1846, w/m, burglary, 3y. Gardner worked in the tailor shop at the pen and was pardoned 4 April 1847.[525]

John W. Scott (aka Wesley W. Scott), born MD, received 16 January 1846, w/m, forgery/larceny, 4y.[526]

Ignatius Grimes, received 26 January 1846, b/m, larceny, 1y6m. Grimes stole a $5 gold piece, 1 Mexican silver dollar, 1 U.S. silver dollar, and 58 silver half dollars, property of Daniel Chew.[527]

John Angel, received 23 January 1846, assault with intent to kill, 2y. Angel was pardoned 12 June 1846.[528]

Thomas Johnson (aka Thomas Williams), received 6 March 1846, b/m, larceny, 2y. Around 18 January 1846, Johnson stole two pair of shoes ($2), property of William Noyes & Sons (William Noyes, William Noyes, Jr., and Albert Noyes), and was pardoned 13 June 1846.[529]

George Kendall, received 6 March 1846, mu/m, larceny, 1y.[530]

Mary Davis (aka Mary Baltimore), received 15 March 1846, mu/f, larceny, 1y. Davis stole a shawl ($40), property of Levin M. Powell on 29 January 1846.[531]

John Giles (aka John Robinson), received 25 March 1846, w/boy, assault with intent to kill Benjamin Young on 23 February 1846, 3y. Giles was a broom maker in the pen and was pardoned 21 April 1847.[532]

JB, received 13 April 1846, b/m, larceny, 2y.[533]

JL, received 25 April 1846, felony, 7y.[534]

John Young, received 19 June 1846, b/boy, larceny, 1y. On 25 March 1846, Young stole one large leather trunk ($10), one gold chain ($10), one gold finger ring ($2), 14 linen shirts ($28), and 6 pair cotton drawers ($3), all property of James M. Brown.[535]

George Gaines, received 27 June 1846, b/m, larceny, 1y. On 29 April 1846, Gaines stole one satin vest ($60), one cap ($1), and 2 linen handkerchiefs ($1.25), property of Philander Gould.[536]

Henrietta Butler, received 8 July 1846, b/f, larceny/obtaining goods on false pretenses, 1y. Butler forged a $4 orders for goods from John E. Carter on 13 April 1846, by signing Walter Smoot's name to a letter that read: "Mr. Carter, sir, please send Walter Smoot 6 yards of book muslin. 2 yards of pink cambric. One pair of white stockings and 2 yards of lace. Walter Smoot."[537]

JB, received 20 November 1846, w/m, forgery, 2y. JB was a blacksmith.[538]

GP, received 20 November 1846, b/m, larceny, 1y.[539]

Christy A. Brown, born Georgetown, received 12 December 1846, b/f, larceny, 1y. Brown stole the following goods of Elizabeth Dover on 12 September 1846: 4 dresses ($2), 1 night cap (6 cents), 3 shawls ($3), 4 petticoats ($1), 1 chemise (37 cents), 1 under flannel shirt (25 cents), 3 white capes (37 cents), 1 yd. muslin (25 cents), 2 handkerchiefs (25 cents), 3 muslin cuffs (6 cents), 1 pr. silk stockings (50 cents), 1 pr. mitts (12 cents), and 1 quilt (20 cents).[540]

William Carpenter, born VA, received 18 December 1846, mu/m, larceny, 3y. On 12 October 1846, Carpenter stole 2 yards of cloth ($8), 2½ yards thread ($1.87), 2 patterns ($8), and 1 pattern ($3.75), goods of William Eckloff.[541]

William Lacey, b. VA, received 24 December 1846, b/m, horse stealing, 3y. Lacey stole 2 horses and one mare ($400 total), property of Allison Nailer on 20 April 1846.[542]

Chapter Twenty-four

INTAKE 1847

Peter Hanley, received 5 March 1847, w/m, larceny, 1y3m. Hanley stole one cloak ($12), property of William W. Seaton and was pardoned 2 June 1848.[543]

Arthur P. Brown, born VA, received 12 March 47, w/m, burglary, 3y. Brown broke into the house of George Brower at 11 p.m. on 24 December 1846.[544]

Joseph de la Fountaine, born France circa 1811, received 15 March 1847, w/m, larceny, 6y. De la Fountaine was found guilty on 15 December 1846 of stealing 1 bank note ($20), 1 promissory note ($240), 1 promissory note ($50), and other notes and money of William Wells. Prior to imprisonment, Fountaine was a confectioner.[545]

David W. Dixon, born VA circa 1800, received 22 March 1847, b/m, larceny/receipt of stolen goods, 9y. Dixon was found guilty on 19 December 1846 on the following receipts of stolen goods: on 9 November 1846, 100 yards of painted canvas ($12.50) belonging to Johnathan T. Walker; on 5 November 1846, 3 candlesticks (60 cents), 1 ballot box (12 cents), 1 pitcher (25 cents), and 1 stove + pipe ($6), all belonging to the Washington Benevolent Society; on 5 November 1846, 20 reams paper ($15 each), 1 case steel pens ($200), 1 gross paper folders ($36), 1 ream parchment paper ($30), 6 gross black lead pencils ($30), 30 reams note paper ($60), 50 pieces of red tape ($2), 30 lbs. of sealing wax ($32), 12 boxes wafers ($12), 20 blank books ($100), and 50 reams of cob paper ($200), belonging to John T. Sullivan; on 5 November 1846, 3 pr. shoes ($5.25), 1 monocco skin (62 cents), 1 shoe knife (12 cents), 3 packs nails (33 cents), 1 pr. pincers (25 cents), 1 shoe hammer (50 cents), and 2 awls (10 cents) belonging to Charles Collier; on 5 November 1846, 1 pr. venetian blinds ($9), 1 lot of split blinds ($2), 1 lot of worsted cord (75 cents), one lot of worsted tassels (75 cents), 1 shaving case ($1), and 1 ax ($1.25), and 1 hammer (37 cents), belonging to William H. Prentiss; on 5 November 1846, one plane (25 cents), one gauge (25 cents), and one small square (31 cents), property of Francis Mohun; on 5 November 1846, 6 knit shirts ($6 value), 2 pair knit drawers ($2 value), 2 vests ($6 value), 2 vest patterns ($3 value), 2 pieces drilling ($3.75 value), and 10 silk handkerchiefs ($10 value) from Abner H. Young and Phineas J.

Steer; and on 5 November 1846, one piece of black cloth ($8), property of W. C. Eckloff. Dixon was pardoned 28 April 1855.[546]

Eli Wheeler, received 29 March 1847, b/m, forgery, 1y. Wheeler altered numbers on a lottery ticket from 46*58*61 to 29*58*61 to obtain $5.31.[547]

Hosea Hildreth Smith, received 30 March 1847, w/m, forgery, 8y. Smith was accused of forging powers of attorney; one on 4 February 1847, purportedly signed by Charles T. Ford, executor for Thomas Ford, deceased in Philadelphia ($1091.50); another purportedly signed by Ebenezer Burd, executor for Edward Shippen, deceased in Philadelphia ($86); another on 29 February 1847, purportedly signed by Casper Wistar, executor for Dr. Casper Wistar, deceased in Philadelphia ($120); another on 18 February 1847, purportedly signed by Abigail Chollett, executrix for Samuel Chollett, deceased in Philadelphia ($202.50); another purportedly signed by Peter Adams Dorey on 18 February 1847, executor for Peter Dorey, deceased in Philadelphia ($200); one purporting to be signed on 18 February 1847 by Joseph Shaw, executor for Joseph Shaw, deceased in Philadelphia ($75.69); and one signed on 18 February 1847 purportedly signed by John Anderson, executor for John Anderson, deceased in Philadelphia ($190), all to obtain money fraudently from the U.S. Smith was pardoned 29 June 1848.[548]

SH, received 27 April 1847, w/m, counterfeiting coin, 3y.[549]

Isaac Prine, born VA circa 1784, received 27 April 1847, w/m, counterfeit coin, 6y. Prine was pardoned 3 February 1851.[550]

William Dean, born DC circa 1826, received 25 June 1847, b/m, burglary/larceny, 4y. Dean broke into Edward Hale's house with the intent to steal and also broke into Edward Simms' store around 20 April 1847 and stole a silver watch ($10), property of Samuel Walker.[551]

Daniel Hunt, received 25 June 47, b/boy, larceny, 2y. On 30 May 1847, Hunt stole one gold coin ($80) and 8 gold pieces ($10 ea.), property of Grafton Hanson.[552]

JH, received 1 July 1847, b/m, assault/battery with intent to kill, 2y.[553]

Nelson Sims, received 9 December 1847, b/m, larceny, 2y. On 2 December 1847, Sims stole one silver watch ($10), property of William Williams. This was his second offense, the first being a larceny conviction in June 1846.[554]

Richard Bays, received 9 December 1847, b/m, larceny, 1y. On 16 August 1847, Bays stole one $6 tweed coat, and three pass books (37 cents), property of Charles Homillen.[555]

Hannah Turner, received 11 December 1847, b/f, larceny, 1y. On 25 July 1847, Turner stole one $5 frock, one $1 frock, one $1.50 frock, one $2.50 lady's sack, and one 75 cent cotton sheet, property of Hazel Benezet (?).[556]

Asbury Tyler (aka Asbury Bush), born DC circa 1825, received 13 December 1847, b/m, larceny, 1y6m. Tyler stole one bridle and one martingale ($1 total value), property of Edward Sims, on 2 August 1847.[557]

John Henry Butler, received 13 December 1847, y/m, larceny, 1y6m. On 19 November 1847, Butler stole one washing tub ($1.25 value), one iron pot ($1.50 value), one bucket (25 cents), and one pair of potholders (12½ cents), property of Fortune Norton. This was his second offense, the first being for larceny in December 1844. Butler died 23 December 1848 in the penitentiary from tubercular phthisis.[558]

James Diggs, received 14 December 1847, b/m, larceny, 2y. On 30 August 1847, Diggs stole one $50 horse, one $3 saddle, and one $1 bridle, property of Richard Mason.[559]

Chapter Twenty-five

INTAKE 1848

N. Leeds (aka Noah M. Lee), received 6 January 1848, w/m, forgery/counterfeit money, 4y. Lee passed a forged and counterfeit note for $10 on John West on 4 December 1847. An affidavit taken 31 December 1847 from Thurston Lee said that about 20-22 years ago, Noah Lee received a head injury that "produced a disarrangement of his mind." He [Noah] was once "a man of considerable property the most of which he has wasted by foolish contracts and gifts that the remainder of his property his friends have felt constrained to take charge of to prevent him from wasting and destroying." Before the head injury, Lee was a man of good character. He was a broom maker in the pen and was pardoned 4 March 1849.[560]

William Thomas, born DC circa 1820, received 15 March 1848, b/m, assault/battery with intent to kill, 4y. Thomas was pardoned 13 March 1852.[561]

John Martin, received 16 March 1848, b/boy, larceny, 1y. Martin stole $8 worth of goods.[562]

Mordecai Carpenter, received 16 March 1848, b/boy, larceny, 1y.[563]

Isabella Brown, born VA, received 23 March 1848, b/f, larceny, 2y.[564]

Georgiana Humphreys, received 10 April 1848, b/f, larceny, 1y. Humphreys stole one $6 gold ring, and one $4.75 gold ring, goods of Isaac S. Ball, on 30 March 1847.[565]

Jacob Sharer (?), born VA, received 24 April 1848, w/m, counterfeiting U.S. coin, 1y.[566]

William Patterson (aka William Jackson), received 24 June 1848, b/boy, larceny, 2y. On 26 January 1848, Patterson stole one $9 cloth cloak, property of Wm. E. Bomford.[567]

Elizabeth Beckett, received 1 July 1848, b/f, larceny, 1y. On 29 May 1848, Beckett stole one $5.50 scarf, one $6 silk scarf, one $1.50 scarf, one $2 pair silk stockings, one $5.50 dress, one $5.50 muslin dress, one $3 lawn dress, one $2 pair of gator boots, two pair of blankets ($13 value), and ten sheets ($10 value).[568]

William Ford, born MD, received 15 July 1848, b/m, larceny, 1y6m. On 28 January 1848, Ford stole a $50 gold watch, property of W. E. Bomford.[569]

Robert Rose, born VA, received 21 August 1848, b/m, larceny, 1y. On

18 July 1848, Rose stole one $5 half eagle and $8.50 worth of half dollars from Henry Wilson.[570]

William Childers, born VA, received 20 September 1848, w/m, passing counterfeit coin, 2y.[571]

William James, born DC, received 9 December 1848, b/m, larceny, 1y6m. On 22 October 1848, James stole one box of candles ($5.68 worth) and 26 bars of soap ($2.25 value), property of Bates and Brother (William Bates and Frederick Bates).[572]

James Oliver (aka James McKane), born MD circa 1824, received 28 December 1848, w/m, larceny, 2y. On 19 October 1848, Oliver stole one $5 bank note, 3 silver dollars, 3 silver half dollars, and 4 silver quarter dollars, property of George Caton.[573]

Randolph Bean, born DC circa 1829, received 28 December 1848, w/m, larceny, 2y. On 19 October 1848, Bean stole one $5 bank note, 3 silver dollars, 3 silver half dollars, and 4 silver quarter dollars, property of George Caton. Randolph was a boatman prior to imprisonment.[574]

Chapter Twenty-six

INTAKE 1849

Ferdinand Diggs, born VA, received 10 March 1849, mu/m, larceny, 1y.[575]

Ellen Lindsley (aka Mary Shepherd), received 12 March 1849, b/f, larceny, 1y3m. On 13 January 1849, Lindsley stole four pots of preserves ($3.50), one 25 cent pillow, one 50 cent blanket, one $2 gown, and one $1 quilt, property of Benjamin Lee.[576]

Joseph Dockhart, received 16 April 1849, w/m, perjury, 4y. On 23 October 1848, Dockhart falsely swore before Justice of the Peace, John P. Van Tyne that he [Dockhart] was August Goetz. Dockhart died in the penitentiary on 9 February 1850 from diarrhea contracted in Mexico where he was a soldier in the Mexican War.[577]

John D. Fenton, born VA circa 1827, received 30 May 1849, w/m, felony, 4y. Fenton was a store clerk before imprisonment.[578]

Jacob Shuster (aka Tom Hand), born PA circa 1807, received 13 June 1849, larceny, 3y. On 8 November 1848, Shuster stole the following property of the United States: one $1000 gold snuff box studded with diamonds, one $2000 bottle of alter (?) of roses, one $500 gold scabbard, one $3000 pearl necklace, two pearls ($100 each), one $50 German gold medal, and one $25 South American gold medal. Shuster's was married to a woman named Eliza.[579]

John P. Stone, born MD circa 1824, received 13 June 1849, w/m, felony/passing counterfeit money, 3y6m. On 1 March 1849, Stone passed a counterfeit note on H. H. McPherson, Jr. Prior to imprisonment, Stone was a druggist.[580]

Milly Davis, received 23 June 1849, b/f, larceny, 1y. On 10 April 1849, Davis stole $85 in gold coin, property of Ann Nesbit.[581]

Joseph West (aka J.Snyder), born Switzerland circa 1824, received 11 July 1849, w/m, perjury, 4y. On 6 April 1849, West lied under oath claiming to be the brother and only living heir of Lewis B. West who reportedly had died in Contreras, Mexico around 20 August 1847, when, in fact, Lewis left a widow Abigail A. West and three daughters--Ellen Irene West, Sarah Eleanor West and Louisetta B. West, who was born shortly after her father died. Joseph West sought to obtain monies that might be due Lewis West; however, Joseph was neither a brother nor an heir. West was a baker in the pen.[582]

Richard Bays, born DC circa 1816, received 12 July1849, b/m, larceny, 1y6m. On 28 June 1849, Bays stole 200 lbs. of old iron ($5), 3 sets of horseshoes ($1.50), one 25-cent bucket, and one 75-cent shoeing box, property of Michael Cavinaugh.[583]

Thomas A. Stickleman, born VA circa 1824, received 16 October 1849, w/m, mail robbery, 2y. Stickleman was pardoned on 9 October 1851.[584]

Alice C. Haney, born MD circa 1810, received 5 December 1849, w/f, larceny, 1y. On 10 August 1849, Haney stole one $2.50 coat, 18 towels ($1.50), a $1 bundle of sewing, one 75-cent pair of gator boots, and four wine glasses (62½ cents), property of James W. Davis.[585]

Asbury Tyler (aka A. Burk), born DC circa 1825, received 6 December 1849, b/m, larceny, 2y.[586]

George Handy, born DC circa 1836, received 14 December 1849, b/boy, larceny, 2y. On 26 November 1849, Handy stole 5 pistols, ($120), property of William Voss.[587]

Lavinia Overton, born DC circa 1823, received 14 December 1849, b/f, receipt of stolen goods, 1y6m.[588]

Catherine Allen (aka Harriet Jones aka Harriet Smith), born DC circa 1820, received 14 December 1849, b/f, larceny, 1y6m. This was the third time Allen had been convicted of larceny. The first was on 19 October 1831, and the second in March 1833. On 21 August 1849, Allen stole two $4 shirts; one $1.50 shirt; one 37-cent shirt; one 25-cent bucket; one 37-cent gown, one 12-cent towel; one 18-cent butter kettle; one 25-cent bag of old clothes; two 50-cent baskets; one 25-cent crock; four aprons (total value 50 cents); one 18-cent broom, and one 75-cent iron pot, all property of John McMann.[589]

Seymour Hooe, born VA circa 1780, received 14 December 1849, b/m, larceny, 1y. On 29 August 1849, Hooe stole one gold Eagle ($10), property of Richard R. Goldin.[590]

Eliza Simms, born MD circa 1834, received 14 December 1849, mu/f, larceny, 2y. On 29 August 1849, Sims stole three $10 gold Eagles, four $5 gold Eagles, two $2.50 gold quarter Eagles, and five $1 gold pieces, property of Richard R. Goldin.[591]

Francis West (aka Thomas or Francis Gray), born DC circa 1837, received 14 December 1849, mu/boy, larceny, 2y. On 26 November 1849, West stole five pistols (total value $12), property of William Voss, and on 26 November 1849, he stole three pistols ($6 total value), property of John H. T. Werner.[592]

John Seitz, born Germany circa 1825, received 17 December 1849,w/m, larceny, 1y6m. On 5 October 1849, Seitz stole one barrel of flour worth $5.37½, property of George W. Hughes.[593]

Mary Butler, born DC circa 1826, received 21 December 1849, b/f, larceny, 2y. On 4 September 1849, Butler stole the following goods belonging to Mary Eckles: one 6-cent purse; one Mexican silver coin worth $1 US money; ten U.S. half dollars ($5 value); ten Mexican half dollars ($5 U.S. value); seven silver Spanish half dollars ($3.50 value); ten U.S. silver quarters ($2.50); ten silver Spanish quarter dollars ($2.50 U.S. value); and 9 silver Mexican quarter dollars ($2.25 U.S. value). Butler was convicted of larceny in June 1848, also, and died in the penitentiary from consumption on 12 July 1851.[594]

Elizabeth Butler, born MD circa 1827, received 24 December 1849, b/f, larceny, 1y6m. On 10 December 1849, Butler stole one $10 silk mantilla, one 50-cent veil, and one 37-cent pocket handkerchief, property of Mary Pilling.[595]

Sarah Johnson, born MD circa 1822, received 26 December 1849, b/f, larceny, 2y. On 7 August 1849, Johnson stole one $10 gold coin, and one $5 gold coin, property of Mary Heisler.[596]

Charles Brown, born MD circa 1826, received 26 December 1849, b/m, larceny, 3y. On 20 August 1859, Brown stole 2 shirts ($1 value), one pair pantaloons ($4), one 75-cent vest, one 50-cent vest, and one $2.50 vest, property of Charles Williams.[597]

James Williams, born DC circa 1829, received 27 December 1849, b/m, burglary, 4y.[598]

Arton Savoy, born MD circa 1799, received 27 December 1849, b/m, larceny, 3y. On 30 October 1849, Savoy stole two oil cans worth 50 cents each, property of Joseph Hilton.[599]

Samuel Adams, born DC circa 1825, received 28 December 1849, b/m, assault/battery with intent to kill, 2y. Prior to imprisonment, Adams was a hackdriver.[600]

Chapter Twenty-seven

INTAKE 1850

William Adams, born MD circa 1807, received 2 January 1850, mu/m, larceny, 1y. On 20 June 1849, Adams stole one 50-cent shovel, one 50-cent grub hoe, one $1 pick, one 50-cent crow bar, property of James F. Scott.[601]

George Henderson (aka J. T. Wethelay, aka J. T. Wetherley, aka John T. Warren, aka John T. Weatley, aka John T. Watson), born England circa 1828, received 7 January 1850, w/m, larceny, 2y6m. On 29 December 1849, Henderson stole one $40 cloak, property of William M. McPherson. Prior to imprisonment, Henderson was a druggist.[602]

Thomas Jones (aka William Carpenter aka Bill Jett), born DC circa 1818, received 11 January 1850, b/m, larceny, 4y. On 31 December 1849, Jones stole four $6 vests, property of Michael Shanks and Williams Wall (partners). Jones was convicted of larceny in March 1841 also.[603]

James Smith, born Ireland circa 1819, received 16 March 1850, w/m, larceny, 1y. On 25 January 1850, Smith stole one cloak ($5), property of Bonavendur Shadd.[604]

Michael Bateman, born Ireland circa 1826, received 16 March 1850, w/m, larceny, 1y. On 25 January 1850, Bateman stole one cloak ($5), property of Bonavendur Shadd.[605]

John Barrett (aka John Forrester), born Ireland circa 1800, received 16 March 1850, w/m, larceny, 1y6m. On 9 January 1850, Barret stole one $20 cloak, property of Moses Menger.[606]

George Evans, born VA circa 1822, received 18 March 1850, b/m, larceny, 3y. On 5 March 1850, Evans stole seven watches ($125 value), 3 lockets ($22), one watch key ($2), and one vinaigrette ($2), property of Francis and Vincent Masi. Evans was a baker in the pen.[607]

John McMonegle, born Ireland circa 1809, received 22 March 1850, w/m, making, passing, and attempting to pass counterfeit money, 4y. McMonegle attempted to pass counterfeit coin worth 50 cents to Richard Eaton on 17 January 1850 and to make, forge, and counterfeit seven half dollar coins on 17 January 1850.[608]

Sarah Langster, born PA circa 1831, received 25 March 1850, mu/f, larceny, 1y. Langster, a spinster, stole two bank notes ($10 each) from John Howard Payne. Langster was 3 months pregnant when she was received at the penitentiary.[609]

Charles Maddin, born Ireland circa 1813, received 29 March 1850, larceny, 1y6m. On 17 March 1850, Maddin stole 2 coats ($12 value) and one 12½-cent handkerchief, property of Samuel Wollard. Madden once hit a fellow prisoner on the head with a piece of iron taken off the bedpost. In two other instances, he attacked a prison officer and another prisoner. The prison doctor said Maddin exhibited an "insane impulse."[610]

William Pennington, born VA circa 1834, received 5 May 1850, w/boy, stealing from mail, 10y.[611]

Mary McPherson (aka Mary Ellis), born MD circa 1829, received 29 June 1850, b/f, larceny, 1y. McPherson had a stillborn child on 18 September 1850.[612]

William Noland, born DC circa 1820, received 6 July 1850, w/m, larceny, 2y. Noland stole 6 pieces of leather ($35 value), and 80 yards of damask ($32 value) on 22 June 1850.[613]

John Brown, born VA circa 1837, received 6 July 1850, mu/boy, arson, 1y.[614]

Elizabeth Beckett, born MD circa 1830, received 6 July 1850, b/f, larceny, 1y6m. Beckett had a baby on 16 September 1850.[615]

Frederick Noliean, born Germany circa 1820, received 18 July 1850, w/m, larceny, 1y6m. On 5 July 1850, Noliean stole one $2 watch from William Voss. Prior to imprisonment, Noliean was a brewer.[616]

Thomas Cook, born VA circa 1816, received 19 July 1850, w/m, larceny, 2y. Prior to imprisonment, Cook was a barkeeper. Cook was accused of stealing a $10 coat, a $2.50 pair of pantaloons, a 50 cent handkerchief, and a 50 cent pair of pantaloons, all the property of Theodore Hurley.[617]

Christy Ann Brown, born DC circa 1827, received 23 July 1850, b/f, larceny, 1y.[618]

Archibald Sterritt (aka Alexander Sterritt), born VA circa 1833, received 29 July 1850, w/boy, larceny, 1y6m.[619]

Thomas Heise, born DC circa 1832, received 29 July 1850, w/boy, arson, 2y. On 7 May 1850, Heise set fire to Samuel Bryan's stable and out house and also to the stable and out house of John P. Ingle. Heise was pardoned on 11 April 1851.[620]

Cordelia Diggs, born DC circa 1828, received 29 July 1850, b/f, forgery, 2y. Diggs presented a false written order on 17 December 1849 for Mary Suter, ordering 12 yards Alpaca ($4.50 value), 3 yards fringe ($1.32 value), and hooks and eyes ($2 value); Diggs presented a false order from Mary Suter on 17 December 1849 for one pair of shoes ($1.25 value).[621]

Isaiah Contee, received 12 December 1850, b/boy, larceny, 2y. Contee worked in the blacksmith shop at the pen.[622]

Bable Seymour, received 16 December 1850, b/m, assault and attempted rape, 3y.[623]

Thomas Harry, born DC circa 1819, received 28 December 1850, w/m, assault/battery with intent to kill, 6y. Harry was pardoned 11 August 1855.[624]

Harriet Johnson, received 28 December 1850, mu/f, assault/battery with intent to kill, 2y. Johnson was pardoned 23 January 1851.[625]

Henry Young (given name Henry Frazier, aka Henry Cox), received 31 December 1850, w/m, larceny, 3y. Young was convicted in NJ under the name of Henry Cox. He was in the NJ Penitentiary at Trenton for 3y, beginning 24 December 1846. Just before the end of his term, Young murdered his cellmate John Sherman by cutting his throat. Young was transferred to the NJ Lunatic Asylum from where he escaped on 11 May 1850.[626]

Chew Dorsey, received 31 December 1850, b/m, larceny, 1y6m. Dorsey stole a coat ($3.50), property of Patrick Moran on 14 November 1850.[627]

Chapter Twenty-eight

INTAKE 1851

William Brown, received 2 January 1851, b/m, larceny, 1y.[628]
Ellen Lindsley (aka Mary Ellen Shepherd), born MD circa 1813, received 2 January 1851, b/f, larceny, 6y.[629]
Samuel Hall (aka James Hall, aka George King, aka Joseph Abel), born DC circa 1831, received 7 January 1851,w/boy, forgery, 3y.[630]
Patrick Finegin, received 7 January 1851, w/m, larceny, 1y6m.[631]
Mary Francis Wheeler, received 7 January 1851, b/f, larceny, 1y. According to Matron Marceron, Wheeler "has some letters and marks on her arms, and a scar under the eye."[632]
Joanna Proctor, received 7 January 1851, mu/f, larceny, 2y.[633]
Frederick Rickman (aka Frederick Reckmeyer), received 9 January 1851, w/m, larceny, 2y. Rickman worked in the carpentry shop at the pen.[634]
Mary Mason (aka Mary Ann Mason, aka Mary Ann Thomas), received 13 January 1851, b/f, larceny, 1y. Mason stole a bonnet (62 cents) and one sack ($1.50), property of Charles E. Sherman on 18 October 1850.[635]
John Hall, received 16 January 1851, b/m, larceny, 2y.[636]
Sandy Spriggs, born MD circa 1806, received 16 January 1851, b/m, assault/battery with intent to kill, 8y. Spriggs was convicted of assault/battery on John Hutchinson with intent to kill and rob Hutchinson, on the highway, of one silver half dollar, one silver quarter dollar, one silver 1/8 dollar, one silver dime, one silver ½ dime, and five cents in copper coins; Spriggs cut and wounded Hutchinson with a knife.[637]
John Thomas (aka William Thomas), born MD circa 1805, received 16 January 1851, b/m, larceny, 3y.[638]
Joseph Allemander, born LA circa1814, received 17 January 1851, w/m, larceny, 10y. On 2 June 1854, Allemander escaped with fellow inmate Frank Camper. A reward of $100 was offered for his capture. On the reward poster,[639] Allemander is described as being of "moderately fair complexion," gray eyes, light brown hair, about 40 years old. He stood at 5 ft. 7⅛ in. tall and his foot measured 10¼ inches. He had a scar under his right eye, had broad shoulders, and had lost the end of his second right toe.[640]
Joseph Brown, born MD circa 1826, received 17 January 1851, w/m, larceny, 10y.[641]

Franklin Camper, born MD circa 1826, received 27 January 1851, w/m, manslaughter, 8y. Camper worked in the carpentry shop at the pen. Camper escaped from the penitentiary about 6:30 a.m. on 2 June 1854 using an iron bar with a hook fashioned on one end to escape over the wall with fellow inmate Joseph Allemander. A reward of $100 was offered for Camper's capture. He was described as having sallow skin, black hair, hazel eyes, a scar on his upper lip from his right nostril to his mouth, and one missing upper front tooth. He was about 28 years old, had tattoos on both arms—one of the crucifixion on his right arm in red and blue. He was 5ft. 5½ in. tall and his foot was 9 ⅞ in. long. (Note: the actual reward poster is in the files.) On 3 June 1855, Camper wrote Warden Thornley a letter, inscribed across the top with the words "I am about." In the letter he told Thornley to give his [Camper] sister Angeline his things—rings and studs that were in the warden's safekeeping. He added "if you are well, I don't know how long you will be so if you don't give Angeline those things of mine. I am not so far from you that I can't git holte of your cate tale. I have seen you twice within the last too weeks. I will make som of you smell hell an the only way you can escape it is to give those things up to my sister. I have some bitter enemies in Washington."[642] Camper and Allemander were captured in Hagerstown, MD. They had apparently made off with a horse and buggy which they had taken from Birch's Livery Stable, saying that they were riding to Georgetown. They were pursued from the livery stable by Mr. Southron and Mr. Hicks who found them in a hotel in Hagerstown, registered as James Johnson and brother.[643]

WF, received 31 January 1851, b/m, larceny, 3y. WF was a broom maker at the pen.[644]

Mary Lawson (aka Mary Benedict), born VA circa 1823, received 15 February 1851, w/f, perjury, 4y. Mary testified she was with Joseph Brown in Washington between 2-3 p.m. on 24 December 1850, when she actually was in Alexandria, VA at that time.[645]

George Wilson, received 11 March 1851, b/boy, larceny, 1y.[646]

Patrick Rady, received 11 March 1851, w/m, arson, 2y.[647]

Richard Bays, born DC circa 1805, received 18 March 1851, w/m, larceny, 3y.[648]

Addison Brown, born MD circa 1798, received 18 March 1851, w/m, larceny, 3y.[649]

John Rady, born DC circa 1822, received 18 March 1851, assault/battery with intent to kill, 6y. Rady worked in the blacksmith shop at the pen.[650]

Charles Weidig, born Germany circa 1828, received 1 April 1851, w/m, perjury, 4y.[651]

Charles Bentz (aka Charles Brandt), born Germany circa 1821, received 1 April 1851, w/m, perjury, 4y. Bentz was pardoned 23 March 1855.[652]

August Hannchild (aka Augustus Houschild aka Heinrig Russ), born Germany circa 1815, received 1 April 1851, w/m, perjury, 4y. Hannchild purported himself to be Joseph McLoughlin, the brother and heir of Andrew McLoughlin, a Marine private in Colonel Watson's Battalion, killed while storming Chapultepe in Mexico. In an effort to acquire McLoughlin's bounty land and thus defraud the US government, Hannchild signed the name of Patrick Clousky, who really did know the deceased, to a paper saying that Joseph McLoughlin was Andrew's sole heir.[653]

William Adams, born MD circa 1805, received 23 June 1851, b/m, larceny, 3y. On 9 April 1851, Adams stole one $5 robe of William Lollers.[654]

John Meyer (aka Jacob Meyer), received 24 June 1851, w/m, forgery, 4y.[655]

Harry Beute, received 5 July 1851, w/m, perjury, 4y. Beute was pardoned 26 January 1854.[656]

Alfred Brest, received 5 July 1851, w/boy, larceny, 3y. On 16 May 1851, Brest stole twenty $1 bills, seven $10 bills, one $5 bill, five $5 bills, several other bills and one 50-cent pocketbook, all property of William Marshall. Brest was pardoned 20 June 1854.[657]

Albert H. Beach, received 7 July 1851, w/m, obtaining money under false pretenses, 1y6m. On 10 May 1851, Beach obtained $20 under false pretenses from Charles Thomas.[658]

Jacob Rowles, received 19 July 1851, w/m, larceny, 2y. On 16 May 1851, Rowles stole one $15 cream jug, one $25 coffee pot, and 16 tumblers ($5), property of Harriet Nesbit.[659]

Elias J. Mothershead, received 21 July 1851, w/m, bigamy, 3y. Mothershead married wife #1, Maria Shelton on 1 July 1828 in Alexandria and wife #2, Elizabeth Lomax on 10 May 1851. He worked in the carpentry shop at the pen.[660]

Noah W. Lawrence, born SC, received 13 August 1851, w/m, larceny, 3y. On 18 July 1851, Lawrence stole eleven tablespoons ($11), twelve dessert spoons ($12), and nine forks ($9), all property of John F. May. Lawrence was a barber in the pen.[661]

Frank Bell, received 29 September 1851, b/boy, larceny, 1y. On 16 Jun 1851, Bell stole 14 chickens ($1.75 value), property of Buckner Bayliss.[662]

James Diggs, received 5 December 1851, b/m, larceny, 3y. On 4 Aug 1851, Diggs stole one dish ($1.50 value), property of the U.S.[663]

George Lee, received 11 December 1851, b/m, larceny, 2y. On 14 February 1851, Lee stole a $7 coat belonging to Moses Leiblich.[664]

George Regalan, received 19 December 1851, b/boy, larceny, 2y. On 12 November 1851, Regalan stole $20 and 400 cents that were in a shot bag, and $10-12 in half- and quarter-dollars, property of free black, J. Brooks, Jr.[665]

Elias Matthews, received 20 December 1851, mu/boy, larceny, 2y6m. On 30 September 1851, Matthews stole a $3.50 coat, a $1 jacket, a $1 pair of pantaloons, a 50-cent vest, a 25-cent comb, a $1 horse brush, a 50-cent sponge, a 50-cent chamois skin, and two bags (30 cents), all property of Richard S. Hill.[666]

William Umberfield, received 27 December 1851, w/boy, larceny, 2y. On 26 September 1851, Umberfield stole a $60 wagon, a $100 mule, a $5 harness, and two $3 milk cans, property of Henry H. Willard.[667]

Chapter Twenty-nine

INTAKE 1852

Asbury Taylor, born DC circa 1825, received 10 January 1852, b/m, larceny, 6y. On 2 January 1852, Taylor stole a $5.50 saddle, a $1.25 bridle, and a 25-cent bag, all property of William Choppin (?).[668]

Richard Davis (aka Richard D. Lane, aka Richard Dilano aka Richard Delane), received 15 January 1852, w/m, larceny, 2y4m. Davis stole 25 yards of cassinett ($18) from Thomas N. and George J. Johnson.[669]

Leonard Zimmermacher, received 17 January 1852, w/boy, larceny, 2y. On 21 October 1851, Zimmermacher stole a $40 cow from James Frazier and two cows worth $25 from Joseph B. Hall. Zimmermacher was pardoned 31 December 1853.[670]

William Lee, received 27 January 1852, b/m, larceny, 1y8m. Lee stole a $15 violin and bow and a $1.25 fan from Garrett and Eliza Anderson, and 12 hams ($15) from Thomas Oxley and Samuel Stott.[671]

Frank Allor, received 17 March 1852, w/m, larceny, 2y.[672]

Charles Fisher (aka Sebery), received 17 March 1852, w/m, larceny, 2y.[673]

Charles Campbell (aka Charles Piermont), received 17 March 1852, w/m, larceny, 1y6m. Campbell picked oakum in the pen.[674]

Nace Bell, received 17 March 1852, b/m, larceny, 1y. On 20 December 1850, Bell stole two pigs from Edward Brooks.[675]

William Kingsley, received 27 March 1852, w/boy, larceny, 2y.[676]

Mary McPherson, received 2 April 1852, b/f, assault/battery with intent to kill Hannah Wilson on 27 March 1852, 4y.[677]

Johannah Foley (aka Johannah Connell, aka Johannah O'Connor), received 20 April 1852, w/f, bigamy, 2y. Foley was pardoned 22 April 1852.[678]

William Wells, born MD circa 1817, received 23 April 1852, w/m, murder, life in prison. Wells, a Marine, loaded a gun, held it in both hands, and fatally shot Samuel Mundell in the left neck on 17 September 1851. Mundell died instantly. Wells was sentenced on 9 February 1852, and when the judge asked him if he had anything to say, Wells replied that everything had already been said. In his case, the death sentence was commuted to life in prison through a presidential pardon.[679]

Henry A. Naglee, received 25 May 1852, w/m, government fraud, 4y. In an effort to obtain money from the government, Naglee presented vouchers which he falsely claimed were authorized by William Quail (of Pittsburgh), Captain of Co. H, 2nd PA Regiment. Naglee was pardoned 8 August 1854.[680]

George Kendall, received 25 May 1852, b/m, larceny, 2y. On 18 October 1851, Kendall stole a $2 coat and a $1.25 pair of slippers. Kendall picked oakum in the pen.[681]

JS, received 29 May 1852, w/m, mail robbery, 3m. JS worked in the blacksmith shop in the pen.[682]

William H. Haines, received 29 May 1852, w/m, mail robbery, 10y. Haines was pardoned 2 January 1854.[683]

William Walker, received 28 June 1852, w/m, larceny, 2y.[684]

John Day, Jr., born DC circa 1828, received 23 July 1852, w/m, manslaughter, 8y. Day was a bricklayer before imprisonment. Day shot his wife, Catharine Virginia Day, on 12 May 1851, in her left side with a pistol. The wound was 10 inches deep and ½ inch wide. She lived for forty minutes and died. Ann Wood, wife of John W. Wood, and former wife of John Day, Sr., was John Day's mother. (Her maiden name was Padget and she had a sister Sally (Padget) Rudd.) It was claimed John had been mentally unstable long before he killed his wife, and because of his mental instability, he was "under the influence of a diseased mind" and not deemed guilty of murder. Catherine married John Day on 4 June 1850, and three months later on 18 September 1850, gave birth to a child. John Day lost esteem and character among his friends and became mentally diseased after the birth. He was pardoned 19 July 1860.[685]

Richard Smith, received 3 August 1852, b/m, larceny, 1y6m. Smith picked oakum in the pen.[686]

George W. Lightfoot, born DC circa 1829, received 3 August 1852, mu/m, receipt of stolen goods, 5y. Lightfoot worked in the carpentry shop at the pen. Lightfoot escaped on Saturday night, 22 September 1855 and was described as being 5 ft. 7 in. tall with a foot that measured 10¼ in. He had a dark complexion, dark brown hair, hazel eyes, heavy eyebrows, and red/blue tattoos on each arm. On one arm was a crucifixion. On the other arm was the word "Ceceiela" in a wreath, and the bust of a woman with the word "Mary" underneath it. His initials were tattooed on the inside of both calves, and several scars were on his back. He was described as being supposedly white but looking like a "bright mulatto." He had once worked on ships and in long boats. A $100 reward was offered for his capture.[687]

Charles Calvert, received 3 August 1852, mu/boy, larceny of a coat ($4.50), 1y6m.[688]

William Patterson (aka William Jackson aka William Miner), received 3 August 1852, b/m, larceny, 3y.[689]

Mahala Duvall, received 5 August 1852, w/f, larceny 2y.[690]

Frances Penny, received 13 August 1852, b/girl, larceny 2y. Penny was pardoned 29 December 1852.[691]

Hannah Wilson, received 14 August 1852, b/f, larceny of $5 worth of goods, 3y.[692]

Thomas Whitmore (aka Thomas Dobob), received 14 August 1852, b/m, larceny, 2y.[693]

John Holly (aka John Prosser), received 14 August 1852, mu/m, larceny $5 worth of goods, 4y.[694]

Thomas Humphrey, received 16 August 1852, b/m, larceny, 2y. Humphrey picked oakum in the pen.[695]

James Ferguson, received 16 August 1852, b/boy, larceny, 3y6m.[696]

Henrietta Magruder, received 23 August 1852, b/f, larceny, 7y6m.[697]

Spencer Day, received 23 August 1852, b/m, larceny, 3y. Day picked oakum in the pen.[698]

Patrick Kernan, received 24 August 1852, w/m, larceny, 1y6m.[699]

Walt Edwards, born IL circa 1825, received 4 October 1852, w/m, mail robbery, 10y. Edwards was a stage driver before imprisonment.[700]

NKG, received 16 October 1852, w/m, mail robbery, 2y.[701]

John McComb, born SC, received 11 December 1852, w/m, larceny, 3y. On 8 July 1852, McComb stole a horse/buggy ($300 value), property of Robert Rainey.[702]

Ellen Story, received 18 December 1852, w/f, larceny 1y6m.[703]

Matthew Green, received 21 December 1852, w/m larceny, 2y.[704]

Charles Roach, received 26 December 1852, w/m, larceny, 1y6m. Roach picked oakum in the pen.[705]

William Noland, received 26 December 1852, w/m, larceny, 2y.[706]

George Dunbar, received 29 December 1852, mu/m, larceny, 1y6m.[707]

Chapter Thirty

INTAKE 1853

James Shields, received 6 January 1853, w/m, larceny, 1y6m. Shields stole a watch and was pardoned 5 June 1854.[708]

Nelson Simms, received 10 January 1853, b/m, larceny, 2y.[709]

George Williamson (aka Henry Cummings), received 13 January 1853, w/m, larceny, 1y.[710]

David Lewis, received 13 January 1853, b/m, larceny, 1y6m.[711]

Lucretia Gibbs, received 14 January 1853, b/f, larceny of one dress $2 and not guilty of stealing the other items listed in the indictment, 1y.[712]

Gustavus Heisler, received 19 January 1853, w/m, arson, 5y. Heisler was pardoned 16 November 1855.[713]

Anthony Lucasey, received 19 January 1853, w/m, receipt of stolen goods, 3y. Lucasey worked in the carpentry shop at the pen and was pardoned 17 January 1856.[714]

Silas Tucker, received 20 January 1853, w/m, bigamy, 2y. Tucker waspardoned 2 March 1853.[715]

James Bowie, received 30 January 1853, b/boy, assault/battery with intent to kill John Lee, 3y.[716]

Joseph W. Morgan (aka Robert Walton, aka Harry Fritze), received 1 February 1853, w/m, forgery, 6y. On 18 May 1852, Morgan presented to John King "a suspicious draft" dated 15 May 1852 for $155 purported to have been signed by E. I. Dupont Nemours. Morgan was pardoned 14 November 1856.[717]

Thomas Harper, received 2 February 1853, w/m, larceny, 1y6m. Harper stole a $10 gun from Samuel Shepherd.[718]

William J. Shaw, received 3 February 1853, w/boy, assault/battery with intent to kill, 4y. As a result of a drunken fracas, Shaw, about 16 years old, made an assault with intent to kill on a boy named Moore in Georgetown. He was pardoned 6 November 1854.[719]

Frances Penny, received 14 February 1853, mu/girl, larceny, 2y.[720]

Edward Johnson, received 18 February 1853, w/m, larceny, 2y.[721]

John Williams (aka William Williamson), received 19 February 1853, w/m, attempt to pass forged bank notes, 2y6m. Williams was pardoned 2 March 1855.[722]

Edward Mooney, received 19 February 1853, w/boy, mail robbery, 10y. Mooney was pardoned 14 April 1856.[723]

Alfred H. Green, received 1 March 1853, b/boy, larceny, 4y. Green and Penny (following entry) stole together.[724]

Joseph Penny, received 1 March 1853, mu/boy, larceny, 4y.[725]

Jane Prosser (aka Jane Holly, aka Jane Johnson), received 13 May 1853, mu/f, receipt of stolen goods, 2y.[726]

William Coale, received 24 May 1853, mu/m, larceny, 1y6m.[727]

George Holland, received 23 June 1853, b/boy, larceny, 1y. Holland stole a pocketbook and $5, and on 1 May 1853, he also stole a 25-cent pocketbook; a $5 gold coin; 2 notes ($1 ea.); a piece of silver (25 cents); and a piece of silver (12½ cents), all the property of Ellen L. Evans.[728]

Robert Andree, received 27 June 1853, w/m, larceny, 5y. Andree was charged with four cases of theft and sent to four months in the jail, followed by 5 years in the penitentiary.[729]

Asbury Lansdale, received 27 June 1853, mu/m, burglary, 4y6m. On 16 January 1853, Lansdale broke into the house of James Wallace about 11 p.m. and stole $63 in bank notes, a $5 pistol, a purse and beadbag ($5), a $1 powder flask, and two pieces of tobacco.[730]

William Burke, received 29 June 1853, mu/m, larceny, 1y.[731]

Charles Gorman, received 9 July 1853, w/m, larceny, 2y. Gorman picked oakum in the pen.[732]

Vandora Otis, born Havana, Cuba received 11 July 1853, mu/m, larceny, 2y.[733]

Elias Simms, received 11 July 1853, mu/m, assault/battery with intent to kill, 3y.[734]

Mary Gray, received 13 July 1853, mu/girl, larceny of two $5 notes and one gold dollar, 1y.[735]

Christine Ann Brown (aka Christiana Brown aka Christy Brown) received 15 July 1853, b/f, larceny, 3y.[736]

John Runnells, received 26 July 1853, mu/m, larceny, 1y. Runnells stole a $7 wheelbarrow and a $4 wheelbarrow from W. P. Drury. Runnells was sentenced to serve 6 months in jail for the theft of the $4 wheelbarrow, to be followed by one year in the penitentiary upon his release from the jail.[737]

Jack Shepherd (aka John Fisher), born MD circa 1836, received 2 August 1853, mu/m, arson, 12y. Shepherd worked in the carpentry shop at the pen and was pardoned 31 December 1861. Shepherd and West (following entry) committed crime together.[738]

John F. West, born DC circa 1835, received 16 August 1853, b/m, arson, 12y. West was pardoned 10 November 1862.[739]

John Thomas, received 19 August 1853, b/m, obtaining goods under false pretenses, 2y.[740]

William Meinkin, received 16 December 1853, w/m, receipt of stolen goods, 2y6m. Meinkin was a clothing store owner indicted for stealing two coats, an overcoat, a pair of pants, a vest, and one gold pen (total value $45.50) from R. Colledge about 16 May 1853. Colledge was staying a room on Missouri Avenue and when he returned from work, the goods were missing. Colledge had not locked the door of his room. In July 1853, two months after the theft, one of Colledge's friends asked him to appraise the value of a certain gold pen. Colledge recognized the pen as his own, and with information from the friend, tracked the theft to Meinkin. Meinkin said he had purchased the pen from some man. Found guilty of receiving stolen goods but not of stealing them, Meinkin was sentenced on 8 December 1853. He was pardoned on 28 September 1854.[741]

Chapter Thirty-one

INTAKE 1854

Alice Smith, received 6 March 1854, w/f, 2 cases of larceny, 6y. Smith behaved "outrageously"and had to be taken out of court when she was sentenced. She accused the judge of killing Dr. George Gardiner, a man who had recently committed suicide when sentenced to the penitentiary. (See Chapter 40).[742]

William Moody, received 9 March 1854, mu/boy, larceny, 1y6m.[743]

Charles Carr, received 10 March 1854, w/m, burglary, 4y6m. Carr's mother, Mary, lived in Philadelphia.[744]

Henrietta Reed, received 10 March 1854, mu/f, larceny, 1y.[745]

John Netter (?), received 18 March 1854, b/m, larceny 1y.[746]

Thomas E. Bartley, received 20 March 1854, w/m larceny, 2y6m. Bartley worked in the carpentry shop at the pen and was pardoned 10 May 1854.[747]

Richard Biddle, born MD, received 20 March 1854, w/m, mutiny, 1y7m+1day. Biddle, a seaman under naval court martial, was pardoned 21 July 1855.[748]

Samuel Kays, born PA, received 20 March 1854, w/m, mutiny, 2y6m+7days. Kays, a seaman under naval court martial was pardoned 21 July 1855.[749]

John Baptiste, received 21 March 1854, w/m, larceny 1y6m.[750]

JCH received 26 April 1854, w/boy, mail robbery, 6m from 6 April 1854.[751]

Newton G. Shreeve, received 26 April 1854, w/boy, mail robbery, 10y from 31 March 1854. Shreeve robbed a post office at Buckhannan, VA and was sentenced in the U.S. Court for Western District of Virginia. Shreeve received several letters from his father, John Shreeve, and some from his brother John Allen Shreeve who was living in Marysville, CA. (see Chapter Seven) Shreeve was pardoned 25 January 1856.[752]

John Connor, received 16 May 1854, w/m, manslaughter, 4y. Connor was tried for the murder of Patrick Hurley. Connor said he had no guns at home, but there was a gun and ammunition under his bed. The District Attorney said had it not been for whiskey, Hurley might still be alive. Ratcliff, Connor's lawyer, said Mr. Hurley had refused to have his wounds treated. On 5 May 1854, Hurley's death was ruled a manslaughter.[753]

Penuel Hendricks, received 17 June 1854, w/m, passing counterfeit gold coin, $2500 fine + 10 y from 2 November 1853. Hendricks was transferred from the Raleigh, NC jail to the penitentiary because there was no penitentiary in Raleigh where he was sentenced by the U. S. District Court of North Carolina. Hendricks received several letters from his brother George Hendricks and father Reuben Hendricks, assuring him [Penuel] of efforts being made to have him pardoned. (See Chapter Seven). He was pardoned 12 August 1859.[754]

William Carpenter (aka Bill Johnson), received 5 July 1854, mu/m, larceny, 1y6m.[755]

Alexander A. Thompson, received 5 July 1854, w/m, kidnapping, 4y +$50 fine. On 20 June 1854, Thompson kidnapped a Negro boy, Charles Barnes, and took him to Richmond with the intent of selling him. Thompson said a Mr. Hevner had shown him a bill of sale such that Thompson believed Barnes to be Hevner's slave and said Hevner authorized him to sell Barnes for $800.[756]

George Montgomery, received 7 July 1854, w/m, forgery, 4y. Montgomery's sister was Sarah A. Donnelly of Baltimore. He pardoned 3 March 1857.[757]

CG, born Ireland, received 9 July 1854, w/m, larceny, 2y. CG died 26 November 1854.[758]

Charles Rosa, received 10 July 1854, w/m, receipt of stolen goods, 2y.[759]

Robert Wagner, received 10 July 1854, w/m, larceny, 2y.[760]

George R. King, received 14 July 1854, w/m, larceny, 2y.[761]

Matthew Butler, received 25 July 1854, b/m, larceny, 1y.[762]

Patrick Butler, received 25 July 1854, b/m, larceny, 1y.[763]

Robert Holloway, received 25 July 1854, b/m, larceny, 1y.[764]

William Dant, received 28 July 1854, w/m, assault with intent to rape Mrs. Eliza Ann Fernandis on 14 February 1852, 4y. Mrs. Fernandis was about 25 years old, a resident of the Petersburg, VA area. Early on the morning of 14 February 1852, she arrived by mail boat in Washington and hired a hack to take her to a hotel. Dant, the driver, took her out Seventh Street, nearly to Cross Keys, and tried to rape her. When his attempt failed, he left her on the road. She walked back to town and reported the crime to some postal workers coming in to work. As soon as Dant was seen in town, he was arrested.[765]

Martin King, born DC, received 28 July 1854, w/m, larceny, 2y. King was pardoned 17 July 1855.[766]

Christian Krouse, received 29 July 1854, w/m, assault with intent to rape Ruth Ann Worthington, 2y. Krouse was pardoned 16 November 1855.[767]

William H. Mortimer, received 31 July 1854, w/m, larceny, 1y.[768]

John Rollins (aka Whit Cissell), born DC circa 1830, received 1 August 1854, w/m, arson/larceny, 6y. (Rollins was sentenced to 2y for the larceny and 4y for the arson). Prior to his imprisonment, Rollins was a boatman. In a letter to his uncle Washington Rollins who lived in Washington, DC, John confessed to stealing the money from Mrs. Carrey (?), but claimed innocence in the Swampoodle fire. He was pardoned 30 July 1860.[769]

Henry Williams, received 7 September 1854, mu/boy, larceny, 1y6m. Williams was sentenced to 6 months in jail in March 1854, the jail sentence to be followed by 1y6m in the penitentiary.[770]

George Simms, born MD circa 1814, received 14 December 1854, mu/m, rape of his daughter on 26 July 1854, 15y.[771]

Chapter Thirty-two

INTAKE 1855

Stephen F. Lucas, born Kentucky, received 2 January 1855, w/m, false pretense, 4y.[772]
John Kelly, born PA, received 16 January 1855, w/m, larceny, 1y6m.[773]
Charles O'Donnell, born PA, received 30 January 1855, w/m, passing counterfeit money, 4y. O'Donnell was pardoned 15 August 1855.[774]
GB, born DC, received 7 February 1855, w/m, arson, 4y.[775]
GS, born DC, received 7 February 1855, w/m, arson, 4y.[776]
Henry Byrle (aka Henry Murphy), born VA, received 26 February 1855, mu/m, larceny, 1y6m. Byrle was pardoned 7 June 1855.[777]
Martha A. Safford, born Scotland, received 26 June 1855, w/f, larceny, 3y.[778]
Andrew Kidwell, born DC, received 30 June 1855, w/m, larceny, 1y4m.[779]
Samuel Sheckells, born DC, received 30 June 1855, w/m, larceny, 1y4m.[780]
George Evans, born VA, received 30 June 1855, b/m, burglary, 4y.[781]
GM, born DC, received 7 July 1855, b/m, larceny, 1y3m.[782]
George A. Watson, born DC, received 14 July 1855, w/m, larceny 1y3m. Watson was pardoned 13 September 1856.[783]
JW, born DC, received 17 July 1855, b/m, larceny, 2y.[784]
Joseph Hutt (aka Joseph Williams), born DC, received 17 July 1855, b/m, false pretense, 2y.[785]
John Brown, born VA, received 20 July 1855, mu/m, larceny, 1y. Brown stole a coat and pantaloons from George S. Taliaferro.[786]
Washington Taylor, born MD, received 23 July 1855, b/m, false pretense— obtaining groceries under false pretenses, 1y.[787]
John F. Bell, born DC circa 1819, received 22 September 1855, b/m, assault/battery, 5y.[788]
John M. Weeks, born VA, received 19 October 1855, w/m, mail robbery, 10y. Weeks was convicted by the U.S. Court for the Western District of VA) and worked in the carpentry shop at the pen. He was pardoned 3 April 1858.[789]
John W. Moore, born MD, received 13 December 1855, w/boy, larceny, 1y.[790]
Joseph Kershner, born Germany, received 17 December 1855, w/boy, horse stealing, 5y.[791]
William Dent, born VA, received 19 December 1855, b/m, 2 cases of larceny, 2y6m.[792]

John Francis Jones (aka John Sheaks), born DC, received 22 December 1855, w/boy, larceny of patrie monnaie and a $5 note, 1y.[793]

Sarah Dorsey, born DC, received 22 December 1855, b/girl, larceny of a pair of stockings, a pair of drawers, a handkerchief, and a bracelet (total value $7.50), 1y.[794]

Mary Butler, born DC, received 23 December 1855, b/f, larceny, 1y.[795]

Charles White, born Vermont, received 28 December 1855, w/m, larceny, 2y6m.[796]

Lewis Bell, born DC, received 29 December 1855, b/m, 2 cases larceny, 2y6m.[797]

John Mager, born Ireland, received 29 December 1855, w/m, larceny, 1y.[798]

William Eliason (aka Bill Lawrence), received 29 December 1855, b/boy, larceny, 1y6m.[799]

John Bashler, born Germany circa 1838, received 17 December 1855, w/m, horse stealing, 5y, convicted by the U.S. Court for the Western District of VA).[800]

Chapter Thirty-three

INTAKE 1856

Adele Williams, born DC, received 1 January 1856, b/girl, larceny, 1y. Williams was pardoned 3 September 1856.[801]

John Jones, born MD circa 1834, received 4 January 1856, w/m, arson, 5y. Jones was a bricklayer before his imprisonment. His wife's name was Sophia, and he had a sister named Henrietta.[802]

George Raglan, born DC, received 15 January 1856, mu/m, manslaughter, 8y.[803]

John T. Russell, born MD, received 26 January 1856, w/m, forgery, 3y. Russell was pardoned 15 March 1856.[804]

Hezekiah Walker, born MD, received 24 January 1856, w/m, assault/battery with intent to kill, 4y. Walker worked in the carpentry shop at the pen.[805]

Charles P. Parker, born DC, received 11 March 1856, b/m, larceny, 1y6m.[806]

Vandora Otis, born Havana, Cuba, received 12 March 1856, assault/battery with intent to kill Henry E. Robinson, 4y, Otis died in the pen of general scrofula which had attacked both lungs in 1858.[807]

John Anderson, born VA, received 16 March 1856, b/boy, larceny, 1y.[808]

William Moody, born DC, received 24 March 1856, b/boy, larceny, 1y.[809]

William W. B. Edwards, born England, received 25 March 1856, w/m, manslaughter, 7y. On 11 Oct 1857, Edwards tried to escape with convict Demaine. As a result, he was "now in the dungeons." He was pardoned 13 April 1861.[810]

Caleb Barton, born MD, received 23 June 1856, b/m, larceny, 1y. Barton was found guilty 24 March 1856 of petit larceny and sentenced to 3m in jail and also guilty of grand larceny and sentenced to 1y in pen after his jail time was completed.[811]

John Foreman, born DC, received 24 June 1856, b/boy, larceny, 1y. Foreman had ulcers and died at the pen on Thursday, 8 October 1857. He was buried in the cemetery "attached to prison."[812]

David Dunigan, born DC, received 26 June 1856, w/m, assault/battery with intent to kill Officer A. E. L. Keese, 3y. Dunigan was pardoned 3 March 1857.[813]

George Humphreys, born DC, received 28 June 1856, b/m, larceny, 1y.[814]

Bridget Curtis, born Ireland, received 30 June 1856, w/f, larceny of $14 worth of goods, 1y.[815]

John Brandt, born DC, received 27 June 1856, w/boy, 2 cases larceny, 2y6m.[816]

James W. Smallwood, born VA, received 8 July 1856, b/m, larceny, 1y.[817]

William Lyons, born DC circa 1830, received 30 July 1856, w/m, burglary, 4y. Prior to imprisonment, Lyons was a midshipman in the Navy. He was 24 when he was convicted of stealing a watch and sentenced to 4y in the pen. Shortly after he joined the Navy, he got drunk and stole the watch. He was a stubborn and unruly prisoner, frequently in irons for insubordination. On 13 July 1857, Warden Thornley wrote the penitentiary physician of his concern about Lyons who "has frequently said he would plunge a knife in the heart of any one who would detain him in prison." Dr. Garnett replied that he felt Lyons to be both mentally and physically fit for work.[818]

George Watson (aka William H. Taylor), born MD circa 1820, received 3 August 1856, w/m, false pretense, 4y. Prior to imprisonment, Watson was a stonecutter.[819]

John E. Bailey, born DC circa 1820, received 8 August 1856, w/m, larceny, 6y. Bailey stole from John E. Latham's store on 24 March 1856 and George W. Hinton's store 19 October 1855.[820]

Thomas (Henry) Croggin, born DC, received 8 August 1856, larceny, 6y. Croggin stole goods (vests, coats, pantaloons, silk suspenders, vest patterns, umbrellas, etc.) from George W. Hinton's store 19 October 1855 and also from M. Hoffa. Croggin had been one of the most daring of the Nailor gang of burglars. He died in the penitentiary on 3 July 1859. He was about 24 years old. Rev. George W. Dorrance officiated at the funeral which was held in the chapel at the penitentiary. The body, in a "handsome" walnut coffin was given to relatives after the service and they buried him in the Methodist Burying Ground. Croggin's mother lived in Baltimore.[821](See also Chapter Seven)

John W. Demaine, born VA circa 1836, received 10 August 1856, w/m, larceny, 6y. Demaine was guilty of robbing John E. Latham's store on 24 March 1856 and of stealing from George W. Hinton's store 19 October 1855. Demaine was an engraver before imprisonment, and was the son of W. W. Demaine. On 11 October 1857, Demaine tried to escape and was reported by Warden Thornley to be "now in the dungeons." Demaine was pardoned 30 September 1861.[822]

Richard Thomas, born DC circa 1837, received 31 August 1856, b/m, larceny, 5y.[823]

J. Contee, born DC, received 12 September 1856, b/m, larceny 1y6m.[824]

Thomas Kernan, born Ireland, received 6 December 1856, w/m. larceny, 1y.[825]

William Chase, born DC, received 9 December 1856, b/m, assault with intent to kill, 2y.[826]

Mary F. Wheeler, born VA, received 9 December 1856, larceny, 1y6m.[827]

Thomas Johnson, born Ireland, received 19 December 1856, w/m, larceny, 1y6m. Johnson worked in the carpentry shop at the pen.[828]

TM, born VA, received 20 December 1856, b/m, larceny, 1y6m.[829]

Charles Campbell, born VA, received 20 December 1856, w/m, larceny, 1y6m.[830]

Lorenzo (Loza) P. Burke, born VA circa 1833, received 22 December 1856, w/m, manslaughter, 5y. Burke and George Cornwell (following entry) were accused of murdering Pasqual DeFalco on 2 September 1856. Testimony in the case indicated that DeFalco asked Burke and Cornwall for the time. Burke and Cornwell had been drinking and started beating DeFalco, a musician in the Marine band. Dr. Miller visited DeFalco on 3 September 1856, the day after the assault, and his head and face were very bruised. A small wound was behind his left ear, and severe wounds were on the left side of his head and on his left breast. Burke was a U.S. Marine before imprisonment and was pardoned 14 October 1861.[831]

George Cornwell, born NY circa 1831, received 22 December 1856, w/m, manslaughter, 5y. (Accused of murdering Pasqual DeFalco. See Lorenzo Burke, previous entry, for details.) Cornwell was a U.S. Marine before imprisonment and was pardoned 14 October 1861.[832]

John Barkman, born DC, received 30 December 1856, w/m, larceny, 1y6m. Barkman robbed Peddicord's bacon stall in Centre Market.[833]

John Wroe, born VA, received 30 December 1856, w/m, larceny, 1y6m. Wroe robbed Peddicord's bacon stall in Centre Market.[834]

Phillip Killian (aka William Johnson), born Ireland, received 30 December 1856, w/m, larceny, 1y6m. Killian robbed Peddicord's bacon stall in Centre Market.[835]

Chapter Thirty-four

INTAKE 1857

John Kelly, born VA circa 1827, received 6 January 1857, w/m, larceny, 4y. Kelly was a barber and a broom-maker in the penitentiary.[836]

Jacob Brieberg, born Germany, received 6 January 1857, w/m, horse theft, 2y.[837]

Richard Davison, born VA, received 16 January 1857, w/m, larceny, 2y. Davison worked in the carpentry shop in the penitentiary.[838]

Henry F. Koss, born Sweden, received 14 March 1857, w/m, larceny, 3y. Koss was guilty on 3 charges of stealing from the stores of Taylor, Maury, R. Farnham, and J. Shillington.[839]

John Robertson (aka John Roberts), born PA, received 14 March 1857, w/boy, larceny 1y. Robertson was about 15 yrs. old when convicted of stealing several brass cocks from the Georgetown Gas Company.[840]

Pink Coakley, born MD, received 14 March 1857, b/m, larceny, 1y.[841]

William F. Johnson, born DC, received 19 March 1857, b/boy, larceny, 1y6m.[842]

James Wilson, born Ireland circa 1828, received 20 March 1857, w/m, larceny (3 cases of burglary), 6y. Prior to imprisonment, Wilson was a ship carpenter. Wilson escaped 22 October 1860. A $250 reward was offered for his capture. He was described as 32 years old, 5 ft. 6⅛ inches tall, and having a 10¼" long foot. He had a flesh-colored mole on his left calf.[843]

JW, born NY, received 20 March 1857, w/m, larceny, 6y.[844]

Laura Turner, born DC, received 1 April 1857, b/f, larceny of $7 mantilla, 3y. Turner had a baby on Sunday, 6 October 1857 while incarcerated at the penitentiary.[845]

George W. Mahoney, born DC, received April 1857, b/boy, larceny, 1y.[846]

John Small, born Philadelphia, PA circa 1836, received 6 June 1857, w/m, larceny, 4y. Prior to imprisonment, Small was a brick maker. Small was sentenced on 6 December 1856 to serve six months in jail before going to the pen. On 22 October 1860, Small escaped and a $100 reward was offered for his capture. He was described as being 5 ft. 6⅝ inches tall, and having a foot that measured 10⅛ inches. His father, Patrick Small, reportedly lived in Indiana, and his mother lived in Philadelphia. A "J" was tattooed on his right arm at the elbow, and he had scars on his head caused by "blows from a club."[847]

James Gavin, born PA circa 1835, received 6 June 1857, w/m, larceny, 4y. Prior to imprisonment, Gavin was a brick maker. Gavin was sentenced on 6 December 1856 to serve six months in jail before going to the pen.[848]

William Carpenter, born VA, received 18 June 1857, b/m, larceny, 1y. Carpenter stole a $6 piece of gingham from Jacob C. Gibson.[849]

Thomas Fletcher, born VA circa 1836, received 22 June 1857, b/m, assault/battery with intent to rape Ellen Bruce (b/f), 3y.[850]

Joseph Penny, born DC, received 22 June 1857, b/m, larceny, 1y6m. Penny stole a $6.50 pair of boots, a $2.50 pair of shoes, $3.50 gaiters, all property of Francis Thomas, shoemaker. Penny had previously served in the penitentiary for larceny.[851]

Emily Bryant, born VA, received 3 July 1857, b/f, larceny, 1y6m. Bryant stole two silver spoons and a silver cup, property of Charles and John Abert.[852]

John Butler (aka John Williams), born DC circa 1838, received 28 July 1857, b/m, larceny of several hundred dollars from R. W. Carter, 3y.[853]

Richard P. Jones (aka Wrangy), born MD circa 1833, received 23 September 1857, w/m, assault/battery with intent to kill Rose Bell, 4y. Mr. Ward, the jailor, said Bell and Elizabeth Staples came to the jail on 17 April 1857 and asked for Jones. He was brought to them and when Ward turned, he heard a scream. Looking back, Ward saw Bell on her knees, bleeding. As Bell had prepared to leave, Jones asked her for a kiss. When she bent to get the kiss, he took a razor from his pocket and cut her throat. He would have killed her had her breastpin not interfered with the razor. Ward asked Jones why he did that, and he said that he loved her and had asked her to marry him and she had refused. Bell (aka Rebecca Martin) said that Jones often acted mentally unstable around her and hadn't asked her to marry him. He was just jealous. John Sullivan, a fellow jail mate, said Jones bit his nails constantly, and in Sullivan's mind, that confirmed Jones' insanity. In March 1859, the penitentiary doctor, Dr. Alexander Y. P. Garnett, Warden Sengstack, and Deputy Warden Sengstack all agreed that Jones was insane and dangerous and he was sent to the insane asylum. He escaped from the insane asylum later that same year and was caught after being at large for several months. Officers at the jail where he was briefly held awaiting return to the asylum, disputed his insanity, feeling that he was as sane as anybody. The *Evening Star* reported on 27 June 1859 that Jones escaped from the insane asylum again. Convinced he was cured, doctors at the asylum planned to return Jones to the penitentiary. Even though they tried to keep this information secret, Jones found out and escaped before he could be sent back. He was caught, however, and returned to the pen where he was pardoned by President Lincoln on 27 June 1861.[854]

William W. Cline, born PA circa 1817, received 23 September 1857, w/m, felony/counterfeiting coin in Wheeling, WV, 10y. Cline was a blacksmith in the penitentiary and was pardoned 6 March 1861.[855]

John Thompson, born DC, received 12 December 1857, b/m, larceny, 1y. On 4 August 1857, Thompson stole clothes ($20.62 value) from the house of Dr. Owen Munson, 338 Pennsylvania Avenue. The clothes were taken to the store of Mr. Mela on Louisiana Avenue and sold for $4.[856]

Matthew Butler, born DC, received 12 December 1857, b/m, larceny, 1y. Butler stole a $10 banjo from William H. Baum on 16 August 1857.[857]

GN, born NC, received 12 December 1857, w/m, passing counterfeit coin, 3y.[858]

George Handy, born DC circa 1836, received 17 December 1857, b/m, larceny, 1y6m. Handy stole $14 worth of clothes. Handy died on 15 August 1858 of an enlarged heart and general dropsy.[859]

Robert Cross, born DC circa 1834, received 22 December 1857, w/m, assault/battery with intent to kill Officer Thomas H. Robinson of the 6th Police District on 30 June 1857, 8y. According to Officer B. Donnelly, a member of the Auxiliary Guard, he [Donnelly] went into Middleton's Restaurant on 9th and C Streets where Cross asked him to drink with him. Donnelly refused and, knowing there was a warrant for Cross' arrest, went to George H. Phillips, Deputy Marshall of DC, and told him that Cross was in town. Officers were sent to arrest Cross, and after chasing Cross for several blocks, the Guard caught up to him in an alley. Cross drew a pistol and said he'd kill whomever tried to arrest him. The chase resumed and Officer Robinson was shot his forefinger, cheek, and near his ear. Dr. Dunhamel extracted the bullets. Cross was a plasterer before imprisonment. He was pardoned 23 October 1860. While in prison, he wrote a poem about trying to escape (see Chapter Seven).[860]

Thomas Richards, born MD, received 22 December 1857, b/m, larceny, 1y. Richard stole a $7.50 pair of boots, property of August Burchell on 3 November 1857.[861]

Edward Mahoney, born Ireland, received 22 December 1857, w/m, larceny, 1y. Mahoney stole a coat and a revolver from Hillery Hutchins.[862]

Charles Brown, born Ireland, received 22 December 1857, w/m, larceny, 1y. Brown stole a coat and a revolver from Hillery Hutchins.[863]

William Jones, born VA, received 24 December 1857, b/m, larceny, 1y. Jones stole a $5 note, property of Frederick Stinger.[864]

Catherine O. Rose, born Canada, received 28 December 1857, w/f, larceny, 2y. Rose stole three $20 gold pieces and three $1 gold pieces, property of William G. Phillips.[865]

Chapter Thirty-five

INTAKE 1858

Joseph Cunningham, received 6 January 1858, w/m, two cases of larceny, 6y. One case involved the theft of 8 hats ($12). On 26 April 1859, Cunningham was a victim of a gunshot wound while in the penitentiary. When prisoner William Lyons broke the rules and scuffled with prison personnel, Cunningham was caught between Lyons and Deputy Warden Sengstack, Jr., who fired his gun and accidentally hit Cunningham. Cunningham was pardoned on 13 October 1859 as he had been an obedient prisoner and had come to the warden's aid in the April 1859 prison fray.[866]

Isaac Lambert, born VA circa 1835, received 6 January 1858, w/m, larceny, 6y. Prior to imprisonment, Lambert was a stage driver. Lambert was pardoned 20 June 1862.[867]

George W. Humphries, born DC, received 6 January 1858, mu/m, larceny, 1y.[868]

William Ewing, born Ireland, received 6 January 1858, w/m, burglary, 4y.[869]

James Thompson, born DC, received 7 January 1858, b/m, larceny, 2y. Thompson stole 10 bushels of wheat and 2 bushels of corn, property of William T. Aud.[870]

John Holly, born DC, received 7 January 1858, b/m, larceny, 2y. Holly stole 4 hogs ($40 value), property of Bruce Dent, on 4 October 1857.[871]

Samuel Blewett, born VA circa 1841, received 10 May 1858, w/m, mail robbery, 10y. Blewett was convicted at the Western District of VA US District Court. Blewett was a mail rider before imprisonment and worked in the prison tailor shop. On 22 August 1861, Blewett was pardoned by President Lincoln.[872]

Caleb Batson, born DC, received 7 January 1858, b/m, larceny, 2y. Batson stole 4 hogs ($40 value), property of Bruce Dent, on 4 October 1857.[873]

Gusty Price, born DC, received 7 January 1858, b/m, larceny, 2y. Price stole 10 bushels of wheat and 2 bushels of corn, property of William T. Aud.[874]

William H. Douglass, born VA, received 8 January 1858, b/m, larceny, 1y3m. Douglass stole a $20 coat and a 25-cent handkerchief, property of Henry A. Bills. Douglass was moved to the insane asylum 3 March 1859.[875]

George Gaines, born DC, received 8 January 1858, b/m, larceny, 1y. Gaines stole an $8 gentleman's shawl.[876]

George Krauss, born VA circa 1830, received 15 January 1858, w/m, intent to kill George E. Hillery, 5y. Before imprisonment, Krauss was a fisherman. Krauss was pardoned 6 March 1861.[877]

Mary McPherson, born DC circa 1832, received 30 January 1858, b/f, manslaughter of Nancy Buchanan, 6y. On 7 September 1857, McPherson beat Buchanan so as to cause her death approximately two weeks after the beating. According to witness Polly Buchanan, about 9 a.m. on a Monday, McPherson entered the house, went directly to the kitchen, got a piece of wooden sleeper from under the floor, struck it on the wall to break it, and took a piece of the board and hit Nancy over the head with it. Then McPherson hit Buchanan over the head with a chair which split in two as it hit Buchanan's head. Buchanan fell, skull split open, and asked McPherson why she was beating her again.

At the time of this beating, Buchanan was recuperating from a recent illness. She was about 25 years old, single, small, delicate, and of frail health. She suffered bowel problems, headaches, and piles, and was pregnant enough to feel movement, until a few days before she died when she noticed there was no longer any movement of the child within her.

Witness Dr. John E. Willet who attended Buchanan after the beating said she had a number of wounds on the right side of her head, several bruises, no use of her right arm, a fracture of the right skull, and her hair was mashed on to her brain.

Witness Ann Brown, who lived in the same house as Buchanan, said McPherson had brought some clothes for Buchanan to wash. When McPherson discovered that Buchanan had torn some of the clothing, she beat Buchanan over the head with a board. Buchanan said she tore the clothes up because her mother had no money to buy liquor for her.[878]

Joseph Ward, born DC c. 1839, received 16 January 1858, b/m, mayhem, 4y. Ward put out the left eye of Lorenzo Seymour with a knife on 29 November 1857. Ward escaped from the penitentiary on 24 July 1861, was returned on 12 October 1861, and discharged 12 April 1862. He was a blacksmith in the penitentiary.[879]

John Ogden, born DC, received 16 January 1858, b/m, larceny, 2y. Ogden stole 4 hogs, property of Bruce Dent.[880]

Nathan Allen, born MD, received 19 January 1858, b/m, grand larceny, 1y6m.[881]

Thomas Humit, born Germany circa 1833, received 8 April 1858, w/m, burglary, 3y.[882]

Jacob Keppell, born Germany, received 27 January 1858, w/m, larceny, 2y. Keppell stole a gold watch and gold chain (total value $50), property of James I. Lawn. Lawn, a citizen of Baltimore, had stopped at Keppell's hotel at the old rail depot on Pennsylvania Avenue, because he was sick. Lawn's friends moved him to another place shortly after the theft occurred and Lawn died a day or two later. Keppell was about 60 years old when sentenced to the pen.[883]

Benjamin Woods, born DC circa 1834, received 29 January 1858, w/m, manslaughter of Samuel Brown on 17 September 1857, 8y. Prior to imprisonment, Woods was a plasterer. He was pardoned 10 June 1861.[884]

James Kearney, born Ireland, received 30 January 1858, w/m, larceny, 1y. Kearney stole a $5 cloak, property of Col. H. R. Craig.[885]

Michael McIntire, born Ireland, received 1 February 1858, w/m, larceny, 1y3m. McIntire stole an infant's embroidered dress and two shirts. He was an invalid while in the penitentiary.[886]

Charles Davis, born DC, received 3 February 1858, b/boy, larceny, 1y4m. Davis stole a $15 watch and a $25 gold chain, both property of Samuel Samstag on 21 January 1858.[887]

Benjamin Robinson, born DC circa 1839, received 8 February 1858, w/m, manslaughter of Thomas Turner, 3y. Robinson and Turner were playing "bandy" when an argument ensued. Robinson dared Turner to hit him, and when Turner did, Robinson took a stone the size of a paving stone and hit Turner in the side of the head behind his ear. A few days later, Turner died.[888]

GL, born NY, received 10 February 1858, w/m, larceny, 1y.[889]

William Garner, born DC, received 12 February 1858, w/m, assault/battery with intent to kill Otto Sherman, 4y. Sherman, a Marine, was walking along with two sailors and two Marines when he got separated from them and saw his friend being beaten by three men, one of whom was Garner. Sherman tried to help and Garner threw a brick at him, breaking Sherman's nose, wounding his cheek, and knocking him out. As he was throwing a rock at Marine Timothy McCarty, Garner told Officer Joseph Williamson he "was only killing Marines."[890]

On 11 February 1858, Dr. A. J. Semmes forwarded penitentiary physician Dr. Garnett, a request from Garner's mother that Garner be supplied with warm underclothing which she would provide, if necessary. In 1856, Garner had suffered a "severe attack of inflammatory rheumatism," and she hoped to prevent a recurrence by seeing that he was warmly dressed. Garner was pardoned on 10 February 1860.[891]

John Cunningham, born MD circa 1842, received 2 April 1858, w/boy, assault/battery with intent to kill on two counts, 8y. Cunningham committed an assault/battery on a Negro boy and was sentenced on 9 March 1858 to 3y in the penitentiary. On 10 March 1858, he was convicted of assault/battery with intent to kill Edward Burnham. Burnham was an out-of-towner who was in Mr. Kirby's Restaurant when Cunningham came in, provoked a fight, and shot Burnham with a pistol. Two bullets went through the breast of Burnham's overcoat. For this crime, Cunningham was sentenced to serve 5y in the penitentiary to begin after his 3y sentence (above) ended. Prior to imprisonment, Cunningham was a barkeeper.[892]

Robert Richardson, born VA, received 2 April 1858, b/boy, larceny, 1y3m.[893]

Sonny Jackson, born DC, received 2 April 1858, b/boy, larceny, 1y3m.[894]

Charles Dalman (aka Charles T. Ellman), born Ireland, received 2 April 1858, w/m, larceny, 2y. On 17 March 1858, Dalman stole two pistols, two swords, one scabbard, one clock, one hat, etc., property of Dr. Edward Maynard.[895]

CH, born Germany, received 8 April 1858, w/m, burglary, 3y.[896]

Louisa Parker, born VA, received 10 April 1858, b/f, assault/battery with intent to kill, 2y.[897]

Thomas Connelly, born MD circa 1842, received 12 April 1858, w/m, assault/battery with intent to kill Henry Brooks, 3y.[898]

Frances Penny, born DC circa 1838, received 26 April 1858, mu/f, assault/battery with intent to kill Julia Bigley (w/f), 3y. Penny's husband was John Johnson.[899]

Benjamin Ogle, born DC circa 1829, received 3 May 1858, w/m, manslaughter of Johnny Webb in January 1858 in Georgetown. 8y. Ogle's lawyers sought to prove Ogle innocent by reason of insanity. Witness Anna Harrison, Ogle's mother-in-law, said he was acting odd the day of the murder—like he was in another world. Witness George Ellis, trying to corroborate Ogle's insanity plea, testified that Ogle's aunt tried to hang herself; however, witness John Clemenson, married to this particular aunt for 37 years, testified that she never acted insane or tried to hang herself. Clemenson and his wife had 12 children. None were insane nor was there any record of insanity in the family. After four hours of deliberation, the jury found Ogle guilty of manslaughter. Prior to imprisonment, Ogle was a painter. He was pardoned 22 June 1861.[900]

Charles Hoffman, born Germany, received 5 May 1858, w/m, rape, 15y. Hoffman, along with seven others was charged with raping Victoria Fugleman on 14 April 1858. Fugleman was not so much a victim as it seemed, as she had expected payment for her services. She testified that she knew three or four of the men and had had "liaisons" before with one or two of them. She considered the whole thing a joke and only decided to file charges when the police became involved. Hoffman was pardoned 21 March 1860.[901]

John A. Sitzer, born Germany, received 5 May 1858, w/m, rape, 12y. Sitzer, along with seven others was charged with raping Victoria Fugleman on 14 April 1858. Fugleman was not as much a victim as it seemed, as she had expected payment for her services. She testified that she knew three or four of the men and had had "liaisons" before with one or two of them. She considered the whole thing a joke and only decided to file charges when the police became involved. Sitzer was pardoned 21 March 1860.[902]

David Franck, born Germany, received 5 May 1858, w/m, rape, 12y. Franck, along with seven others was charged with raping Victoria Fugleman on 14 April 1858. Fugleman was not as much a victim as it seemed, as she had expected payment for her services. She testified that she knew three or four of the men and had had "liaisons" before with one or two of them. She considered the whole thing a joke and only decided to file charges when the police became involved. Franck was pardoned 21 March 1860.[903]

William Schmidt, born Germany, received 5 May 1858, w/m, rape, 12y. Schmidt, along with seven others was charged with rape on Victoria Fugleman on 14 April 1858. Fugleman was not as much a victim as it seemed, as she had expected payment for her services. She testified that she knew three or four of the men and had had "liaisons" before with one or two of them. She considered the whole thing a joke and only decided to file charges when the police became involved. Schmidt was pardoned 21 March 1860.[904]

Herman Julius, born Germany, received 5 May 1858, w/m, rape, 12y. Julius, along with seven others was charged with raping Victoria Fugleman on 14 April 1858. Fugleman was not as much a victim as it seemed, as she had expected payment for her services. She testified that she knew three or four of the men and had had "liaisons" before with one or two of them. She considered the whole thing a joke and only decided to file charges when the police became involved. Julius was pardoned 21 March 1860.[905]

John Hughes, born Ireland, received 6 May 1858, w/m, larceny, 2y. Around Christmas 1857, Hughes stole eight $5 notes; one $20 gold piece; four $2.50 gold pieces; three gold dollars; one fifty-cent piece, and a pocketbook, all property of Patrick Hand.[906]

Joseph Bulger, born DC, received 8 May 1858, b/m, larceny, 1y3m.[907]

LB, born VA, received 10 May 1858, w/boy, mail robbery, 10y.[908]

George Kreiger (aka George Williams), born MD circa 1839, received 18 May 1858, w/m, manslaughter of William Farrell on 22 February 1858, 8y. Witness Patrick Farrell, William's brother, testified that on 22 February 1858, he and his brother were returning home after work around 3 p.m. and met Berry Knight and a friend of Knight's on the road. The Farrell brothers were invited for a drink and all stopped at Vulcan House for the drink. While there, two men, one of whom was Kreiger, came in to the bar. William Farrell and Knight's friend left the room and conversed in private. Kreiger hit one of his drinking buddies and William Farrell then hit Kreiger. Kreiger stabbed William Farrell in the back with a 7" long Bowie knife and ran. William Farrell died at his home on 23 February 1858 around 11:30 p.m. Witness James Holmes testified Kreiger worked at the Baltimore and Ohio Railroad with him and that he had known Kreiger for eight years. Witness Scott Holmes, Kreiger's brother in law, testified that he had known Kreiger for 10 years, and Kreiger was nicknamed "the preacher" due to his quiet living. At some time prior to his imprisonment, Kreiger was a cigar maker. He was pardoned 12 August 1862.[909]

James Starbuck, born England circa 1824, received 5 June 1858, w/m, mail robbery, 10y. Prior to imprisonment, Starbuck was a physician.[910]

Clinton Smith, born VA, received 2 June 1858, mu/m, larceny, 1y. Smith stole a set of harnesses from wood merchants, Messrs. Galt.[911]

JP, born MD, received 6 June 1858, w/m, larceny, 1y.[912]

Johanna Hornsburg, born MD, received 9 July 1858, b/f, larceny of a dress, 1y.[913]

William Rawlings, born DC circa 1836, received 9 July 1858, b/m, larceny of two sets of harnesses ($60), property of George M. Boatman, 2y.[914]

Richard Thomas, born DC circa 1834, received 9 July 1858, b/m, larceny of two sets of harnesses ($60), property of George M. Boatman, 2y.[915]

James P. Devlin, born DC, received 19 June 1858, w/m, manslaughter, of Thomas G. Berry, 4y. James P. Devlin and his brother John S. Devlin were charged with the 6 April 1858 murder of Thomas Berry. James P. Devlin, the younger Devlin, stabbed Berry five times--once through the lung and heart, once in the shoulder blade, twice in the ribs, and once through the left arm above the elbow-- with a Spanish dirk knife while John Devlin held him. In addition, Berry's left eye and left temple were bruised, according to the doctor who examined him after he was shot. Berry was about 5ft. 9 inches tall, 160 lbs., and had well-developed muscles. Witness Mary Berry testified that she married Berry in August 1851 in Philadelphia where, at the time of the trial on 1 July 1858, she still lived. On 23 August 1851, Berry left Mary to go to Washington, saying that he would send for her in four weeks. He returned the following February and then left again without her. According to Mary Berry, Thomas Berry was a large man, fair-skinned, sandy-haired, and blue-eyed, who professed to be a U.S. Senate messenger. The day before he left Philadelphia the second time, he had wounded Mary on her breast with a knife and threatened to kill her, so she never went to DC after him. She stayed in Philadelphia where she made caps to support herself. Mary Berry further testified that Thomas Berry married Fanny Devlin 19 August 1852 in Washington after a four-month acquaintance. Witness Mary A. Devlin, Fanny's mother, said she didn't consider Thomas Berry to be her real son-in-law because he had another wife in Pennsylvania. Thomas Berry came several times to see Fanny and on 6 April 1858, Berry accused Fanny's brother James of mistreating her. After Congress had adjourned for the day on April 6th, Berry went to Hamlin's Restaurant on Capitol Hill where the stabbing took place. James and John Devlin were there. John Devlin was not a drinking man, and to many seemed weak-minded, according to witness William Wharton. [John] "could never connect two sentences together."[916] Witness Dr. A. W. Miller testified that he was often called to treat John for restlessness/nervous diseases, etc., and said he had a medical disorder called "nervous sanguinous,"[917] which meant he was "easily excited, quick to take offence." On 8 July 1858, James P. Devlin was charged with manslaughter. At his sentencing, he spoke of his mother, saying he had no one but her to live for, and he would be miserable if sent away from her.

August Heissler, born at sea (German descent) circa 1833, received 6 August 1858, w/m, manslaughter/robbery, 15y. On 3 April 1858, around 9 p.m., Marcellus Stoops and Frederick Manyette were walking on NY Avenue near 9th Street when they were accosted by a party of young men, and Stoops, around 20 years old, was shot and killed by a bullet wound in his right chest. Police arrested William Johnson (who supposedly fired the gun), George Johnson, Van Loman Johnson, Augustus Heissler, and Robert Squibb.

Earlier that same evening, a gang, two of whom Cornell identified as William and George Johnson, robbed Cornell. Cornell testified that as he was going out 14th Street, he saw two men coming who he thought were college students. As he approached them, they separated so he could pass between the two of them. When he reached the Catholic cemetery, he turned to notice they were following him. They asked him for some chewing tobacco and chatted a moment. As he was about to enter the college grounds, one of the men stepped in front of him and asked him if he were associated with the Northern Liberties Fire Engine. When he said "no," three other men who were nearby, said "yes, he is." The two who had followed Cornell, then asked him for a quarter for a drink, which he gave them. Then they wanted more money and held a pistol to Cornell's head while reaching into his pockets and taking $2-$3, his $15 watch, and his breastpin. Cornell testified that Van Loman Johnson and his father offered to give him $250 to leave town and not testify against George Johnson. Heissler and Johnson were sentenced to 8y in the penitentiary for manslaughter of Stoops and 7y for robbing Cornell. On hearing the sentence, Heissler smiled indifferently as he left the courtroom. He was pardoned 15 April 1862.[918]

George W. Johnson, born DC circa 1839, received 6 August 1858, w/m, manslaughter/robbery, 15y. (An accomplice of August Heissler, see preceding entry). Johnson took the sentence very hard. He escaped 23 October 1860 and was captured on 15 November 1860 in Philadelphia. The $500 reward for his capture described him as 21 years old at the time of escape, and a carpenter by trade. It was noted that his parents and brothers lived in DC. On his right arm was tattooed a "wreath" inscribed with "JTJ" and a small heart and small circle. On his left arm was tattooed a crucifix and "GWJ," and on his left knee, a small dot was tattooed. He had sandy hair, light eyebrows, was 5 ft. 2½ inches and his foot measured 9⅞inches.[919]

Henry Williams, born Germany circa 1835, received 6 August 1858, w/m, manslaughter of Reeve Lewis, 8y. Williams and Charles Barrett were charged with the shooting murder of Reeve Lewis. on 27 March 1858 between 12-1 a.m. on Capitol Hill. Witness Dr. Noble Young testified that Lewis had a bullet in his right buttock which could not be found until the autopsy was performed. The bullet had severely fractured Lewis' hipbone. There was no evidence that Williams fired the gun; consequently, he was charged with manslaughter rather than murder. Charles Barrett, on the other hand, was charged with murder and burst into tears at the verdict. Later in the jail, Williams went to Barrett to console him, putting his arm around his shoulder. Barrett cried some more, was said to be "unnerved" and in much agony.

Williams was brought from the penitentiary in January 1860 and tried for assault/battery with intent to kill Mr. Entwistle who was badly wounded the night Lewis was killed and had to be confined to bed for several months. Williams was found guilty and sentenced to another 8y in the penitentiary, time to begin following the completion of his present eight-year term.[920]

John Roach, born Ireland, received 7 August 1858, w/boy about 13 years old, assault/battery with intent to kill Thomas C. Magruder, 3y. Roach was pardoned by President Buchanan on 2 March 1861.[921]

Thomas Hanahan, born Ireland, received 7 August 1858, w/boy about 16 years old, assault/battery with intent to kill Thomas C. Magruder, 3y. Hanahan was pardoned by President Buchanan on 2 March 1861.[922]

W. G. Williams, born VA, received 5 October 1858, w/m, assault/battery with intent to kill, 3y.[923]

John P. Millard, born OH, received 5 October 1858, w/m, convicted at Wheeling for passing counterfeit coin and sentenced to 2y in the pen. Millard was formerly of Marietta, OH. A letter from O. L. Clarke of Marietta, OH was written to the warden on behalf of Millard's mother who wished to know what she had to do to get her son pardoned. Clarke mentioned that Millard was once Deputy Sheriff in Marietta, and once collected money for "some of the heaviest business firms,"[924] always totally responsible and proper with the money.

Charles H. Barrett, born MD, received 4 November 1858, w/m, murder, Life. In the early morning hours of 27 March 1858, Reeve Lewis was murdered on Capitol Hill. Henry Williams (see 6 August 1858, above) and Charles Barrett were charged with the murder. Trial witness Dr. Noble Young testified that Lewis had a bullet in his right buttock which could not be found until the autopsy was performed. The bullet had severely fractured Lewis' hipbone. Barrett was charged with murder and burst into tears at the verdict. Motion was made for a new trial; however, no reason could be found to justify a new trial, and the verdict stood. Barrett was sentenced to be hung on 22 October 1858. His sentence was later commuted to "Life in prison."[925]

Thomas H. Dunbar, born MD, received 10 December 1858, b/m, larceny 2y.[926]

Thomas Pormley, born Ireland, received 10 December 1858, w/m, horsetheft.[927]

William Hooper (aka William Jones), born DC, received 19 December 1858, w/m, larceny of a $125 horse belonging to James B. Greenwell, 4y.[928]

Moses Mozine, born DC, received 20 December 1858, w/m, larceny of a $12 shawl, property of George M. Arth, 2y6m. Mozine and John Carberry agreed to drive Arth to his home at the Navy Yard, with a stop on Capitol Hill, for $1. After making the stop at Capitol Hill, they wanted another $1 to go the rest of the way. Mozine and Carberry grabbed Arth by the neck and ripped the shawl off him. Arth, trying to get it back, fell down and was knocked unconscious. When the came to, Mozine and Carberry were gone.[929]

Anthony Ducket (aka Arthur Duckt), born MD, received 20 December 1858, w/m, horse stealing, 3y.[930]

Lewis Franck, born Prussia, received 23 December 1858, w/m, larceny of gold and silver coins, jewelry and clothing of Charles Erbach, 2y6m. Franck was an invalid in the penitentiary.[931]

John Dandridge, born DC, received 23 December 1858, b/m, grand larceny of coats, etc of N. J. Porter and Mr. Fay, 1y3m.[932]

John D. Baptiste, born France, received 24 December 1858, w/m, larceny of coats, etc. of N. J. Porter ($6 coat) and Mr. Fay at a ball on the Island, 2y6m.[933]

Benjamin Gwinn, born PA, received 27 December 1858, w/m, larceny, 2y6m.[934]

Benjamin Gant, born MD, received 27 December 1858, b/m, larceny of $20 coat of William Tower, 2y6m.[935]

JB, born DC, received 27 December 1858, b/f, larceny, 4y.[936]

Chapter Thirty-six

INTAKE 1859

Fred Betz, born MD circa 1831, received 7 January 1859, w/m, larceny of money of J. C. Reynolds, 2y6m. Prior to imprisonment, Betz was a sailor.[937]

George Bryant, born VA, received 8 January 1859, w/boy, larceny of $40 of jewelry and cash of John Kaiser, 1y.[938]

Alfred Green, born DC circa 1841, received 10 January 1859, b/m, larceny of property of C. Cole and larceny of various hats and coats of Alfred W. Carter, 2 days in jail to be followed by 5y in penitentiary.[939]

Thomas Smith, born CT circa 1842, received 18 January 1859, w/m, pick-pocketing at the railroad depot in Dec 1858, 3y. Prior to imprisonment, Smith was an upholsterer.[940]

John Smith, born NY circa 1830, received 18 January 1859, w/m, pick-pocketing at the railroad depot in Dec 1858, 3y. Prior to imprisonment, Smith was a painter.[941]

David Van Pelt, born Germany circa 1829, received 18 January 1859, w/m, pick-pocketing at the railroad depot in Dec 1858, 3y. Van Pelt was pardoned 31 December 1859.[942]

Gus Gassenheimer, born Germany circa 1839, received 18 January 1859, w/m, larceny of boots, 18m.[943]

Terence Corrigan, born Ireland circa 1822, received 18 January 1859, w/m, larceny of $8 of iron, property of Samuel R. Brick, 3y. Corrigan was an invalid in the pen.[944]

William Dent, born VA circa 1831, received 24 January 1859, b/m, larceny of two blankets and counterpane ($13.50 total value), 1y6m.[945]

Edgar (Eddie) Patterson, born DC circa 1842, received 27 January 1859, w/boy, manslaughter of Andrew Bowlen (b/m) in Georgetown, 4y. Witness Joseph Libby saw Bowlen walking on the street by Mr. Wheatley's lumberyard. Patterson was following Bowlen softly, and when he got close, Patterson threw a large stone (approximately 1-1½ pounds) at Bowlen. Bowlen fell down and Patterson started kicking him. When Libby asked Patterson why he was doing that, Patterson told him because Bowlen had hit him the previous week. Witness Dr. Cragin testified Bowlen had a large cut over his right eye and a wound on the back of his head. Dr. Cragin prescribed treatment and was called again that same day as Bowlen was bleeding from his ear. Bowlen died the next day around noon. Dr. Cragin testified that the probable cause of death was compression of the brain. Prior to imprisonment, Patterson was a huckster. He was pardoned on 30 December 1861.[946]

Peter Searchfield (aka John Searchfield), born Ireland circa 1826, received 12 March 1859, w/m, larceny of 2 coats ($20 ea.) on 31 January 1859, property of George Poe, 1y9m. Prior to imprisonment, Searchfield was a machinist.[947]

Louis Bell, born DC circa 1835, received 14 March 1859, b/m, manslaughter, 4y. Bell was pardoned 30 December 1861. Prior to imprisonment, Bell was a plasterer.[948]

WFW, born DC, received 4 April 1859, w/boy, larceny, 2y.[949]

William Patterson, born DC circa 1842, received 19 March 1859, mu/boy, larceny, 2y. On 21 December 1858, Patterson was found guilty of two cases of larceny. In the first, he stole a hat and an umbrella from Charles P. Pope, and in the second, he stole 2 hats, a coat, and an umbrella from Anna LeCompte. He was sentenced in the first to 3 months in jail to be followed by 2y in the penitentiary. Prior to imprisonment, Patterson was a waiter.[950]

A. Blake, born Greece circa 1829, received 20 April 1859, w/m, larceny, 1y. Prior to imprisonment, Blake was a sailor.[951]

Cornelius Lee, born MD, received 17 May 1859, b/m, larceny of paper from the Capitol, 2y.[952]

John H. Ray, born MD circa 1830, received 22 June 1859, w/m, felony, 6y. Prior to imprisonment, Ray was a blacksmith/machinist, an expert at making skeleton keys. Ray had just finished serving 2y at the Richmond, VA penitentiary. As officers brought Ray to Washington to stand trial here, he told them that in 1856, he had made keys to get into the U.S. Treasury and the Bank of the Metropolis. He was one of five members of the Nailor gang, who planned to use the keys in a robbery; however, the plan failed when Ray refused to participate because the watchman would most likely be killed in the attempt. Ray was tried in DC for stealing goods from Hinton's clothing store in 1855, for participating with the gang in stealing $50 of dry goods from John A. Latham's store on Easter, and for robbing Hoffa's jewelry store on Pennsylvania Avenue. After the robbery, the gang took the goods to gang member Bailey's house and divided the spoils. He was convicted on three counts and sentenced to 2y in the pen for each conviction, a total of 6y. In sentencing Ray, the judge remarked that Ray was a married man and he was surprised that that was not enough to keep Ray straight. On his way back to the jail before going to the pen, Ray told the officers that he was pleased with the sentence. He had expected to get 15y for his crimes. He also said that he was going to try to escape from the pen and when he got out of the pen in 6 years, he planned to rob a certain (unnamed) bank. He said there was "never a lock he could not pick," and he planned to die rich or die in the pen.[953]

Jane Brown, born VA circa 1841, received 24 June 1859, b/f, larceny of a $5 watch, 1y. Brown was involved in gardening at the pen and was a house servant at the pen.[954]

Amy ?, born VA circa 1838, received 27 June 1859, b/f, larceny, 6y. Amy was from Richmond.[955]

Frank Shandy (?), born VA circa 1817, received 27 June 1859, b/m, larceny, 1y.[956]

Major S. McDonald, born Portland, ME circa 1833, received 27 June 1859, w/m, assault on the high seas, 2y. Prior to imprisonment, McDonald was a sailor. On 22 October 1860, McDonald escaped. A reward of $250 was offered for his capture. He was described as being 5 ft. 6⅜ inches tall, with his foot measuring 9½ inches. He was 27 years old at the time of escape. He had small circular tattoo on his right arm. His wife Harriet M. McDonald, his mother, and three brothers reportedly lived in Maine. One brother lived in California.[957]

Michael ("Mitch") Quinn, born Ireland circa 1820, received 27 June 1859, w/m, mail robbery, 2y.[958]

William Boston, born DC circa 1829, received 27 June 1859, mu/m, assault/battery at sea, 3y.[959]

Hillery Hutchins, born MD circa 1825, received 6 July 1859, w/m, larceny, 1y. Prior to imprisonment, Hutchins was a fisherman. Hutchins was a large, "powerful-looking"[960] man, rather good-looking and sported a black goatee.

Emanuel Miller, born DC circa 1810, received 6 July 1859, w/m, larceny of a calf, property of Michael Homiller, 1y. Prior to imprisonment, Miller was a wheelwright.[961]

Lewis Arthur, born Leone circa 1826, received 7 July 1859, w/m, manslaughter, 8y. Arthur was a cabinetmaker.[962]

Michael Glascow, born VA circa 1824, received 11 July 1859, b/m, larceny of, and killing of, a cow, property of Mrs. Foley, 1y.[963]

George Fisher, born MD circa 1841, received 12 July 1859, b/m, larceny, 1y6m.[964]

L. Shamblin, born KS circa 1839, received 18 July 1859, w/m, larceny, 2y.[965]

Michael (Mitch) Doyle, born NY circa 1841, received 20 July 1859, w/m, burglary/arson, 7y. Doyle was found guilty of stealing groceries/dry goods from Hugh Leddy's house on 31 May 1859. He was also found guilty of setting fire with Robert Binnix (below) to two stables belong to Mr. Ward. Prior to imprisonment, Doyle was a stonecutter. Doyle was pardoned 12 February 1862.[966]

James Keenan, Jr., born Ireland circa 1842, received 20 July 1859, w/m, arson, 3y. Keenan set fire to an out-house and stable of David Windsor (owned by George E. Kirk). Prior to imprisonment, Keenan was a stonecutter. He was pardoned 18 January 1862.[967]

Robert Binnix, born MD circa 1841, received 20 July 1859, w/m, arson, 8y. Binnix set fire to an out-house and stable of David Windsor (owned by George E. Kirk). He also set fire to two of Mr. Ward's stables and to Thomas Potentini's icehouse on B Street. Binnix was pardoned 12 October 1861. Prior to imprisonment, Binnix was a stonecutter.[968]

William (James) Looney, born NY circa 1839, received 20 July 1859, w/m, arson, 3y. Looney set fire to an out-house and stable of David Windsor (owned by George E. Kirk). He was pardoned 15 November 1861. Prior to imprisonment, Looney was a stonecutter.[969]

George Williams (aka George F. Pocket), born DC circa 1829, received 20 July 1859, b/m, larceny, 2y.[970]

Ann Brown, born DC circa 1807, received 22 July 1859, b/f, grand larceny of $7.50 in gold coin, 1y.[971]

James Keenan, Sr., born Ireland, received 17 August 1859, w/m, perjury, 4y. Keenan was a weaver. Keenan's son, James Keenan, Jr., was tried and convicted of arson (see above). James Keenan, Sr., testified at his son's trial, saying that on the night of the fire his son was at his [Keenan, Sr.] house. Keenan, Sr. who had lived in the Washington area for many years was of unblemished character up to the moment when he "permitted his regard for the safety of a worthless son to overcome his sense of integrity."[972] Keenan was pardoned 16 August 1860.

John R. Darling, born GA circa 1825, received 26 August 1859, w/m, mail robbery, 2y. On 26 August 1859, after a nine day trip, J. S. Gonzales, Esq., U.S. Deputy Marshal of the Northern District of Florida, arrived in Washington from Pensacola, FL, with Darling and 5 other prisoners to be incarcerated in the U.S. Penitentiary.[973]

John French, born GA circa 1828, received 26 August 1859, w/m, manslaughter, 2y. On 26 August 1859, after a nine day trip, J. S.

Gonzales, Esq., U.S. Deputy Marshal of the Northern District of Florida, arrived in Washington from Pensacola, FL, with French and 5 other prisoners to be incarcerated. Prior to imprisonment, French was a farmer.[974]

William Thomas, born NY circa 1835, received 26 August 1859, w/m, manslaughter, 3y. On 26 August 1859, after a nine day trip, J. S. Gonzales, Esq., U.S. Deputy Marshal of the Northern District of Florida, arrived in Washington from Pensacola, FL, with Thomas and 5 other prisoners to be incarcerated. Prior to imprisonment, Thomas was a sailor.[975]

James Gill, born Ireland circa 1830, received 26 August 1859, w/m, mutiny, 7y. On 26 August 1859, after a nine-day trip, J. S. Gonzales, Esq., U.S. Deputy Marshal of the Northern District of Florida, arrived in Washington from Pensacola, FL, with Gill and 5 other prisoners to be incarcerated pardoned 28 March 1862. Prior to imprisonment, Gill was a sailor.[976]

William Wetherilt, born Canada circa 1827, received 26 August 1859, w/m, mutiny, 7y .On 26 August 1859, after a nine day trip, J. S. Gonzales, Esq., U.S. Deputy Marshal of the Northern District of Florida, arrived in Washington from Pensacola, FL, with Wetherilt and 5 other prisoners to be incarcerated. Wetherilt was pardoned 28 March 1862. Prior to imprisonment, Wetherilt was a sailor.[977]

Charles Price, born VA circa 1826, received 1 October 1859, w/m, felony/counterfeiting, 5y. Convicted at the Western District of VA U.S. District Court in September 1859, Price received a pardon from President Lincoln on 22 August 1861. Prior to imprisonment, Price was a farmhand. His wife's name was Susan.[978]

MD, born Ireland, received 1 December 1859, w/m, felony, 2y. MD was released 23 November 1861.[979]

Thomas King, born PA circa 1837, received 1 December 1859, w/m, felony, 2y. King was released 23 November 1861. Prior to imprisonment, King was a sailor.[980]

John Summers, born VA circa 1840, received 9 December 1859, b/m, larceny, 2y. Summers was a plasterer.[981]

Thomas Keenan, born Ireland circa 1819, received 10 December 1859, w/m, larceny, 2y.[982]

Thomas Barnett, b. NY circa 1847, received 1859, larceny.[983]

Levi M. Smith, born NY circa 1835, received 1859, b/m, larceny. Prior to imprisonment, Smith was a carpenter.[984]

Charles Stewart, born DC circa 1837, received 1859, w/m, intent to kill, waiter.[985]

James W. Kelly, born VA circa 1834, received December 1859, w/m, larceny of a $3.50 silver watch, $10 gold piece, $2.50 gold piece, one gold dollar, and one $5 note, property of James W. Parkes, captain of an oyster boat. Kelly and Brown had been on board talking with Parkes until 12 o'clock. Parkes left and went to another nearby boat. He left a servant in charge of his boat. When he returned, Parkes found his watch and money, which he had left in a cupboard, gone. Kelly had $16 of the money on his person when he was arrested, and the watch and part of the money was found under a rock in an alley near a house Kelly had visited. 1y6m.[986]

George Humphreys, born DC circa 1833, received 1859, b/m, larceny of a coat, property of Frederick Wilson.[987]

James Davis, born DC circa 1833, received 1859, b/m, larceny.[988]

Isaiah Wormsley, born DC circa 1834, received 1859, b/m, larceny. Prior to imprisonment, Wormsley was a butcher.[989]

William Henry Chandler, born DC circa 1841, received 1859, b/m, Larceny. Chandler was a blacksmith.[990]

Eli Legg, born VA circa 1838, w/m, received 1859, larceny. Prior to imprisonment, Legg was a clerk.[991]

James Bryant, born DC circa 1845, received 1859, b/m, larceny of thirty half- and quarter-dollars, 1y3m. Reported as "unusually smart looking."[992]

William H. White, born PA circa 1839, received 1859, w/m, larceny of gold studs ($9 value), property of William S. Roberts, 1y.[993]

Bartlett Lipscomb, born DC circa 1832, received December 1859, w/m, larceny, 1y6m. Lipscomb stole two pair of pants, two coats, one shirt, one pair of boots, gold studs, and gold sleeve buttons ($21.50 total value), property of George Morgan, tailor. Lipscomb was a "well-known hard character."[994]

Sonny Jackson (aka Alexander Jackson), received 31 December 1859, b/m, larceny of a gun, property of George Semmes, 1y.[995]

John Newcomb, born MA circa 1838, received 1859, w/m, felony.[996]

Ed Graham, born MA circa 1835, received 1859, w/m, felony. Graham was a sailor prior to imprisonment.[997]

M. C. H. Graham, born OH circa 1836, received 1859, w/m, felony. Graham was a sailor prior to imprisonment.[998]

Chapter Thirty-seven

INTAKE 1860

Thomas E. Kirkley, born MD circa 1831, received 4 January 1860, w/m, subornation of perjury, 4y. On 23 June 1859, Kirkley appeared in criminal court facing a charge of assault/battery with intent to kill Charles H. Dent, a black boy who lived with Kirkley and was bound to him. Dent was found tied up by his neck in a dark room with his toes barely on the floor, after he had allegedly been beaten with a cowhide. His hands were tied behind him, and he was nearly dead when he was found. Kirkley also had another apprentice, Frederick Peters (born circa 1842). Peters was an uneducated orphan from Baltimore and didn't know whether he was indentured to Kirkley or not. On 18 January 1859, the grand jury reported that they felt Peters was also abused by Kirkley and recommended he be taken away from Kirkley and placed elsewhere. Kirkley tried to get Peters to lie for him and say he hadn't committed such an assault/battery on Dent. Kirkley was found guilty of assault/battery only and sentenced to 6 months in jail and a $20 fine. On 29 June 1859, a letter to the editor of the *Star* entitled "The Very Last Case" stated the opinion that Kirkley may have gotten off too easily. The writer of the editorial appealed to the "public functionary" to try Kirkley for subornation of perjury for trying to get his apprentice to lie for him. "He [Kirkley] should be prosecuted for the subornation—he should be prosecuted as a cruel and improper master to his white apprentice." Signed H.L.S., 25 June 1859.[999] Prior to imprisonment, Kirkley was a bricklayer. Kirkley was pardoned 20 June 1862 for good conduct and because the testimony that convicted him was not deemed credible.

Aaron "Pink" Coakley, born MD circa. 1830, received 5 January 1860, b/m, larceny of a $6.60 cart wheel, property of Henry Whitsel, 1y. Coakley was a "frequent customer" of the Auxillary Guard, usually for fighting and disorderly conduct.[1000]

David Christopher Bohlayer, born DC circa 1831, received 5 January 1860, w/m, assault/battery with intent to kill Officer Holden at the Navy Yard on 5 November 1859 by shooting him with a pistol, 8y. Bohlayer had been wanted by the police for over a year and had managed to dodge arrest all that time. He was wanted for assault and battery with intent to kill. When police spotted him on 5 November 1859 (he was known by the police and he was familiar with them such that he could recognize some of the officers from a distance), a chase ensued. Bohlayer drew a pistol and shot it at Officer Holden, shooting Holden in the upper right arm. Officers Irving and Scarff continued in the chase and captured Bohlayer. Holden, a stonecutter by trade, was a quiet and courteous man, well-respected in the community. Though the bone in his arm was broken in several places, amputation proved unnecessary, and he recovered. On 4 January 1860, Bohlayer was sentenced to two days in jail for assaulting and resisting Officer Scarff and for assaulting and resisting Officer Irving. For assault and battery with intent to kill Officer Thomas Holden, Bohlayer was given 8y in the penitentiary. The judge told Bohlayer he should be thankful that Holden was not dead or he [Bohlayer] would be up for murder and added, "It was the duty of all classes to bow to the law. It is our master, no matter who or what we are."[1001] After the sentence was given, "Bohlayer then impudently remarked that 'there would be a day of Judgment when all would get justice; he hoped so, anyhow.'"[1002] He was pardoned 10 August 1861. Prior to imprisonment, Bohlayer was a butcher. His mother's name was Ann.[1003]

James Baedley, born England circa 1837, received 7 January 1860, w/m, felony, 1y.[1004]

William Hamelin, born KY circa 1837, received 7 January 1860, w/m, felony, 1y.[1005]

Andrew King, born DC circa 1844, received 9 January 1860, b/boy, larceny of gold and silver coin ($10.50 value) from a fellow servant, and of a $7.50 revolver, property of N. O. Driver, 2y (1y each offense). King was released 13 April 1862. Prior to imprisonment, King was a butcher.[1006]

Clinton Smith (aka John Brown), born VA circa 1839, received 11 January 1860, b/m, larceny of a $10 cloak of Thomas John Foster, 1y6m.[1007]

Cesarino Cesalto, born France circa 1829, received 14 January 1860, w/m, larceny of $40 carriage, $50 horse, and $10 set of harness, property of W. A. Hopkins, 2y3m.[1008]

Thomas Robbins, born PA circa 1843, received 18 January 1860, w/m, larceny of twelve pair of boots ($18 total value), property of Francis Pratt, 1y.[1009]

Sarah Weems, born Rockville, MD, circa 1830, received 18 January 1860, b/f, obtaining groceries under false pretences, 1y. Weems was a house servant. She had a scar from a burn on the back of her left hand, a scar over her right eye, and one on her right breast.[1010]

John W. Mahoney (aka George Mahoney), born VA circa 1837, received

25 January 1860, b/m, two cases of forgery/obtaining goods under false pretences, 3y.[1011]

Emanuel Dodson, born DC circa 1841, received 27 January 1860, b/m, larceny of eight bushels of corn, eight more bushels corn, and six more bushels of corn, 3y.[1012]

Michael ("Mitch") Pfeifer, born Germany circa 1826, received 31 January 1860, w/m, bigamy, 4y. About 6 September 1846, Pfeifer was married in Baltimore, MD to Catherine Dill in St. Alphonsus Church. After they were married, witness George Baunstock testified that the couple lived in Baltimore about six years. On 3 November 1859, he married Mrs. Jane Ann Jones in Georgetown. She was a widow who had known Pfeifer for about four months before they were married in the Methodist Church in Washington by Rev. Royland. At time of the trial, Mrs. Catherine Pfeifer and the Pfeifer's four little children were still living in Baltimore. Prior to imprisonment, Pfeifer was a butcher.[1013]

J. W. Harney, born GA circa 1836, received 7 February 1860, w/m, mail robbery, 15y. Prior to imprisonment, Harney was a farmhand.[1014]

Dr. William Boyd, born Ireland circa 1820, received 10 February 1860, w/m, larceny, 14y. Boyd was found guilty on two charges of stealing slaves, and on two charges of transporting slaves to a free State. Boyd was pardoned 2 October 1861.[1015]

Thomas Fagan (aka James Fagan), born Ireland circa 1804, received 7 March 1860, w/m, larceny of two coats and a comfort ($9 total value), 2y.[1016]

Bishop A. Tyler, born DC circa 1824, received 7 March 1860, b/m, larceny of a $60 cow, property of Ephraim French, 3y.[1017]

John Fletcher, born DC circa 1830, received 7 March 1860, b/m, larceny of a $60 cow, property of Ephraim French, 3y.[1018]

John Sullivan, born Ireland circa 1825, received 9 March 1860, w/m, assault/battery with intent to kill Margaret Sullivan, his wife, 2y. He knocked her down many times with his fist and a stick and kicked her in the head and face, threatening to kill her. He was released 8 March 1862.[1019]

Thomas Brent, born England circa 1835, received 9 March 1860, w/m, larceny of watch, property of Dennis Lafferty, 1y6m. Lafferty was a servant in Willard's Hotel, and Brent, his coworker had been let go a few days before the theft. Brent had spent the night in Lafferty's room, leaving before Lafferty got up. Brent was released 8 September 1861.[1020]

Richard ("Rich") Ellis, born DC circa 1833, received 9 March 1860, b/m, larceny of chickens, property of Timothy Mahar, 1y6m. Ellis was released 8 September 1861.[1021]

John Meyer, born PA circa 1817, received 10 March 1860, w/m, larceny of an overcoat, property of Richard H. Laskey, Esq., 1y6m. Meyer was released 9 September 1861.[1022]

James (Tobias) Fletcher, born VA circa 1841, received 10 March 1860, b/m, larceny, 2y. Fletcher stole three dozen bricklayer's trowels ($38 value when new), property of Paulus Thyson. Fletcher sold them for 25 cents each.[1023]

George King, born DC circa 1842, received 10 March 1860, b/m, larceny, 2y. King aided Fletcher (above) in stealing the trowels.[1024]

George Taylor (aka Washington Taylor), born MD circa 1832, received 14 March 1860, b/m, false pretenses, 3y. Taylor was tried on two cases of obtaining a number of hams of bacon from Mallard & Co., saying he was a servant of Major Sutherland and getting the hams for Sutherland. Prior to imprisonment, Taylor was a brickmaker.[1025]

G. F. Cloy, born France circa 1838, received 16 March 1860, w/m, murder, 7y. Prior to imprisonment, Cloy was a sailor.[1026]

Daniel Barry, born Ireland circa 1840, received 13 March 1860, w/m, arson of an empty house belonging to Emily Boscoe, 3y. Barry went to Boscoe's house and asked to borrow three cents. She refused to loan it to him. Later that day, a fire was set with pieces of trellis on the back porch of a home Boscoe owned. Barry walked with a cane and a crutch. He was an old soldier with one leg. He was pardoned 10 November 1862.[1027]

Joseph Goldsmith, born Germany circa 1839, received 13 March 1860, w/m, larceny of goods belonging to Emanuel Kauffman, 1y.[1028]

William Hall, born VA circa 1800, received 13 March 1860, w/m, larceny of a $6 pair of pants, 1y6m. Prior to imprisonment, Hall was a sailor.[1029]

John Doherty (aka John Dougherty), born VT circa 1838, received 20 March 1860, w/m, rape of a German woman, Laura Schwingman, 10y. Through an interpreter, Schwingman testified that she had only been in town a few weeks and was looking for a job when Eberling, a

Marine (see below), offered to help her if she would come with him. When the carriage they were riding in stopped and picked up two other men, one of whom was Doherty, Schwingman wanted to get out, but was threatened with a knife and then raped by all three of the men. The rape occurred in an isolated area of town, so there was no one around to come to her aid. James Hawkins, a Marine, testified that Eberling and Hickman (see below) admitted having had sex several times in a carriage with a German woman and that it had been a struggle in which one had had his finger bitten. They had been drinking. At sentencing, Doherty denied his guilt. Prior to becoming a Marine, Doherty was a potter. Doherty enlisted 12 December 1859 in the Marines.[1030]

James Eberling, born PA circa 1836, received 20 March 1860, w/m, rape of a German woman, Laura Schwingman, 10y. Through an interpreter, Schwingman testified that she had only been in town a few weeks and was looking for a job when Eberling, a Marine, offered to help her if she would come with him. When the carriage they were riding in stopped and picked up two other men, Schwingman wanted to get out, but was threatened with a knife and then raped by all three of the men. The rape occurred in an isolated area of town, so there was no one around to come to her aid. James Hawkins, a Marine, testified that Eberling and Hickman (see below) admitted having had sex several times in a carriage with a German woman and that it had been a struggle in which one had had his finger bitten. They had been drinking. At sentencing on 19 March 1860, Eberling had nothing to say. Prior to imprisonment, Eberling was a house painter. He enlisted December 1859 in the Marines.[1031]

John Hickman, born MD circa 1837, received 20 March 1860, w/m, rape of a German woman, Laura Schwingman, 10y. Through an interpreter, Schwingman testified that she had only been in town a few weeks and was looking for a job when Eberling, a Marine, offered to help her if she would come with him. When the carriage they were riding in stopped and picked up two other men, one of whom was Hickman, Schwingman wanted to get out, but was threatened with a knife and then raped by all three of the men. The rape occurred in an isolated area of town, so there was no one around to come to her aid. James Hawkins, a Marine, testified that Eberling (see above) and Hickman admitted having had sex several times in a carriage with a German woman and that it had been a struggle in which one had had his finger bitten. They had been drinking. At sentencing, Hickman denied his guilt. Prior to imprisonment, Hickman was a plasterer. Hickman enlisted 2 December 1859 in the Marines. Through an interpreter, Schwingman testified that she had only been in town a few weeks and was looking for a job when Eberling, a Marine, offered to help her if she would come with him. When the carriage they were riding in stopped and picked up two other men, Schwingman wanted to get out, but was threatened with a knife and then raped by all three of the men. The rape occurred in an isolated area of town, so there was no one around to come to her aid. James Hawkins, a Marine, testified that Eberling and Hickman (see below) admitted having had sex several times in a carriage with a German woman and that it had been a struggle in which one had had his finger bitten. they had been drinking.[1032]

Anthony Kidwell, born DC circa 1829, received 20 March 1860, w/m, larceny of a buffalo robe and other property of William R. Edes of Georgetown, 1y6m. Prior to imprisonment, Kidwell was a dyer.[1033]

John Larner (aka John Maher), born Ireland circa 1833, received 20 March 1860, w/m, larceny of a buffalo robe and other property of William R. Edes of Georgetown, 1y6m.[1034]

Herman Jaeger (aka Herman Jurowitz aka Count Jerowitz), born Germany circa 1832, received 20 March 1860, w/m, false pretenses, 2y. Jaeger defrauded Charles Duchanoy with a valueless draft for 5000 francs. Witness John Glass testified that he knew Jurowitz in Germany where Jurowitz was a forest attendant named Frederick Yager and a soldier in the army. Glass knew Jurowitz in Wittemberg, and said Jurowitz had been in prison in Germany. Glass further testified that Jurowitz said he was the illegitimate son of Count Norman and Countess Kisfaludi in Germany and had been placed in the Jaeger family where he was raised as a common citizen. Jurowitz called himself Count Herman De Jurowitz Nalietty, Major in the French army, a refugee. Count Jerowitz, who arrived without baggage and lived in Charles Duchanoy's house for three weeks, had Duchanoy convinced he was royalty.[1035]

James Ford, born VA circa 1838, received 21 March 1860, w/m, larceny, 1y. Ford stole a $10 gun from John W. Sothoron of Georgetown and also stole two pair of pants from John S. Shackleford of Georgetown. Ford was sentenced 8 March 1860 to two weeks in jail for stealing the pants and 1y in the penitentiary for stealing the gun. Ford was a barber.[1036]

James Walsh (aka James Wallace), "the curtain thief," born Ireland circa 1831, received 24 March 1860, w/m, larceny, 11y. Walsh was convicted on four counts of grand larceny. For stealing a piano cover from Susan Prince, he was sentenced to one week in jail; for stealing articles from the house of James C. McGuire, W. P. Browning, and Buckner Bayliss, he was sentenced to 6y (2y on each count); and, for breaking into the house of Hugh McLaughlin in February 1860 and stealing $20 worth of curtains, he was sentenced to 5y in the penitentiary, a total sentence of 11 years. At sentencing, Walsh denied his guilt and delivered a long speech when asked if he had anything to say. Walsh, a private in the U.S. military, came to Washington in January 1860 from Governor's Island, NY. He was with the Regulars, 4th Artillery, Co. B. "He is an accomplished housebreaker."[1037]

Frank Hair, born VA circa 1839, received 14 April 1860, b/m, mail robbery, 2y. Hair was pardoned 23 October 1861 to go to insane asylum.[1038]

Mary Williams, born VA circa 1844, received 26 April 1860, b/f, larceny, 3y. Williams stole two dresses, a shawl, etc. of Eliza DeCamp and Elizabeth Everett. Williams' baby was Incarcerated with her.[1039]

Augustus Price, born DC circa 1830, received 26 April 1860, b/m, larceny of goods of Patrick Gavin, 3y.[1040]

William H. Moody, born DC circa 1837, received 26 April 1860, b/m, larceny, 2y. Moody stole a harness set ($11.50 value) and a $17 dress. Prior to imprisonment, Moody was a cart driver.[1041]

Ed A. Henivery, born FL circa 1840, received 27 April 1860, w/m, mail robbery, 1y. Henivery was released 16 April 1861. Prior to imprisonment, Henivery was a machinist.[1042]

Henry Weasner, born VA circa 1837, received 29 April 1860, w/m, horse theft ($75 horse) property of John Jones, 3y.[1043]

James Brayley, born England, received 11 May 1860, w/m, misdemeanor, 3y. Prior to imprisonment, Brayley was a sea captain. He was pardoned 3 July 1862.[1044]

Ed Anderson, born Ireland circa 1834, received 17 May 1860, w/m, larceny, 6m. Anderson was released 12 October 1860. Prior to imprisonment, Anderson was a farmer.[1045]

W. P. Wright, born PA circa 1840, received 17 May 1860, w/m, larceny, 1y. Wright was released 7 May 1861. Prior to imprisonment, Wright was a farmer.[1046]

Patrick Keenan, born Ireland, received 10 June 1860, w/m, aiding Eberling/Hickman/Dougherty (above) in the rape of Laura Schwingman, 10y. While in jail awaiting trial, Schwingman was reported to behave indecently, asking men to kiss her. At sentencing, Keenan denied his guilt.[1047]

Paul Henry (aka E. M. Chandon), born France, received 19 June 1860, w/m, forging the name of Charles Gautier on a check made to Marshall Brown to pay a bill, 3y.[1048]

Hugh Atwell, born VA, received 22 June 1860, w/m, larceny of six pair of boots, property of Mathias Natli, 2y. Atwell escaped from the pen at 4:30 p.m. on 7 March 1861 with prisoner Fugett. They were under officer Wm. B. Maxwell's watch and disappeared while taking broomcorn scraps to a compost heap outside the prison. Maxwell found them waist deep in the swamp and brought them back.[1049]

William Alexander, born VA, received 23 June 1860, b/m, larceny, 1y6m.[1050]

AJ, born DC, received 20 June 1860, b/m, larceny, 1y.[1051]

Mathias Butler, born DC, received 25 June 1860, b/m, larceny of $6 worth of chickens, 1y.[1052]

Charles Perez, born Mexico, received 30 June 1860, w/m, larceny, 2y.[1053]

Edward Hurley, born VA, received 2 July 1860, b/boy, larceny, 3y. Hurley escaped from the penitentiary on 15 April 1861. Warden Hiram I. King offered a $50 reward in addition to what the Board of Inspectors offered. Hurley escaped on the 15th and was captured on the 18th.[1054]

Isaac Contee, born DC, received 3 July 1860, b/m, larceny, 1y6m.[1055]

Lemuel Harris, born VA, received 3 July 1860, b/m, larceny, 1y6m.[1056]

Marion Ward, received 11 July 1860, 4y (beginning 2 July 1860).[1057]

Richard Merriman, born MD, received 11 July 1860, b/m, larceny of $5 worth of property, 3y. Merriman was a baker in the pen and was pardoned 10 November 1862.[1058]

Phillis Smith (aka Eliza Smith), born DC, received 13 July 1860, b/f, larceny of a pair gold spectacles, 1y.[1059]

Louisa Bowen, born DC, received 13 July 1860, b/f, larceny of a silk dress and half-dollar, property of Henry Wilson, 1y.[1060]

John J. Simmons (aka John King), born DC, received 18 July 1860, w/m, larceny of $20 note of James Needle, 1y10m.[1061]

Charles Morrell, born MO, received 20 July 1860, w/m, passing counterfeit coin, 1y. Morrell was brought in from Kansas and was from Ft. Scott.[1062]

James McCormick, born MO, received 20 July 1860, w/m, larceny, 8m. McCormick was brought in from Kansas and was released 4 February 1861.[1063]

Joseph Gray (aka Joseph Reed), born VA, received 20 July 1860, w/m, counterfeit coin, 3y. Gray was convicted by the Second Judicial

District of Kansas for passing counterfeit coin and sentenced to 3y in the penitentiary on 6 June 1860. He was pardoned 28 January 1862.[1064]

Asbury Scribner, born DC, received 24 July 1860, w/m, larceny, 1y3m.[1065]

John Campbell, born NY, received 24 July 1860, w/m, larceny, 2y.[1066]

John W. Fischer, born DC, received 28 July 1860, b/m, larceny of money drawer and contents, property of Mr. Miller, 1y6m.[1067]

George Lomax, born DC, received 28 July 1860, b/boy, larceny of money drawer and contents, property of Mr. Miller, 1y6m.[1068]

Ann Clark, born DC, received 6 August 1860, w/f, larceny of jewelry of Mrs. Thompson, 2y. On 17 November 1860, Matron Marceron wrote the warden a letter requesting baby items for Clark, who was to deliver soon after the letter was written.[1069]

William Fugitt (aka General Fugitt), born DC, received 6 August 1860, w/m, horse theft, 3y. Fugitt stole a horse from J. B. Grinnel around 1858.and had been on the run since then. On his way from the jail to the courthouse in 1860, Fugitt escaped but was captured. He was pardoned 24 September 1862.[1070]

AC, born DC, received 17 August 1860, b/m, larceny, 1y6m.[1071]

LJO, born OH, received 8 September 1860, w/m, passing counterfeit coin, 10y.[1072]

JGW, born VA, received 8 September 1860, w/m, felony, 2y. JGW was released 6 September 1862.[1073]

Johnathan Bush, born MD, received 8 September 1860, w/m, felony, 2y. Bush was pardoned 9 April 1862.[1074]

Laurence Dent, born MD, received 5 December 1860, b/boy, larceny, 1y6m. Dent stole gold and silver coins, silver watch, brass checks, a pistol, and a razor, property of George M. Miller.[1075]

Joseph Robbins (aka Dolly Dobbins), born DC, received 7 December 1860, w/m, larceny of lead, property of H. I. Offut, 1y6m.[1076]

John Urle, born Germany, received 7 December 1860, w/m, larceny, 1y.[1077]

Charles Newman, born Prussia, received 8 December 1860, w/m, larceny, 6y. Newman stole clothes and jewelry, property of Lewis Kurtz (3y) and stole jewelry and money, property of Mary Platz (3y). Newman was a blacksmith at the pen.[1078]

John Reutzell (aka John Peeps), born DC, received 10 December 1860, b/m, larceny of $6 in silver coin, property of S. A. Schloss, 1y3m.[1079]

Levi Barrett, born MD, received 10 December 1860, b/m, larceny of $20 gold piece of James F. Gordon, 1y.[1080]

Henry Taylor, born VA, received 11 December 1860, b/m, larceny of one gold watch and chain ($125 total), property of Jesse B. Haw, 1y6m.[1081]

Philip Strobel, born Switzerland, received 13 December 1860, w/m, larceny of gold and silver ($272.74 value), property of Michael Fredenburger, 3y.[1082]

George Davis, born DC, received 14 December 1860, w/m, larceny of a variety of clothing of Wm. F. Armstrong, 1y.[1083]

Simon Meyers, born Germany, received 14 December 1860, w/m, larceny of clothing and money, property of Wymer Miller, 1y.[1084]

John Williams, born DC, received 19 December 1860, b/m, larceny of two gold watches and chain, property of Mr. Lange, 3y.[1085]

Thomas Fletcher, born VA, received 20 December 1860, b/m, larceny of 79 lbs. of beef and basket (total $5.78), property of John H. Hurley, 1y.[1086]

Michael Kein, born Bavaria, received 20 December 1860, w/m, larceny, 2y3m. For stealing a coat, vest, pair of pants, and pistol, property of Jacob Paes, Kein was sentenced to 1y3m, and for stealing a pistol from Frederick Fink, Kein was sentenced to 1y.[1087]

Elizabeth Hamilton, born VA, received 21 December 1860, b/f, larceny of overcoat and handkerchief of John Potts, 1y.[1088]

William Henry Selby (aka William Henry), born DC, received 22 December 1860, b/boy, larceny of money drawer from barroom at restaurant kept by George M. Miller, 1y6m.[1089]

Daniel Miller, born MD, received 26 December 1860, w/m, larceny of $6 coat, property of Daniel Radcliffe, 1y6m.[1090]

Anna Boyle, born MD, received 28 December 1860, w/f, larceny of two cloaks, shirt, wrapper, bedspread, tablecloth and china vases ($56 total), property of Charles McNamee, 1y. Boyle was pardoned 9 December 1861.[1091]

William Johnson (aka William Lammon), born DC, received 31 December 1860, w/m, larceny, 2y. Johnson stole 60 dozen eggs, chickens, geese, turkeys, property of John L. Wilson. Johnson was pardoned 27 July 1862.[1092]

Charles F. Lausman, born Saxony, received 31 December 1860, w/m grand larceny, 3y.[1093]

Chapter Thirty-eight

INTAKE 1861

JR, born Ireland, received 10 January 1861, w/m, mutiny, 10y.[1094]

Hannah Wilson, born VA, received 19 January 1861, b/f, larceny of $6.50 bonnet, property of Samuel Keller, 1y.[1095]

Patrick McCallan, born Ireland, received 19 January 1861, w/m, larceny of property of Mary Ann Grimes, 1y.[1096]

William ("Swyper") Johnston, born DC, received 25 January 1861, w/m, larceny of $14 revolver of Frederick Wessman, 1y9m.[1097]

C. George Porter, born DC, received 1 February 1861, b/m, false pretenses, 1y. Porter obtained $2.50 under false pretences.[1098]

Edward Duffey (aka Edward Ducket), born DC, received 2 February1861, b/m, burglary, 3y. Duffee was discovered under the bed in Mr. Howard's house with the door key of Howard's house in his pocket and a candle, box of matches, skeleton key, etc. He escaped 30 July 1861.[1099]

James Henry (aka John Henry), born Ireland, received 4 February 1861, w/m, larceny of a pair boots, 1y.[1100]

George Sullivan, born MD, received 11 February 1861, w/m, burglary, 5y. Sullivan was a carpenter.[1101]

FB, born VA, received 11 February 1861, b/m, mail robbery 1y.[1102]

ALC, born RI, received 16 February 1861, w/m, forgery, 2y. Prior to imprisonment, ALC was a druggist.[1103]

JS, born Jamaica, received 21 February 1861, b/m, revolt on the high seas, 1y6m. JS was released 7 August 1862.[1104]

EJ, born Bermuda, received 21 February 1861, b/m, revolt on the high seas, 1y6m. EJ was released 7 August 1862.[1105]

EHN, born MD, received 21 February 1861, b/m, revolt on the high seas, 1y6m. EHN was released 7 August 1862.[1106]

TJ (aka JJWP), born Nova Scotia, received 21 February 1861, b/m, revolt on the high seas, 1y6m. TJ was released 7 August 1862.[1107]

Thomas Ferguson, born DC, received 13 March 1861, b/m, larceny of a pair of $8 kid boots, property of John G. Fuss, on 7 February 1861, 1y3m.[1108]

George Evans, born VA, received 14 March 1861, b/m, larceny of $6 coat, property of Wall, Stevens & Co., on 7 February 1861, 1y.[1109]

John Starr (aka John Feig), born MD, received 14 March 1861, w/m, arson, 5y. Starr set fire to the house (which was used as a store) of John

Walsh at 12th St. West and O St. North on 11 December 1860. Witnesses testified Starr told them he set the fire. At sentencing, Starr cursed the court and then thanked the judge for the sentence.[1110]

Joseph Thomas, born DC, received 18 March 1861, b/m, larceny of $15 coat, property of John Waters, on 10 February 1861, 1y6m.[1111]

Jacob Feig, born Germany, received 20 March 1861, w/m, larceny of two kid skins ($7), property of Julius Ring, 1y.[1112]

Antoine Daum, born Germany, received 20 March 1861, w/m, larceny of two kid skins ($7), property of Julius Ring, 1y.[1113]

Noble Grayson, born VA, received 22 March 1861, b/m, arson of James. H. Shreeve's livery stable, 5y. Shreeve testified he raised Grayson for a while until he ran away about 10 years ago. At that time, Shreeve threatened to whip Grayson if he ever caught him. Faunce Grayson, Noble's brother and a witness at the trial, testified that his mother was black, but Faunce had heard his grandmother was white. Officer Gill testified the Graysons lived across from him and Grayson's mother used to wash for Gill's family. The grandmother was old, slim and light-skinned, but was not white. "She used to go …pick up chip on the wharf."[1114] At sentencing on 22 March 1861, Noble Grayson maintained his innocence. He escaped 30 April 1861.[1115]

John Collins, born DC, received 23 March 1861, b/m, larceny of $100 worth of jewelry on board a steamboat, property of Henry Dubois, 2y.[1116]

Patrick O'Neale, born Ireland, received 25 March 1861, w/m, larceny, 2y. O'Neale stole a $20 note, five $5 notes, a $2.50 gold piece and one gold dollar, property of Charles Delano. He was sentenced to serve two months in jail for petty larceny to be followed by 2y in the penitentiary.[1117]

Charles DeVilliers (aka Augustus Beaufort aka Monsieur Augustus Delaroque, born West Indies, received 12 April 1861, w/m, false pretenses, 1y6m. On 19 February 1861, DeVilliers went into the trunk/harness factory of H. S. Johnson and ordered a harness and a small trunk to be paid for upon delivery to 401 Sixth Street. The items were delivered and DeVilliers gave the delivery boy a check for $26. The boy took the check to Riggs Bank where the teller told him "no good," so he found a detective and returned to 401 Sixth Street. DeVilliers was gone. When found, DeVilliers was taken to jail. DeVilliers had a receipt for $35 in furs that he had bought with another bad check at Mr. Stinemetz's millinery shop on Pennsylvania Avenue. The detective found the furs at a pawnshop where DeVilliers had pawned them for $5. While awaiting sentence, DeVilliers sought "mitigation of punishment" due to temporary insanity and also because he did not join in a jailbreak that occurred 2 April 1861, the night before he was sentenced. DeVilliers was pardoned 29 October 1861 by President Lincoln on the condition that he leave the District of Columbia within thirty days and not return for 5 years.[1118]

John Foley (aka James Foley), born Ireland, received 6 June 1861, w/m, murder, 21y. Foley, a soldier in the Regulars, 1st Artillery, Co. D under Major Haskins and stationed on B St. North, Capitol Hill, fatally shot Corporal Murphy on 27 February 1861. Foley was on leave and drunk when he was arrested and put in the guardhouse with his hand tied up. A gun and cartridge box had accidentally been left in the room, unbeknownst to Corporal Murphy, who was guarding Foley. Foley untied his hands and was loading the gun when Murphy went to see what the noise was all about. Foley jumped up and shot Murphy right through the chest. Foley was taken to jail to be held on charge of murder. He was about 25 years old at the time and said to be amiable when sober. Foley showed no feelings of remorse for the deed and said the dead corporal had "abused him, tied his hands, and otherwise treated him with...excessive severity."[1119] Corporal Murphy, who was extremely popular among the officers because of his many good qualities, was buried 28 February 1861 at Mt. Olivet with customary military honors.

On 6 April 1861, Foley was found guilty of murder about 1:30 p.m. He "turned deathly pale" at the verdict. A motion for a new trial was granted because most of the evidence presented had been about the prisoner's mental condition after the murder rather than before. Foley was sentenced on 16 April 1861 to be hanged by the neck until dead, but the sentence was commuted to 21 years in the pen.[1120]

Maria Meyers, born MD, received 22 June 1861, b/f, larceny of a shawl, 1y.[1121]

Matthias D. Rowe, born Germany, received 22 June 1861, w/m, larceny of property belonging to Antoine Kelpler and amounting to $12.50, 1y3m.[1122]

Charles Silver, born IN, received 24 June 1861, w/m, assault/battery with intent to rape Elizabeth Howard, 1y.[1123]

Charles Shorter, born DC, received 22 June 1861, b/m, larceny, 1y6m. Shorter was a cook in the pen.[1124]

Richard Garrison, born DC, received 24 June 1861, b/m, larceny of a $20 gold piece, property of Thomas McLaughlin, 1y6m.[1125]

Joseph Shepherd, born VA, received 24 June 1861, b/m, larceny of six pair of boots, property of Mr. V. Hornbeck, 1y6m.[1126]

Lawrence Finn, born NY, received 1 July 1861, w/m, larceny, 2y. Finn was a soldier in the 14th NY, Co. B.[1127]

John Egan, born Ireland, received 2 July 1861, w/m, burglary, 3y. Egan was a soldier in the 2nd CT, Co. I.[1128]

Mary Bonnett, born DC, received 2 July 1861, b/f, assault/battery with intent to kill, 3y.[1129]

Charles Robinson, born PA, received 6 July 1861, w/m, horse theft, 2y. Robinson was a barber in the pen.[1130]

William Mason, born DC, received 8 July 1861, b/m, larceny, 2y.[1131]

JP, born IN, received 8 July 1861, w/m, counterfeit coin, 1y.[1132]

AS, born PA, received 8 July 1861, w/m, counterfeit coin, 1y6m.[1133]

JB, born NY, received 8 July 1861, w/m, counterfeit coin, 3y.[1134]

JDS, born Switzerland, received 8 July 1861, w/m, counterfeit coin, 3y.[1135]

Samuel Johnson, born NY, received 8 July 1861, b/m, larceny of a gold watch and money, property of Col. McCunn, 2y.[1136]

Alexander Parker, born DC, received 10 July 1861, b/m, larceny, 1y.[1137]

Robert Banks (aka Robert Brooks), born NY, received 13 July 1861, w/m, larceny of gold watch, property of Captain Taylor, 2y.[1138]

GR, born PA, received 15 July 1861, w/m, larceny, 2y.[1139]

GH, born NY, received 16 July 1861, w/m, larceny, 1y. GH was a cooper.[1140]

Daniel McCormick, born PA, received 19 July 1861, w/m, arson, 2y. McCormick set fire to Mary Miller's house on 6 July 1861. McCormick was in the Mozart Regiment, Co. H, Baton Rouge, LA. He enlisted 1 June 1860.[1141]

Henry Boucher, born Ireland, received 20 July 1861, w/m, burglary/larceny of $30 from Charles Nements, 1y6m. Boucher was a soldier in the 2nd District, Co. A.[1142]

James Rankin, born NY, received 25 July 1861, w/m, larceny, 3y. Rankin stole $130 while part of a company of soldiers searching John Frizell's house for concealed weapons. Rankin was a soldier in the 2nd Michigan Regiment, and was pardoned 23 May 1862.[1143]

John H. Murphy, born DC, received 24 August 1861, w/m, manslaughter, 8y. Sergeant J. H. Murphy, along with R. Rawlings, C. Osbourne, J. O. Lusby, W. Nicholson, F. Lowe was indicted for the murder of Cornelius Boyd. According to Mrs. Margaret Boyd, wife of the deceased, her husband came home around 11 p.m. and went to bed. She was awakened by a knocking and woke her husband who went to the window where Mr. A. Grinder and Mr. Wilkinson stood below warning Boyd soldiers were coming to arrest him. Boyd said he had no idea what he had done. Another knock came, and Mrs. Boyd answered and told twelve armed soldiers that her husband lived there but was not there at the moment. Mr. Boyd decided to go out, but before he could get outside, the soldiers had kicked a door panel out of the door and opened fire. Boyd was hit in the left side under his armpit by the first bullet that was fired. Mrs. Boyd called for help from the other people living in the house, but their help was to no avail, and Cornelius died 15 minutes after he was shot. The group of soldiers told Mrs. Boyd that her husband was a secessionist, and that is why they killed him. While awaiting transfer to the pen, Murphy had tried to escape from the county jail by using a saw knife provided to him by one of his friends. The guards found the knife and Murphy was put in irons until he was transferred to the penitentiary.[1144] Note: On 20 August 1861, the day after Murphy was sentenced to eight years in the penitentiary, his sister, who was about 8 or 9 years old and lived in Washington, died. On Friday, 27 September 1861, President Lincoln pardoned Murphy.

JC, born Ireland, received 10 September 1861, w/m, insubordination and assault with intent to kill, 10y. JC was pardoned 2 August 1862.[1145]

William A. Northern, born VA, received 13 March 1861, w/m, mail robbery, 10y. Northern convicted at Richmond, VA of opening letters and stealing the contents. On 4 September 1861, Northern sought release on the grounds that no authority for his imprisonment could be found.[1146]

Thomas J. Getley, born NY, received 18 September 1861, w/m, larceny, 15m. On 26 December 1860, Getley stole a $12 coat, property of Oscar P. Aubert and an $8 coat, property of Francis E. Kane. Getley was sentenced on 19 March 1861 to serve 6 months in the county jail, to be followed by 15 months in the pen.[1147]

Robert McElroy, born Ireland, from PA, received 30 October 1861, w/m, desertion, 3y. Private McElroy, Co. C., 2nd Infantry, disappeared from Camp Turnbull, Virginia around 15 July 1861, shortly before his unit was to fight in the Battle of Bull Run. He was captured in Washington, DC, around 25 July 1861. On 17 August 1861, he was tried in military court for desertion. His remarks: "I have never had the intention to desert. I was drunk from the time I left until the time they took me; all the time my money lasted."[1148] Sentenced to 3y in the penitentiary, McElroy's sentence was remitted on 6 November 1861.

John Hemphill, born NY, received 20 November 1861, w/m, insubordination, 3y. Pvt. Hemphill, Co. D, 1st Artillery (formerly of Company of U.S. Recruits), disobeyed orders on 7 September 1861, by going more than a mile from camp. While he was gone, he trespassed on the farm of Mrs. Hatton, an elderly widow, and threatened her and her family with abusive language and a pistol. He also trespassed on the farm of Joseph C. Hatton, using threatening language and acting as if he were going to shoot into the house. Finally, he was AWOL from camp near Ft. Washington, MD on 9 September 1861. Hemphill was pardoned 4 August 1862 and mustered into the 19th IN Regiment.[1149]

AI, born Sweden, received 23 November 1861, w/m, larceny, 2y.[1150]

DW, born OH, received 23 November 1861, w/m, larceny, 2y.[1151]

James W. Hawkins, born DC, received 9 Dec 1861, b/m, larceny, 1y6m. Hawkins stole three boxes of candles, property of Peter Conlan on or about 24 August 1861.[1152]

George W. Jackson, born DC, received 9 December 1861, b/m, larceny, 1y. Jackson stole twenty-seven pots of flowers, property of John Douglas in April 1861, and was retried as the indictment written for the June term didn't say "free" colored.[1153]

Charles Stephens, born NY, received 14 December 1861, b/m, larceny, 3y. Stephens stole a carpetbag from Allen Pearce on 20 September 1861. The bag contained a $100 gold watch, a $30 silver watch, a $60 ring, a Mexican piné handkerchief (value $50-$60), silver spoons, deeds, mortgages, notes, and other valuable papers. He threw the papers in the canal, and gave the ring to a boy by the canal because it hurt his [Stephens] finger.[1154]

Thomas Gorman, born Ireland, received 14 December 1861, w/m, larceny, 1y3m. Gorman stole a $25 trunk on 9 October 1861 from Henry O. Hood.[1155]

Matthew Riley, born Ireland, received 14 December 1861, w/m, larceny, 1y. Riley stole a $10 silver watch and $3 silver watch chain and $30 from Jeremiah Sheehan.[1156]

Robert Barnes, born DC, received 14 December 1861, b/m, larceny, 1y. Barnes stole a $5 breastpin, a $10 necklace, and a 50-cent "ear-bob" from Brook Mackall on 4 July 1861.[1157]

WP, born MD, received 14 December 1861, b/m, larceny, 3y.[1158]

Thomas Mackey (aka Thomas Michael), born Ireland, received 14 December 1861, w/m, larceny, 2y6m. Mackey entered the house of Joseph Williamson, of the Land Office, on 16 September 1861, and put on a pair of Williamson's "unmentionables, in exchange for his own," took pockets full of jewelry and went into the room next to the one he ransacked and went to bed. Mackey was a soldier in the 2nd MI, Co. D.[1159]

George F. Rhens (aka G. W. Miller), born TN, received 14 December 1861, w/m, larceny, 2y6m. Rhens stole a $125 horse on 12 November 1861, property of Truxton D. Beale. Rhens was a soldier in the Regulars, 2nd dragoons, Co. K.[1160]

Patrick Sullivan, born Ireland, received 14 December 1861, w/m, larceny, 1y4m. Sullivan stole two pistols ($30 total value), property of Mrs. Henrietta Clitz in September 1861. Sullivan was a soldier in the 11th MA, Co. C.[1161]

Chapter Thirty-nine

INTAKE 1862

Note: Inmates marked by a "+" were pardoned and released to serve with the 19th IN Regiment which had suffered a great loss of soldiers in battle and needed reinforcements. Upon release from the penitentiary, several of the new recruits deserted en route to the camp of the 19th IN, were apprehended, and mustered into the 19th.

Patrick Campbell, born Ireland, received 3 January 1862, w/m, larceny of a pair of $6 boots, property of Nathaniel Wells, 1y. Campbell was a soldier in the 62nd NY, Co. C.[1162]

William Plummer, born DC, received 3 January 1862, b/m, larceny, 4y. Plummer stole a $12 barrel of brandy, property of William H. Hoover. The judge warned Plummer he would spend a major part of his life in prison or end up on the gallows if he continued in his thievery. He was sentenced to 3y in the pen for stealing the brandy and 1y for stealing shirts and dresses of Urban Gier.[1163]

Charles Herriman, born Germany, received 4 January 1862, w/m, larceny, 1y2m. Herriman stole a $7 box of tobacco on 10 December 1861, property of Catharine Newman. Herriman was a soldier in the 41st NY, Co. C.[1164]

Richard Evans, born DC, received 6 January 1862, w/m, manslaughter, 6y. Evans was indicted for the murder of George T. Howard in May 1861. Evans' wife was in court with him every day. The jury went out at 3:30 p.m. on 31 December 1861 and returned in an hour with a verdict of manslaughter. Evans was pardoned 10 September 1862.[1165]

Alfred Howard, born MD, received 7 January 1862, b/m, larceny of $60 in gold, property of Robert Newman on 4 October 1861, 2y6m.[1166]

Edward Harmon, born MD, received 7 January 1862, b/m, larceny of two pistols, property of Lt. Robinson and Mr. Matson, 2y6m.[1167]

Thomas E. Miller, born MD, received 7 January 1862, w/m, larceny of cows, 5y. Miller was indicted in two cases of stealing a cow and sentenced to 3y in one case and 2y in the other.[1168]

William Dent, born VA, received 8 January 1862, b/m, larceny of $30 worth of clothing, property of Edward Bebb, on 24 September 1861, 1y6m.[1169]

James Knapp, born NY, received 9 January 1862, w/m, sleeping on post, 2y6m. Knapp was pardoned 29 April 1862. Knapp was a Private in the 17th Reg. NY Volunteers.[1170]

James M. Driscoll, born NY, received 9 January 1862, w/m, sleeping on post, 2y6m. Driscoll was pardoned 29 April 1862. Driscoll was a Private in the 17th Reg. NY Volunteers.[1171]

+Michael Hennessey, born RI, received 10 January 1862, w/m, insubordination, 3y. Hennessey, Co. G. 1st Battalion, 11th Inf., threw a glass bottle at Lt. Evans with intent to kill him on 30 November 1861. He also was charged with using disrespectful and abusive language. He was pardoned on 4 August 1862.[1172]

+James Rea, born Scotland, from Rhode Island, received 10 January 1862, w/m, desertion, 2y7m. Rea deserted at Perryville, MD around 16 October 1861. He was caught in Baltimore about 18 October 1861. He was dishonorably discharged, sentenced to serve out his enlistment in the pen and be branded with a 1½" "D" on his right hip. On 4 August 1862, he was pardoned.[1173]

+Walter T. Bell, born England, received 10 January 1862, w/m, desertion, 2y8m. Bell deserted at Perryville, MD around 16 October 1861. He was caught in Baltimore about 18 October 1861. Bell said he was "under the influence of liquor when I deserted...I would not have done so had I been sober." He was dishonorably discharged, sentenced to fulfill his enlistment term at the pen and branded on his right hip with a 1½" letter "D." On 4 August 1862, Bell was pardoned.[1174]

John Ayers, born MA, received 13 March 1862, w/m, larceny of a $12 watch on 25 February 1862, property of Henry H. Harrison, 1y. Ayers was a soldier in the 19th MA, Co. D.[1175]

Charles E. Fitzgerald, born Ireland, received 15 January 1862, w/m, absent w/o leave, 6m. Fitzgerald, Co. D., 2nd Reg. U.S. Artillery, was absent without leave from about the 12/13th of June 1861 until he was apprehended at Ft. Ellsworth, VA around the 11 August 1861. He had been in the hospital in Georgetown and ordered to rejoin his company at the Washington Arsenal when he deserted. Fitzgerald was released 15 July 1862.[1176]

James E. Dunawin, born MD, received 17 January 1862, w/m, larceny, 3y. Dunawin was well-off, as he had inherited quite a bit of property from his father. He had a wife and three children and was accused of robbing Joseph Travers on 27 December 1861. Dunawin knocked Travers over the head with a cane and stole from Travers' pockets. Dunawin admitted his guilt, saying he was drunk. Dunawin and Travers had been barhopping together.[1177]

Emanuel Rifford, born PA, received 17 January 1862, w/m, larceny of $30 watch, property of John M. Becker on 8 December 1861, 1y3m. Rifford was pardoned 20 May 1862 due to doubt about his guilt.[1178]

Barney Plume, born MD, received 17 January 1862, w/m, larceny of $322.50 from Lewis Seldner on 5 January 1862, 2y6m.[1179]

Benjamin Gant, born MD, received 17 January 1862, b/m, larceny, 1y3m. Gant stole 5 hogs from Terence Boyle.[1180]

Isaac Hall, born MD, received 21 January 1862, b/m, larceny, 1y6m.[1181]

JM, born Ireland, received 27 January 1862, w/boy, larceny, 1y.[1182]

John Cole, born England, received 28 January 1862, w/m, larceny, 1y6m.[1183]

+John F. Beegan, born Ireland, received 29 January 1862, w/m, insubordination, 1y. Beegan, Co. C, 1st Reg. MI, used "contemptuous and disrespectful language" and struck Lt. Amasa J. Finch in the face on 23 October 1861 at Camp Union, MD. On 4 August 1862, Beegan was pardoned.[1184]

Calvin Beckwith, born NY, received 30 January 1862, w/m, desertion, 1y6m. Pvt. Beckwith, Co. A, 25 NY Volunteers, deserted around 8 January 1862 from camp at Hall's Hill, VA was apprehended in citizen's clothes and returned to Hall's Hill 15 January 1862. Beckwith was pardoned 9 July 1862.[1185]

+Charles P. Miller, born OH, received 30 January 1862, w/m, assault, battery, and robbery, 2y. Miller was charged with assault and battery with intent to rob Seymour H. Knight. Miller was pardoned 4 August 1862.[1186]

JC, born Ireland, received 30 January 1862, w/m, assault, battery, and robbery, 1y. JC was pardoned 4 August 1862.[1187]

George Goldsmith, born MD, received 30 January 1862, w/m, larceny of $35 from Thomas A. Hanassey, 1y6m.[1188]

Arni D. Rankin, born NY, received 31 January 1862, w/m, insubordination, 1y. Private Rankin drew a knife on Lt. Benjamin K. Kimberly, made a violent assault on him, and threatened to kill him on 21 January 1862 at Hall's Hill, VA. Rankin was pardoned 2 August 1862.[1189]

Dennis Falby, born VT, received 3 February 1862, w/m, insubordination, 1y. After hearing that he was to be taken to the guardhouse, Private Falby, Stockton's MI Infantry, threw his plate in the air and kicked it when it came down. When Lt. Prentiss told Falby not to smash and throw his plate, Falby said "he would 'lick' him [Prentiss] if he had a chance."[1190] Falby was dishonorably discharged and sentenced to the pen. On 2 August 1862, he was pardoned.

JN, born NY, received 3 February 1862, w/m, forgery, 6m. JN was released 30 August 1862. JN forged orders ($11 value) on paymaster.[1191]

John W. Wilson (aka John Williams), born NY, received 5 February 1862, w/m, larceny, 1y6m. Wilson stole two dresses (one valued at $10 and the other at $5), property of Mrs. Mary Heisler. Wilson was a soldier in the 29th PA, Co. F.[1192]

John Welsh, born Nova Scotia, received 6 February 1862, w/m, larceny of an overcoat, property of Henry Morax, 1y3m.[1193]

WE, born DE, received 7 February 1862, w/m, desertion, 6m. WE was pardoned 4 August 1862.[1194]

Benjamin F. Johnson, born Canada, received 8 February 1862, b/m, larceny of two $20 Treasury notes out of the letters of soldiers of the 1st Long Island Regiment, 4y6m.[1195]

Albert Cantner, born PA, received 10 February 1862, w/m, manslaughter, 8y. Cantner was indicted for the murder of John Bremline. Cantner lived in house with a Mr. Jackson, Anna Light, and Elizabeth ("Lib") McManus. On the night of the murder, John Bremline was in bed with Elizabeth, and Cantner told her to come to him. Bremline would not let her go. Cantner took his pistol and shot Bremline in the left chest. Light testified that Bremline attacked Cantner before Cantner fired. At sentencing on 1 February 1862, the judge lectured Cantner and postponed the start of his imprisonment until 9 February 1862 so that he could see his parents first.[1196]

Daniel O'Callahan, born Canada, received 10 February 1862, w/m, larceny of two $5 notes, a silver half dollar, and a silver quarter dollar, property of Daniel O'Bryan on 18 January 1862, 1y3m. O'Callahan was a soldier in the 2nd District, Co. A.[1197]

William Jones, born DC, received 11 February 1862, b/m, larceny of camp bed and chest, property of Ambrose Carner, 1y.[1198]

WD, born Ireland, received 12 February 1862, w/m, insubordination, 6m. WD was pardoned 4 August 1862.[1199]

Martin Haveren, born Ireland, received 12 February 1862, w/m, insubordination, 1y. On 13 October 1861 at Camp Smith, Haveren, Co. E, 25 Reg. NY, refused to follow orders and return a newspaper he had stolen. He took his musket with the intention to use it, saying "I'll sicken the Captain before he leaves camp...."[1200] Haveren was pardoned 24 February 1862.

TMcD, born Ireland, received 12 February 1862, w/m, insubordination, 6m. TMcD was pardoned 2 August 1862.[1201]

+Orin Keen, born Maine, received 13 February 1862, w/m, insubordination, 5y. Keen, Co. F, 2nd Reg't. ME Volunteers, was AWOL from Camp Jamerson, Hall's Hill, VA, from the morning of 13 November 1861 until the afternoon of 14 November 1861. On 23 November 1861, he was noisy and drunk, insulted and kicked Sgt. Forrest D. Douglass as the sergeant arrested him, and used threatening language against Capt. A. P. Wilson who had had Keen arrested. Keen was pardoned 4 August 1862.[1202]

Railton B. Stalker, born NY, received 14 February 1862, w/m, desertion, 2y6m. Stalker, Co. A, 19th Reg. NY Volunteers, deserted near Rockville, MD about 23 November 1861. He was dishonorably discharged and sent to the pen. On 31 March 1862, he was pardoned.[1203]

D. M. Henderson, born PA, received 15 February 1862, w/m, insubordination, 1y. Henderson, Co. G, 1st PA Rifle Regiment, disobeyed orders by refusing to be quiet and return to his regiment, and he drew two loaded revolvers and fired one at 1st Lt. G. T. Burrough, Regimental Quartermaster, 43rd Regiment NY Volunteers. On 2 August 1862, Henderson was pardoned.[1204]

William Fahey, born Ireland, received 17 February 1862, w/m, insubordination, 3y. Pvt. Fahey, Co. F. 25th Regiment NY Volunteers, disobeyed Captain A. H. Ferguson by refusing to go get wood at camp at Hall's Hill, VA around 26 November 1861. Fahey kicked Ferguson, saying, "[I] enlisted for a soldier, not for a laborer." Fahey was pardoned 4 August 1862.[1205]

Thomas F. Kelly, born Ireland, received 17 February 1862, w/m, insubordination, 2y4m. Private Kelly, Co. G., 40 NY Volunteers, was found guilty of mutinous conduct at Camp Sackett near Alexandria, VA on 9 November 1861. Kelly said, "If you have my head shaved, you will never have another head shaved; you cannot teach me anything...."[1206] Then he hit Lt. George P. Cane with his fist. Kelly was pardoned 9 June 1862.

JH, born Ireland, received 19 February 1862, w/m, insubordination, 6m. JH was pardoned 4 August 1862.[1207]

JS, born Ireland, received 19 February 1862, w/m, insubordination, 6m. JS was pardoned 2 August 1862.[1208]

George Jones, born MD, received 20 February 1862, b/m, manslaughter, 8y. Jones was convicted in the stabbing murder of Theodore Chisley (b/m) on 10 October 1861.[1209]

JOS, born Ireland, received 20 February 1862, w/m, insubordination, 1y. JOS was pardoned 4 August 1862.[1210]

John Jacob Muller, born PA, received 20 February 1862, w/m, insubordination, 6m. Pvt. Muller, Co. B, 35th Regiment PA Volunteers, was drunk when he kicked Captain Kapp on 23 November 1861. Muller was pardoned 4 August 1862.[1211]

George L. Stevens, born Maine, received 21 February 1862, w/m, insubordination, 1y6m. Stevens, Co. C, 10th Regiment ME Volunteers, escaped from a guard tent while serving a sentence there, struck Sgt. Wicks, used disrespectful language against Captain Wm. P. Jordan and 1st Lt. B. M. Redlon, and was drunk at a depot of the Baltimore and Ohio Railroad in Baltimore on 9 January 1862. Stevens was pardoned 4 August 1862.[1212]

PMcG, born Ireland, received 23 February 1862, w/m, insubordination, 6m. PMcG was pardoned 2 August 1862.[1213]

+Samuel Gallagher, born PA, received 24 February 1862, w/m, desertion, 3y. Gallagher, Co. A, 31 Regiment PA Volunteers, deserted camp on Queen's farm around 20 November 1861. As part of Gallagher's sentence, he was branded with a "D" on his left hip, and dishonorably discharged. On 4 August 1862, Gallagher was pardoned.[1214]

+George Smith, born NY, received 24 February 1862, w/m, desertion, 3y. Smith deserted camp on Queen's farm about 20 November 1861. He was pardoned 4 August 1862.[1215]

LM, born Germany, received 25 February 1862, w/m, insubordination, 3y. LM was pardoned 2 August 1862.[1216]

Adolph Grappe, born Germany, received 25 February 1862, w/m, desertion, 1y. Pvt. Grappe, Co. G, 29th Regiment NY Vols., deserted camp around 12 September 1861 and was gone until 9 November 1861 when he was arrested by Lt. Wagner near Alexandria and sent back to camp at Bailey's Cross Roads, VA. Grappe was pardoned 2 August 1862.[1217]

+Epraim Reed, born NY, received 25 February 1862, w/m, insubordination, 1y. Reed was pardoned 4 August 1862.[1218]

+John Colligan, born NY, received 25 February 1862, w/m, insubordination, 1y. Colligan was pardoned 4 August 1862.[1219]

GR, born France, received 26 February 1862, w/m, insubordination, 2y. GR was pardoned 4 August 1862.[1220]

+William H. Tulley, born NY, received 26 February 1862, w/m, insubordination, 1y. Pvt. Tulley, Co. G, 62nd NY Volunteers, spoke disrespectfully to Major Oscar V. Dayton and struck him on

29 January 1862 at Camp Tenally, DC. Tulley was pardoned on 4 August 1862.[1221]

Washington Liscomb, born NY, received 27 February 1862, w/m, insubordination, 2y. Pvt. Liscomb, Co. K, 60th Regiment NY Volunteers, was disorderly, used profane and threatening language, and threw his plate of food into the fire at camp near Baltimore. He refused to obey orders ("I will be damned if I will go. Shoot me, damn you.")[1222] He tried to run from the guards and tried to form a group to leave camp and seize the rifles of the guards. On 2 August 1862, he was pardoned.

Henry A. Whitting, born Maine, received 28 February 1862, w/m, insubordination, 1y. On 6 January 1862, while stationed at Camp California, VA, Private Whitting, Co. C., 5th New Hampshire, was questioned by his sergeant, Joseph H. Harris, after he [Whitting] struck Private Oscar Putnam. In response to why he struck Putnam, Whitting answered: "I struck him because I had a mind to. If you say two words, I will strike you."[1223] When the sergeant warned him to be careful what he said or he would be arrested, Whitting struck the sergeant in the face, knocked him down, and hit him four times while he was down. Whitting was tried for insubordination on 8 January 1862, sentenced to the penitentiary for 1y, and pardoned on 2 August 1862.

DS, born England, received 1 March 1862, w/m, desertion, 1y. DS was pardoned 4 August 1862.[1224]

John Bush, born PA, received 1 March 1862, w/m, desertion, 1y. Bush, Co. K, 9th Regiment of Infantry of PA Reserve, deserted at Fairfax, VA, on 1 January 1862, and returned home to Allegheny City, PA. He had hurt his hand and was given a pass to be off duty but had returned to duty at the time of the desertion. He was returned to camp around 3 February 1862. On 9 April 1862, he was pardoned.[1225]

JD, born PA, received 4 March 1862, w/m, insubordination, 3y. JD was pardoned 9 April 1862.[1226]

JH, born Ireland, received 5 March 1862, w/m, larceny, 1y. JH was pardoned 2 August 1862.[1227]

+Martin J. Burns, born NY, received 5 March 1862, w/m, desertion, 3y. Burns was pardoned 4 August 1862.[1228]

Albert C. Ward, born IN, received 6 March 1862, w/m, assault with intent to kill, 8y. Ward tried to kill James S. Matthews in an attempted robbery of 2 coins ($40), 2 coins ($10), and seven $10 Treasury notes. A pardon was sought for Ward due to the respectability of his family in Indiana. He was pardoned 4 August 1862.[1229]

Montgomery Jones, born MD, received 6 March 1862, w/m, larceny, 1y8m. Jones stole a $30 watch on 15 February 62, property of Charles Herzog.[1230] Jones was a soldier in the 2nd District, Co. C.[1231]

Phelix Mullin, born Ireland, received 7 March 1862, w/m, burglary, 3y .Mullin, a soldier in the 10th NJ, Co. I, broke into the house of a Mr. Adams. Mullin was pardoned 25 July 1862.[1232]

Nathaniel S. Lord, born Maine, received 7 March 1862, w/m, larceny, 1y3m. Lord stole a $15 coat on 17 February 1862, property of Reuben Soloday, a soldier. Lord was pardoned 23 April 1862.[1233]

+William H. O'Dell, born NY, received 7 March 1862, w/m, desertion, 2y. O'Dell, Co. C., 18th NY Reg. Volunteers, deserted around 21 September 1861 and returned in a few days. He was dishonorably discharged, branded with a 2" letter "D" on his left hip, had his head shaved and was sentenced to serve 2y in the penitentiary. On 4 August 1862, O'Dell was pardoned.[1234]

+William C. Ireland, born NY, received 7 March 1862, w/m, desertion, 2y. Pvt. Ireland, Co. C, 18th Regiment. NY Vols., deserted camp around 21 September 1861 and was apprehended in civilian clothes without a pass. Sentenced to the penitentiary, he was branded with a 2 inch "D" on his left hip. Ireland was pardoned 4 August 1862.[1235]

AWB, born NY, received 7 March 1862, w/m, insubordination, 1y. AWB was pardoned 2 August 1862.[1236]

Robert Lovett, born NY, received 7 March 1862, w/m, sleeping on post, 1y. Lovett, Co. D, 5th Regiment NY Vols., fell asleep while on post between 11-12 pm at Camp Federal Hill, Baltimore, MD on 5 December 1861. As punishment, he had half of his head shaved and was sentenced to serve 1y in the penitentiary. Lovett was pardoned 2 August 1862.[1237]

William Griffin, born NY, received 7 March 1862, w/m, desertion, 6m.Griffin, Co. K, 5th Regiment NY Vols., deserted Camp Federal Hill, Baltimore, MD, around 10 December 1861. As punishment, he had half his head shaved and was sentenced to 6m in the penitentiary. Griffin was pardoned 26 June 1862.[1238]

Joseph Affleck, born NY, received 7 March 1862, w/m, desertion, 6m. Pvt. Affleck, Co. F, 5th Regiment NYS Vols., deserted Camp Federal Hill, Baltimore, MD around 5 November 1861. As punishment, half his head was shaved and he was sentenced to 6m in the pen. Affleck was pardoned 4 August 1862.[1239]

John E. Campbell, born NY, received 7 March 1862, w/m, desertion, 6m. Campbell, Co. D, 5th Regiment NY Vols., deserted near Ft. Federal Hill, Baltimore, MD between 8-11 p.m. around 6 January 1862. He had half his head shaved and was sent to the penitentiary where he was pardoned 4 August 1862.[1240]

John James, born PA, received 8 March 1862, w/m, desertion, 3y. Pvt. James, Co. D, 23rd Regiment PA Volunteers, deserted Camp Graham, Washington, DC, from 15 November 1861 until he was brought back on 2 December 1861. James was pardoned 25 March 1862.[1241]

MS, born NJ, received 9 March 1862, w/m, insubordination, 2y. MS was pardoned 2 August 1862.[1242]

+William Fishenden, born England, received 9 March 1862, w/m, insubordination, 2y6m. Private Fishenden, Co D, 1st Regiment U.S. Chasseurs, was charged with being drunk on guard duty on 6 December 1861 at Camp Cochrane, Washington, DC; with "contempt and disrespect towards his superior officers." ("Go to hell you God damn'd pis pot"[1243] was his reply when ordered by Lt. Ellis to "keep quiet."); and, with striking superior officer Corporal William Lutz (Co. I, 1st Regiment) with his fist. Fishenden was pardoned 4 August 1862.

+Dennis Connell, born Ireland, received 9 March 1862, w/m, insubordination, 6m. Pvt. Connell, Co. I, 1st Regiment, Long Island Vols., left camp on 26 October 1861 for twelve hours at Queen's farm in DC without permission. Using disrespectful language, he refused to do his duty as ordered by Sgt. Flagler, and insolently refused to obey Lt. S. M. K. Miles when ordered to do police duty on 28 October 1861. Connell was pardoned 4 August 1862.[1244]

JR, born VT, received 10 March 1862, w/m, insubordination, 6m. JR was pardoned 2 August 1862.[1245]

+William C. McHale, born Ireland, received 10 March 1862, w/m, insubordination, 1y. Pvt. McHale, Co. C, 5th VT Vols., willfully attempted to disable himself by shooting off his right thumb at Camp Griffin, VA while on guard on 4 February 1862. McHale was pardoned 4 August 1862.[1246]

+George W. Curtis, born PA, received 10 March 1862, w/m, insubordination, 3y. Curtis, Co. H, Long Island Regiment, beat and mistreated Pvt. Elias Lomax at camp on Queen's farm between 3-5 p.m. on 21 December 1861. He seized Sgt. Carey by the throat, hit and knocked Sgt. Bishop down, and seized Sgt. Bogart by the collar, calling him "a damned big-headed son of a bitch."[1247] Curtis was pardoned 4 August 1862.

+John Williams, born Ireland, received 10 March 1862, w/m, insubordination, 2y. Pvt. Williams, Co. C, 1st NJ Cavalry, at Camp Curtis near Alexandria, VA on 14 November 1861, struck 1st Lt. John Worsley and exhibited "conduct subversive to good order and military discipline" by saying "If I ever get liberated, I will shoot you, and all such sons of bitches."[1248] Williams was pardoned 4 August 1862.

+August Wolfram, born IN, received 11 March 1862, w/m, assault/battery with intent to kill, 8y. When ordered by his First Sergeant Charles Kronmeyer to get some water, Private Wolfram, Co. C., 52 Regiment, NY Volunteers refused. Kronmeyer told Wolfram to follow him to the guardhouse, and after following for about twenty steps, Wolfram refused to follow any further. Around 5 p.m. on 22 December 1861, at Camp California, VA, Wolfram fired his musket at First Sgt. Charles Kronmeyer and wounded him in the right thigh. Initially Wolfram was sentenced to 2y in the pen for the charges; however, the sentence was deemed inadequate and changed to 8y.[1249]

James Merr, born Ireland, received 13 March 1862, w/m, insubordination, 1y. Merr was charged with assaulting Private Edward Donnelly. Donnelly testified that Merr and McLaughlin (next entry) kicked him so much he was cut in the face and suffered abdominal pain. He was in the hospital a week. Merr was pardoned 2 August 1862.[1250]

Patrick McLaughlin, born Ireland, received 13 March 1862, w/m, insubordination, 2y. Private McLaughlin was in the regular service of the U.S. Army and unattached to any regiment. He was charged with assaulting "with his feet and hands, without provocation, Private Edward Donnelly, acting First Sergeant of a detachment of regulars at Fort Delaware, DE on or about 26 November 1861. McLaughlin was pardoned 2 August 1862.[1251]

John Brady, born Ireland, received 14 March 1862, w/m, insubordination, 4m. Pvt. Brady, Co. A, 4th Regiment NY Vols., threatened to strike Capt. Joseph Henriques with his canteen at Havre de Grace, MD around 30 September 1861.[1252]

JF, born PA, received 14 March 1862, w/m, desertion, 6m. JF was pardoned 4 August 1862.[1253]

+William A. Howard, born VT, received 14 March 1862, w/m, insubordination, 6m. Pvt. Howard, Co. F, 6th Regiment MI Vols., deserted his post as guard around 11 December 1861 at Camp McKim, Baltimore, MD, which allowed his prisoner to escape. When confined to the guard tent for his action, he cut his way out. Howard was pardoned 4 August 1862.[1254]

James H. Brace, born IL, received 14 March 1862, w/m, insubordination, 9m. Pvt. Brace, Co. K, 6th Regiment MI Vols., disobeyed orders to take guard duty on 1 December 1861 at Camp McKim, Baltimore, MD, and used "insolent and abusive language" to the 1st sergeant who ordered him to do so. Brace was pardoned 2 August 1862.[1255]

William Green, born Maine, received 24 March 1862, w/m, desertion, 1y. Pvt. Green, Co. H, 4th Reg. Maine Volunteers, deserted around 26 July 1861 as his company retreated at Bull Run. He was apprehended around 1 October 1861 on the Eastern Shore of MD. Green was pardoned 10 May 1862.[1256]

+Phelix McCrady, born Ireland, received 24 March 1862, w/m, neglect of duty, 6m. Pvt. McCrady, Co. B, 3 NY Vols., neglected his duty at Ft. McHenry, MD around 4 February 1862. McCrady was pardoned 4 August 1862.[1257]

+Henry S. Sager, born NY, received 24 March 1862, w/m, neglect of duty, 6m. Pvt. Sager, Co. C, 3 NY Vols., permitted four enlisted men to go outside the lines while he was on guard at Ft. McHenry, MD around 21 January 1862. Sager was pardoned 4 August 1862.[1258]

+James Lang, born England, received 24 March 1862, w/m, neglect of duty, 6m. Pvt. Lang, Co. G, 3rd NY Vols., allowed men to pass without authority as he stood guard at Ft. McHenry around 10 February 1862. Lang was pardoned 4 August 1862.[1259]

+Thomas H. Cummings, born NY, received 25 March 1862, w/m, insubordination, 10y. Cummings was pardoned 4 August 1862.[1260]

+Samuel Mahon, born NY, received 25 March 1862, w/m, insubordination, 10y. Mahon was pardoned 4 August 1862.[1261]

John H. Chase, born NH, received 29 March 1862, w/m, desertion, 2y. Chase, Co. C, 2nd NH Volunteers, deserted from Camp Beaufort around 24 January 1862 and was apprehended 28 January 1862. Dressed in civilian clothes (except for his socks), Chase denied having deserted. He was ordered to remove his shoes, and it was his government-issue socks that gave him away and forced him to admit he had deserted. Chase was pardoned 2 August 1862.[1262]

Thomas Norris, born Ireland, received 2 April 1862, w/m, manslaughter, 5y. Norris killed Margaret Norris, his wife, on 11 October 1861 between 6-7 p.m. in their home on 3rd Street, south of F Street. Irishman Thomas Norris and his wife Margaret [Kane] Norris occupied the front room on the ground floor of the house. When neighbor Julia

Cahil returned from a shopping trip, Mrs. Norris was dead, or near dead, lying on the floor with blood running from her face and head. Mr. Norris said she had fallen against a chair. He was arrested with blood on his hands and around his fingernails. The only furniture in the Norris' room was two small tables, one broken chair, and a tattered quilt or two. By the time the police arrived, Mrs. Norris' body was wrapped in one of the quilts. There was a pool of blood on the floor and blood was spattered on the wall. A half-full pop bottle of whiskey was in one corner. Dr. Willet found a wound on the left side of Mrs. Norris' nose and a wound over her left eye, both of which had been made with a sharp instrument. She also had a bruise under her left ear. 5y.[1263]

Charles W. Smith, born England, received 2 April 1862, w/m, larceny of five $10 Treasury notes from Patrick and Michael Haley on 24 March 1862, 2y. Smith was a soldier in the 33rd NY, Co. H. He escaped from the pen on 15 July 1862.[1264]

William Connelly, born Ireland, received 2 April 1862, w/m, grand larceny of four coats ($55 value) and one $1 cap, property of George W. McLellan, 2y. Connelly was a soldier in the 43rd NY, Co. B.[1265]

Mary Jane Johnston, born DC, received 2 April 1862, b/m, larceny of $15 from Daniel K. Boswell on 16 March 1862, 2y.[1266]

+John Ryan, born Ireland, received 7 April 1862, w/m, arson of a home owned and occupied by John W. Haynes in Tenallytown, 2y. Ryan was a soldier of the 59th NY Regiment, Co. D, and was a gardener in the pen.[1267]

MMc, born NY, received 9 April 1862, w/m, insubordination, 6m. MMc was pardoned 2 August 1862.[1268]

+Martin Hanley, born Ireland, received 9 April 1862, w/m, desertion, 1y. Hanley was pardoned 4 August 1862.[1269]

+Richard Anderson born England, received 9 April 1862, w/m, insubordination, 2y. Anderson was pardoned 4 August 1862.[1270]

PS born Ireland, received 12 April 1862, w/m, insubordination, 2y. PS was pardoned 2 August 1862.[1271]

John Woodcock, born MD, received 18 April 1862, w/m, larceny, 2y. Woodcock stole $15 from Flint and Johnson on 1 February 1862. He was pardoned 10 November 1862.[1272]

+James S. Maney, born NY, received 3 May 1862, w/m, larceny, 1y. Maney was pardoned 4 August 1862.[1273]

AS, born MI, received 3 May 1862, w/m, larceny, 1y. AS was pardoned 2 August 1862.[1274]

JD, born Germany, received 5 May 1862, w/m, larceny, 6m. JD was pardoned 4 August 1862.[1275]

+Ambrose C. Howland, born MA, received 7 May 1862, w/m, sleeping on post, 5y. Pvt. Howland, Co. G, 1st Battalion, 11th Regiment U.S. Infantry, fell asleep on duty at Camp Winfield Scott near Yorktown, VA on 30 April 1862. He began his shift at 1 a.m. "I was suddenly taken sick…and lied down. I was sick at the stomach and could hardly see, and had a headache." [1276] Howland was pardoned 4 August 1862.

George Hesch, born Germany, received 12 May 1862, w/m, insubordination, 5y. Private Hesch, Co. B, 1st NY Artillery, drew a weapon on Sgt. William Fey, wounding Fey on 27 February 1862 at Camp Duncan, Washington, DC. Fey testified that Hesch was drunk and noisy so he was taking him to the guardhouse. On the way, Hesch stabbed him. Hesch needed an interpreter in the trial as he spoke little English. On 2 August 1862, Hesch was pardoned.[1277]

Peter Meyer, born PA, received 20 May 1862, w/m, larceny/ receipt of stolen goods, 3y. Meyers' house was a "notorious depot for stolen property" [1278] A local mother had been there to admonish Meyers for encouraging her children to participate in crime by buying the stolen things they brought him. He received 3 months in jail plus a $1 fine for the receipt of goods of less than $5, to be followed by 3y in the penitentiary. Meyer was an invalid in the penitentiary and suffering an incurable disease and expected to die, he was pardoned on 6 August 1862 so that the might spend his last days with his family.[1279]

Benjamin J. Fowler, born NY, received 20 May 1862, w/m, insubordination, 3m. Fowler, Co. E, 5th NY Volunteers, left Camp Buchanan, VA, without permission around 10 May 1862 and entered the house of a person of "Burnt District," VA and took letters and books. On 12 May 1862, he entered a house and took an officer's cap and a pair of epaulettes. Fowler was pardoned 4 August 1862.[1280]

+Alfred Stillwell, born DE, received 22 May 1862, violating 54th article of war, 6m. Pvt. Stillwell, Co. G, 3rd Regiment PA Cavalry, took a harness and buggy from a Virginia citizen, Mr. Timberlake, on 14 May 1862. Stillwell was pardoned 4 August 1862.[1281]

William M. Terril, born NY, received 25 May 1862, violating 54th article of war, 6m. Terril, Co. A., 23rd Regt. NY Volunteers, was charged with leaving camp at Upton Hill, VA, on 16 March 1862. As Terril was leaving, Lt. Benjamin Bennett called to him several times to return to ranks, and Terril's "violent and insolent" reply was "What the hell you want?" Lt. Bennett again ordered Terril to return, and Terril said, also in a "violent and insolent manner," "You're putting on your damned airs," all in front of a large group of soldiers. He was also found guilty of calling William B. Rinsey, Orderly Sergeant of the company, "a God damned pis pot" in front of a large number of soldiers. Terril was dishonorably discharged and sentenced to the penitentiary. He was pardoned 2 August 1862.[1282]

+Augustus Juley, born Germany, received 25 May 1862, violating 54th article of war, 5y. Pvt. Juley, Co. G, 22nd Regiment NY Vols., sold blankets for money at Camp Upton's Hill, VA around 13 March 1862 when he was left in charge of the company's property. Then he left camp, dressed in civilian clothes and enlisted in Co. A, 2nd Regiment of Berdan's Sharp Shooters, and got $20 in "soldier clothing". Juley was pardoned 4 August 1862.[1283]

JS, born NJ, received 25 May 1862, violating 54th article of war, 2y6m. JS was pardoned 2 August 1862.[1284]

George W. House, born NY, received 25 May 1862, violating 54th article of war, 3m. House was charged with deserting camp about 17 April 1862. He had been court-martialed before and fined $13 for leaving camp at Falls Church, VA. "When detailed for duty, he always goes, uncomplaining." He was found guilty only of being AWOL and sentenced to 3 months in the penitentiary. House was pardoned 4 August 1862.[1285]

John Percall, born PA, received 25 May 1862, violating 54th article of war, 5y. Percall, Co. D, 35th Regt. NY Volunteers, was charged with desertion near Bristoe Station, VA about 12 April 1862, with theft of a horse about 20 April 1862, with being absent without leave, and with destruction of his military clothing. Percall was pardoned 2 August 1862.[1286]

Frank Pierce, born NY, received 25 May 1862, violating 54th article of war, 5y. Pierce, Co. D, 26th NY Volunteers, was charged for deserting camp on 15 April 1862, with stealing a horse on 20 April 1862, with being absent without leave for twenty days in April 1862 from camp near Alexandria, VA, and with "breach of good order and military discipline" for destroying his uniform while AWOL. Captain George Arrowsmith testified that Pierce had left camp often. "It has been difficult to keep him in camp. As a soldier his reputation is not very good." Pierce was pardoned 2 August 1862.[1287]

Charles F. Williams, born NY, received 26 May 1862, revolt/mutiny, 1y. Private Williams, Taft's 5th NY Battery, was charged with disobeying orders to march on 15 April 1862, and with mutiny. Williams and several others refused Captain Elijah D. Taft's orders to march to Camp Winfield Scott near Yorktown, VA. Williams was pardoned on 2 August 1862.[1288]

Josephus Bond, born NY, received 26 May 1862, revolt/mutiny, 1y. Private Bond, Taft's 5th NY Battery, was charged with disobeying orders to march on 15 April 1862, and with mutiny. Bond and several others refused Captain Elijah D. Taft's orders to march to Camp Winfield Scott near Yorktown, VA. On 2 August 1862, Bond was pardoned.[1289]

Silas Upson, born NY, received 26 May 1862, revolt/mutiny, 1y. Upson, Taft's 5th NY Battery, was charged with disobeying orders to march on 15 April 1862, and with mutiny. Upson and several others refused Captain Elijah D. Taft's orders to march to Camp Winfield Scott near Yorktown, VA. On 2 August 1862, Upson was pardoned.[1290]

William Maxwell, born NY, received 26 May 1862, revolt/mutiny, 1y. Maxwell, Taft's 5th NY Battery, was charged with disobeying orders to march on 15 April 1862, and with mutiny. Maxwell and several others refused Captain Elijah D. Taft's orders to march to Camp Winfield Scott near Yorktown, VA. Included in Maxwell's file are four letters—one from Maxwell's sister, Mrs. Rhodes; one from her husband, William C. Rhodes; one from Maxwell's father, Thomas Maxwell; and one from the six prisoners charged with the mutiny—to President Lincoln, asking for presidential pardon for all who had been court-martialed for the incident. In a letter to his father on 26 May 1862, Maxwell explained that all six men (Upson, Bond, Williams, Thomas, Conklin and himself) had been in service for nine months without any weapons and were within four miles of the enemy at Yorktown when ordered to march. "It is pretty hard after volunteering our services to our country thinking she needed men to support this unholy rebellion and would furnish us with arms, to be cast into a penitentiary for merely asking for our arms. We never refused to do our duty but always was and still are willing."[1291] Ordered to march into enemy territory, unarmed, all six soldiers refused. On 2 August 1862, Maxwell was pardoned.

John Thomas, born NY, received 26 May 1862, revolt/mutiny, 1y. Private Thomas, Taft's 5th NY Battery, was charged with disobeying orders to march on 15 April 1862, and with mutiny. Thomas and several others refused Captain Elijah D. Taft's orders to march to Camp Winfield Scott near Yorktown, VA. On 2 August 1862, Thomas was pardoned.[1292]

+Edward Brooks, born Ireland, received 26 May 1862, desertion, 3y. Brooks was pardoned 4 August 1862.[1293]
JS, born Switzerland, received 28 May 1862, w/m, insubordination, 1y. JS was pardoned 2 August 1862.[1294]
Peleg C. Conklin, born NY, received 2 June 1862, w/m, insubordination, 1y. Private Conklin, Taft's 5th NY Battery, was charged with disobeying orders to march on 15 April 1862 and with mutiny. Conklin and several others refused Captain Elijah D. Taft's orders to march to Camp Winfield Scott near Yorktown, VA. On 2 August 1862, Conklin was pardoned.[1295]
+Samuel Brown, born Canada, received 2 June 1862, w/m, insubordination, 1y. Private Brown, Co. G, 74th NY Reg. Volunteers. Around 19 May 1862, Brown "straggled" on his company's march from Cumberland, VA to Baltimore, MD. When Col. Charles H. Burtis ordered him to rejoin the company, Brown basically said, "I can't and won't march—if the country wants me to work she must feed me—do as you please."[1296] On 21 May 1862, Brown took a musket out of Lt. Charles W. Squires' hands, resisted the uards, refused to be quiet, and told the guards he would "knock hell out of them" if they didn't let him go. Brown was pardoned 4 August 1862.
William L. Oswald, born Scotland, received 2 June 1862, w/m, mutiny, 1y. Oswald was pardoned 23 June 1862. The War Dept. annulled Oswald's sentence. He was a Captain of 34 NY Volunteers.[1297]
JV, born PA, received 10 June 1862, w/m, mail robbery, 3y.[1298]
DD, born VA, received 10 June 1862, w/m, mail robbery, 4y.[1299]
NT, born NY, received 16 June 1862, w/m, larceny, 1y.[1300]
GWP, born TN, received 20 June 1862, w/m, mail robbery, 2y6m.[1301]
EM, born TN, received 20 June 1862, w/m, larceny, 1y.[1302]
Thomas Evans born South Wales, received 20 June 1862, w/m, larceny of silver watch, 1y.[1303]
Charles Brown, born VT, received 22 June 1862, w/m, larceny, 2y6m. Brown stole a $200 horse, a $15 saddle, a $1 bridle, a $1 halter, and a $1 martingale on 11 March 62, property of David Miller.[1304]
Addison Harris, born VA, received 30 June 1862, b/m, larceny, 1y6m. Harris stole 48 napkins from the Willard Hotel.[1305]
Frank Duffy (aka F. J. Harris), born MD, received 1 July 1862, w/m, larceny, 3y. Duffy stole a horse and buggy.[1306]
Samuel Hoffman born Germany, received 3 July 1862, w/m, larceny of money and a silver watch, 1y3m.[1307]
James Hepburn, born MD, received 7 July 1862, b/m, larceny, 2y.[1308]

William F. King, born DC, received 15 July 1862, b/m, burglary, 3y.[1309]
John Cole, born MD, received 15 July 1862, b/m, larceny of an $8 watch property of Jeremiah Diggins, 1y.[1310]
George Birl, born NY, received 15 July 1862, w/m, larceny, 1y6m.[1311]
Henry Williams, born MD, received 19 July 1862, b/m, larceny, 1y6m. Williams stole a coat, property of Thomas J. D. Fuller and a shawl, property of Nathaniel Wells.[1312]
William Ward (aka SB), born MD, received 21 July 1862, w/m, obtaining money under false pretence, 1y. Ward, a soldier and omnibus driver for an Alexandria boat line, took the payroll (approx. $80-90) from a discharged corporal of the regular service, John M. Benjamin, while Benjamin was on the omnibus.[1313]
Columbus Ogle, born DC, received 21 July 1862, w/m, highway robbery, 3y.[1314]
Mary Carter, born VA, received 22 July 1862, b/f, larceny of two $50 Treasury notes, property of Maria S. Nagle, 1y6m.[1315]
WN born MA, received 24 July 1862, w/m, larceny, 1y.[1316]
Dennis Bryan, born MD, received 24 July 1862, b/boy, larceny of a $5 Treasury note, property of John Donoho, 1y.[1317]
Angel Cofen, born Italy, received 24 July 1862, w/m, larceny of a $20 Treasury note, property of Charles Walling, 1y3m.[1318]
Thomas Wilson, born Ireland, received 28 July 1862, w/m, larceny of a $5 Treasury note, 1y.[1319]
Robert Welsh, born NY, received 28 July 1862, w/m, passing $400 in counterfeit money on W. T. Smithson & Co., 5y.[1320]
John Cullen, born Ireland, received 31 July 1862, w/m, mutiny, 1y3m.[1321]
Edward Metternick (aka Edward Leicke), born Germany, received 1 August 1862, w/m, larceny of $975 in Treasury notes, property of Henry C. Willstoff, 3y.[1322]

Hereinafter, the penitentiary was closed. All inmates, excepting one or two females too sick to move, who remained incarcerated on 23 September 1862 were transferred to the penitentiary at Albany, NY. Criminals from the District of Columbia who were sentenced to serve time in the penitentiary after this date, served their time at the penitentiary in Albany or at a federal prison until 1914 when a facility was built at Lorton, VA.

Chapter Forty

PERPETRATORS WHO NEVER MADE IT TO THE PENITENTIARY

McGirk
March 1802

According to Christian Hines in his *Early Recollections of Washington City*, a man named McGirk was the first person to be hung in the District of Columbia around 1803. Found guilty of murder, McGirk holds the distinction of being the first person to be hung in the District of Columbia.

McGirk, a bricklayer, frequently was drunk and quarrelsome with his wife. Mrs. McGirk was pregnant with twins when McGirk beat her so severely that the twins were stillborn and she died soon after their delivery.

McGirk was found guilty of murder, and on 30 March 1802, he was sentenced to be hung on Saturday, 28 August 1802. The gallows were built on Capitol Hill, somewhere on the west side of the Capital among the forest of trees that then stood there. On the day of the hanging, McGirk was taken by cart to the gallows with a priest in attendance. In a final statement, he said, "When a man's character is gone his life is gone."[1323]

After making that statement, McGirk looked skyward and surprised everyone by jumping off the platform. The jack-ketch tried to pull him back on the platform, but before he could, McGirk jumped off again. Someone quickly cut the rope that held the drop, and it fell. McGirk "made three or four convulsive shrugs with his arms and shoulders, his arms being pinioned, and his life was gone."[1324]

McGirk was buried in Holmead's graveyard, just north of the city. Many citizens whose friends and family were buried in the cemetery did not like the idea of McGirk's being buried there, so they dug up the grave and reburied him in a ravine on the opposite side of the graveyard. McGirk's friends found out and moved the grave back to its original spot, only to have the angry citizens secretly return and move McGirk again to a new grave they had dug for him, just east of Holmead's Cemetery, beneath some thorny underbrush near a stream that kept the burial spot consistently wet—"a perfect quagmire."[1325]

Daniel Drayton and Edward Sayres
18 May 1849

Ship captains, Daniel Drayton and Edward Sayres, were convicted on 73 counts of transporting slaves out of the District on board "The Pearl." They were fined $15,000 and required to stay in prison until the fine was paid. Because they could not pay the exorbitant fine, Drayton and Sayres stayed in the Washington County Jail for four years and four months until President Millard Fillmore pardoned them.

Neither the Draytons nor the Sayres had any money, let alone $15,000. Mrs. Sayres went to live with her parents in New Jersey while her husband was imprisoned, and Mrs. Drayton and her four children remained at home in Philadelphia where they were supported by friends.

On 12 August 1852, both men were pardoned from serving jail time; however, they were still held responsible for the fine and court costs. [1326]

Daniel T. Woodward
March 1853

On 27 December 1852, Daniel T. Woodward was arrested for the murder of his wife, Catherine M. Woodward, on 24 December 1852. Woodward shot her in the left side of the head with a pistol. She died instantly. When he was arrested, he told officials he had intended to kill her.

In the March 1853 term of Criminal Court, Woodward was tried for murder, but counsel, seeking to get the sentence reduced to manslaughter, requested a new trial. New evidence had arisen since the first trial in which Woodward's guilt was inferred by a jury that returned a "guilty" verdict much too quickly. On 9 June 1853, at 4:50 p.m., however, Woodward was found guilty of murder. When the death sentence was pronounced on him, Woodward "heard it with a subdued spirit."[1327]

A Congressional act passed 25 January 1853 prohibited public execution, and Woodward was to be hung inside the prison walls or in the yard where only certain spectators were allowed. The law allowed the District Attorney, the prisoner's counsel, two or more doctors, twelve "respectable citizens," three ministers and any relatives the prisoner requested to be in attendance at the execution. No one under 21 was permitted to attend.

Woodward was held in the Washington County Jail awaiting execution. He was the first to be executed since 27 June 1827 when a Mr. Devaughn was executed near Alexandria for the shooting murder of Elias Martin.[1328] As he waited, Woodward's mother, sister, and brother visited him frequently. On 11 July 1853, he said that he "would rather suffer death than a life of imprisonment."[1329] Every effort was made, however, for presidential intervention, but to no avail. On 1 September 1853, the day before he was to be hung, Woodward was asked how he felt. "Never better," he said.[1330]

Rev. John C. Smith and Rev. Scrivener were with him almost all day on the first of September. Woodward shaved that evening and went to bed around 11 p.m., in good spirits. On 2 September 1853, the morning of his execution, he arose about 5 a.m., his leg chains were removed, and he dressed himself in a black suit. By 8 a.m., crowds, hoping they might catch a glimpse of the proceedings, began to gather on the rooftops outside the jailhouse.

As Woodward waited, he paced, prayed, and remained calm. He gave his watch to Rev. Smith to hold until a certain lady came to claim it. "Just before 11 a.m., his arms were pinioned and the black shroud put upon him."[1331] He asked if the shroud would be left on in the coffin. The answer was "No." At 11:05 a.m., Woodward and Rev. Smith entered the jail yard. It was a sunny day, and the breeze was cool. Woodward stepped quickly up the gallows steps. Perfectly calm, he stepped on the trap, and looking at the distance he was to fall, told Marshal Hoover, the executioner, "I think the fall is too great."[1332]

Woodward requested a drink of water and Rev. Smith said a prayer. Then Woodward's feet were tied, the cap put on his head, and the rope adjusted around his neck. He said goodbye to all who were on the stand, and kneeled in prayer. When he got up from praying, the cap was pulled down over his head. When he finished praying, Woodward threw a white handkerchief down, Marshal Hoover touched the spring, and Woodward fell. After he fell, Woodward raised his hand once and his feet several times. After a half an hour, he was pronounced dead and taken down. The shroud was removed and his body was put into the walnut coffin his brother had waiting for him.

James Powers
June 1858

On 26 June 1858, James Powers was hung for the shooting murder of Edward A. Lutz on 7 December 1857.

After the shooting, Powers fled the city and was caught on 8 December 1857 in Bladensburg in the back car of a train. "You have got me," he said to police officer John F. Carter. Lutz died that same evening, and his body was taken home to Baltimore for burial.

Witness Henry Brooders testified that on 23 July 1856, he saw Powers and Lutz fight. Powers was cut and in bed for several weeks of recuperation as a result of the fight. At the time of the fight, Powers was heard to say "I'll kill the son a b----, if it is 20 years hence."[1333]

During the weeklong trial, Powers was calm except for one time when he cried for a few moments when he heard his mother and brothers were in the courtroom. After deliberating for 40 minutes, the jury returned and the foreman burst into tears as he read the "guilty" verdict. Powers was calm, though the sobs of his mother crying in the next room could be heard. Powers was held in the jail to await sentencing and sat there quietly drinking a glass of whiskey and whittling a stick while he waited.[1334]

About 1 p.m. on 17 April 1858, James Powers approached the bench, and when asked if he had anything to say, said, "Nothing, sir, except that I have not had a fair trial. I was hurried into it without due preparation."[1335] The judge told Powers that his guilt was proved by his unprovoked use of a deadly weapon on Lutz without even any words. It was plainly a case of murder. The judge continued to address Powers: "the deplorable condition in which you now stand is traceable to the low drinking houses you frequented, in one of which you took the life of Edward A. Lutz." He then sentenced Powers to be hung by the neck until dead. At the conclusion of reading the sentence, the judge burst into tears as did many other present at the trial.[1336]

James Powers was scheduled to be hung 18 June 1858. He was attended from the time of sentencing by his spiritual advisors, Rev. T. J. O'Toole of St. Patrick's, Rev. Mr. Edelin of St. Dominick's, and the Sisters of Mercy and Sisters of Charity. By 17 June 1858, he was reported to be religiously prepared and resigned to his fate. His mother and relatives visited him frequently.

A rumor of an attempt to rescue Powers led the President to detail a group of Marines to guard the jail around the clock. The gallows were prepared in the jail yard, north of the jail, out of sight of spectators. It was the same gallows built for murderer William Wells but used to hang Daniel Woodward when Wells' sentence was commuted.[1337]

On the day of the hanging (18 June 1858), Powers was resigned to his fate and in good spirits. He had rested well the previous night and felt compelled to apologize to a man, now also a prisoner at the jail, with whom he had argued in the past. Both cried, as did onlookers. A mass was performed early in the morning in Powers' cell. Then the family came. The number of spectators allowed inside the yard was limited by law but included thirty Marines who were there to prevent any rescue. Powers, his family, and friends repeatedly said they knew nothing of a rescue attempt. The execution was on schedule. A final attempt had been made to secure a presidential pardon, but to no avail. At 10:30 a.m., Marshal Selden was headed for Powers' cell, and seeing Powers' 12 year old sister, he said emotionally, "God bless you child. Your brother will not be hung today."[1338] The execution had been postponed until 26 June 1858. The young girl ran to tell her brother the good news.

The week between 18 June and 26 June 1858 was a torturous one for Powers who vacillated between hope and despair about the hanging. However, on the 26th, it became evident that he would indeed be hung. At 12:20 p.m., he was brought into the jail yard. Sandy-haired, fair-skinned, and dressed in black luster pants and coat and a white vest, he was composed as he walked, unassisted, up the scaffold steps. The priest said a prayer as did Powers on his rosary. Marshal Selden (the executor) read a final statement, another prayer was said, and Powers' head was covered with a cap. Another prayer rendered, Powers was given one final moment before the Marshal sprung the trap. An emotional Marshal Selden quickly left the scene after the hanging. Powers' mother and sisters sobbed as did many of the spectators. Powers struggled little and died within a few minutes, seemingly without pain. When death was certain, his body was cut down, put in a coffin, and taken by friends to be buried in Baltimore.[1339]

The coffin was taken to Powers' mother's home on Canal Street in Baltimore where many people came to pay their last respects. Only a slight bruise was evident on Powers' neck. At 5:30 p.m., 2000 people gathered to attend the funeral. Forty carriages were in the funeral procession of family and friends who took the body to the Catholic Cemetery in Baltimore for burial.[1340]

Dr. George A. Gardiner
March 1853

On Monday, 7 March 1853, the trial of Dr. George A. Gardiner convened. It was a trial "without precedent in this land."[1341] Gardiner was indicted for false swearing on 30 November 1849. Gardiner purportedly ran a mine in San Lois Potosi in Mexico and employed 500 workers to clean out the mines, extract ore, build houses, and erect a large and complete refinery of metals. He said he invested $330,392 in the operation and was later driven from Mexico by the Mexican authorities. He received $20,000 per month from his mines. It cost him $10-12,000 to run them. He had extracted around $50,000 of ore when all U.S. citizens were ordered out of Mexico on 21 October 1846. Having only three days to get out, he was forced to leave his business and equipmentbehind. He took as much as he could. Mexican soldiers set fire to the rest, which was totally ruined. Gardiner testified that he never would have ventured a business in Mexico had it not been for a treaty between the U.S. and Mexico that said he would have time (more than the 3 days he was given) to get his belongings out if trouble erupted between the two countries. According to the treaty, the Treaty of 1831, Article 26, he would be allowed to remain in Mexico as long as he did not break any laws and lived peaceably.

Gardiner made a claim against the U.S. because the treaty was broken. He presented a paper, purported to be a memorial of the happenings in Mexico. He falsely swore he was a resident of San Luis Potosi, Mexico from early 1844 to 24 October 1846, during which time he was engaged in mining operations there. Neither did he employ 500 people nor make any investments there. No Americans were expelled, no Mexican soldiers burned anything because there was nothing to burn. Gardiner created the story with intent to defraud the U.S. government.

He had obtained $428,750 from the U.S. Treasury pursuant to his claim, and another $153K from the U.S. Treasury on a claim of Dr. H. Mears, "$83K of which went directly to his [Gardiner] own endowment."[1342] Mears admitted fraud but was safe in Mexico as no extradition laws existed at the time. John C. Gardiner, GeorgeGardiner's brother was a prime witness in the case and corroborated his brother's testimony. John was indicted for perjury on 13 August 1853, and bail was set at $1000.

The trial went on for so long that the court got way behind in trying its cases. The jail was overflowing with people waiting to be tried, and the courtroom was overflowing with spectators waiting to see the outcome of Gardiner's trial.

On 20 May 1853, the jury in the case was discharged as they could not come to an agreement. On 23 May 1853, District Attorney Fendall asked for a continuance until the following term for the trial of George A. Gardiner and his brother. The motion was declined.

Several important papers relevant to this case mysteriously disappeared on 9 January 1854. Mr. May, counsel for the U.S., moved to file a copy of the missing Rio Verde mining title with the signatures in facsimile, and the court granted the motion.

Finally, on 3 March 1854 at 11:25 a.m., the jury agreed on a verdict—"Guilty." Dr. George A. Gardiner was "sentenced to suffer imprisonment and labor in the penitentiary for the District of Columbia for the period of ten years..."[1343] Gardiner seeming slightly agitated upon hearing the verdict, was returned to the county jail where he was to be held awaiting transfer to the penitentiary.

When he got to the jail, he asked for one glass of water and another. He felt faint, so a window was opened. Gardiner was sitting on a chair and fell, chair and all, hitting his head on the corner of a desk. Head bleeding, he was laid on a cot and given a glass of brandy, which he smelled, but would not drink. Dr. E. M. Chapin and jail deputy Isaac Birch were there with him.

Gardiner, "spitting a great deal,"[1344] began to suffer a fit. He took off his overcoat and sat on the bed. John C. Gardiner, his brother, came in and the two conversed briefly in a foreign language, and then in English about New York. John wrote something as George had another spell. Supposedly George had suffered from these types of spells in the past. Dr. Chapin stayed with the prisoner while the deputy prepared a cell for him. Additional doctors were called in as the spasms continued. At 1:20 p.m., Gardiner was asked by Dr.

James C. Hall if he had taken poison. "No," was Gardiner's reply. However, Dr. Miller, also in attendance, later claimed that from all appearances, the death was due to strychnine.

Gardiner had not been ill. The week before his death, he had been seen in church with his fiancée and had been in a good mood.

George Gardiner, a dentist by profession, was born in NY on 19 March 1818 and died in the Washington County Jail on 4 March 1854, a victim of suicide. He was buried in the Congressional Burial ground on Sunday, 5 March 1854. The funeral "took place from a dwelling in F Street, where the deceased boarded."[1345]

John Charles Gardiner, his brother, was born about 1826 in Cuba where the family moved in an attempt to better his mother's health. Indicted for perjury in the trial of his brother, John Charles Gardiner failed to show up for trial on 2 May 1854, and the $8,000 recognizance monies paid by Dr. Thomas Miller were forfeited. Hudson Taylor and George W. Yerby forfeited $4,000 in sureties they paid to guarantee Gardiner's appearance in court.[1346]

A 68-page report as to the recovery of money paid on the claims of Gardiner and Mears was presented on 3 August 1854 by F. P. Stanton, Committee on the Judiciary, entitled "Gardiner and Mears." "And though it must be admitted that the fact of the pretended claim originating in a foreign country, and being supported by documents written in a foreign language, and in some instances, authenticated by the genuine seals of the proper officers in Mexico, and certified by the Mexican legation in this city, was well calculated to deceive those connected with the prosecution of the claim, and even the commissioners themselves; yet it cannot be denied that there were circumstances calculated to arouse suspicion in the minds of vigilant and faithful officers, and to prevent that looseness and negligence which, to use the mildest language proper to the occasion, undoubtedly contributed to the success of this stupendous fraud."[1327]

Congressman Daniel E. Sickles
February 1859

On 27 February 1859, Congressman Daniel E. Sickles shot and killed Philip Barton Key, son of Francis Scott Key, in broad daylight.

The Honorable Daniel E. Sickles of New York City fatally shot U. S. District Attorney Philip Barton Key about 2 pm on Madison Place, near the southeast corner of Lafayette Square on Pennsylvania Avenue. At least three shots were fired.

The shooting occurred a few days after Sickles received an anonymous note dated 21 February 1859:

> ```
> Honorable Daniel Sickles:
> Dear Sir: With deep regret I enclose to
> your address the few lines but an
> indispensable duty compels me to do so,
> seeing that you are greatly imposed upon.
> There is a fellow, I may say, for he is
> not gentleman, by any means, by the ---
> of Philip Barton Key, and I believe the
> District Attorney, who rents a house of a
> Negro man by the name of John A. Gray,
> situated on 15th St. between K and L
> Streets, for no other purpose than to
> meet your wife, Mrs. Sickles; he hangs a
> string out of the window as a signal to
> her that he is in, and leaves the door
> unfastened, and she walks in, and, sir, I
> do assure you. With these few hints, I
> leave the rest for you to imagine. Most
> respectfully, your friend, R.P.G.
> ```[1348]

After the shooting, Sickles, accompanied by Officer Suit, acted calm and normal, waving to a friend as his carriage passed by him on the way to the jail. When Sickles was put in jail that Sunday night, he was put in a cell, especially for murderers, but there were so many bugs in the cell they moved him to the jailor's room until they could clean up another cell for him. He got up early the next morning, smoked a cigar and shaved. He complained about the new cell, but the jailor told him that he had the best one available. Sickles passed his time awaiting trial by reading, writing, and receiving friends. Overall, he was a cheerful prisoner.

In the meantime, at the meeting of the Circuit Court, Key's death was announced and Judge Dunlop said "he [Key] had fine talents and many noble qualities."[1349] Out of respect for the deceased, court was adjourned.

Charles Key, brother of the deceased, was in charge of Key's funeral. The coffin was mahogany with black cloth and silver mounting. Philip was buried in a black cloth coat and pants, white vest, white kid gloves and held a bouquet of flowers. Flower petals were strewn about inside the casket. A silver plate on the lid of the coffin said "Philip Barton Key, died February 27, 1859, aged 39 years."[1350] After the funeral, held at the Episcopal Church, the body was taken to Baltimore where it was buried at Westminster Presbyterian Church, on the corner of Fayette and Green, in the family vault. Key was buried beside his wife and child. He was survived by four children—Lizzie, Mary, James, and Alice—ages four to twelve years old.

On 4 April 1859, Sickles' trial began. A large number of police were present to handle the crowds which were the largest ever present at a trial. Reporters came from Baltimore, New York, Philadelphia, and even from Galesburg, IL to cover the trial that went on for twenty days.

Dr. Richard Cooledge, rooming at 328 H Street on the corner of Vermont, testified that he heard three shots about 2 p.m. on the day of the murder. Pistol shots were common in that neighborhood, especially on Sunday, Cooledge said. Seeing people running, Cooledge went outside and was directed to a room where Barton lay dying. He had been shot in the upper front of his right thigh near the main artery. The second shot had hit him in his left side and passed through his body, lodging under the skin on the right side of his body. The third bullet "glanced" the right side of his body and left a bruise.

Samuel F. Butterworth testified that Key and Sickles met on the street; Sickles said "you scoundrel, you have dishonored me" [1351] or "my family." Sickles fired and Key fell, throwing an opera glass at Sickles as he fell.

Bridget Duffy, the nurse and lady's maid testified that she heard the Sickles' arguing the Saturday night before the murder. Both were crying. The next morning, Mrs. Sickles was still dressed in the clothes she had worn the night before. Mr. Sickles was sitting on the stairs crying, and Mrs. Sickles was sitting on the floor in an upstairs room with her head on a chair.

When Sickles asked her of the affair, Mrs. Sickles said "I am betrayed and lost."[1352] She admitted guilt and pleaded for mercy and forgiveness. Sickles said he would not hurt her, "since he believed her the victim of a scoundrel."

Initially, he asked for her wedding ring back, but he later returned it to her. He told her to have her mother come get her because he never wanted to see her again.

A letter was presented at the trial, written by Mr. G. B. Woolridge that made mention that Key "boasted that he only asked thirty-six hours with any woman to make her do as he pleased."[1353]

Sickles was a New York City native, about 40 years old, originally a printer, "in personal appearance is somewhat of a 'lady-killer.'"[1354] When he married Teresa Bagioli, she was 16. Sickles took her to England where he was Secretary of Legation in London. In London, she was "introduced to the queen" and fashionable society. Their NY home was elegant ($3000 monthly rent), and she was accustomed to riding in splendid carriages and wearing expensive jewels—some worth $5,000.

In Washington, the Sickles' were well known in town and often attended parties and other social functions where Key, the District Attorney, was also in attendance. After receiving the anonymous letter, Sickles accused his wife of having an affair with Key. She fainted, but admitted it, and signed a confession, a copy of which was presented in court and read as follows:

"Confession of Mrs. Sickles"

> I have been in a house on Fifteenth Street with Mr. Key. How many times I don't know. I believe the house belongs to a colored man. The house is unoccupied. I commenced going there the latter part of January, and have been alone and with Mr. Key. I usually stay an hour or more in the front room, second story. There is a bed in it, and I do what is usual for a wicked woman to do. The intimacy commenced this winter when I came from New York, in that house, an intimacy of an improper kind. We have met half a dozen times or more at different hours of the day.

On Monday of this week, Wednesday also. Arranged meetings when we met on the street and at parties. Never would speak to him when Mr. Sickles was home because I knew he did not like me to speak to him. Did not see Mr. Key for some days after I got here. He then told me he had hired the house as a place where he and I could meet. I agreed to it; having nothing to eat or drink there. The room is warmed by a wood fire. Mr. Key generally goes there first. Have walked there together, say four times; I do not think more. Was there on Wednesday last between 2 and 3 o'clock.

I went there alone. Laura was at Mr. Hoover's. Mr. Key took and left her there at my request. From there [Douglas'] I went to 15th Street to meet Mr. Key. From there to the milk woman's. Immediately after Mr. Key left Laura at Mr. Hoover's I met him in 15th Street. I went in the back gate. I went in the same bedroom, there an improper intercourse was held.

I undressed myself. Mr. Key undressed also. This occurred on Wednesday the 23 of February 1859. He has kissed me in this house a number of times. I do not deny we have had connection in this house, last spring a year ago, in the parlor on the sofa. Mr. Sickles sometime out of town and sometimes at the Capitol. I think the intimacy commenced in April or May 1858. I did not think it safe to meet him in this house, because there are servants who might suspect something.

As a general thing have worn a black and white woolen plaid dress, beaver hat trimmed with black velvet, have worn black silk dress there also; also a plaid silk dress, black velvet cloak, trimmed with lace, and a black velvet shawl trimmed with fringe. On Wednesday, I either had on my brown dress or black and white woolen dress, beaver hat, and velvet shawl. I arranged with Mr. Key to go in the back way after leaving Laura at Mr. Hoover's. He met me at Douglas's. The arrangement to go in the back way was either inside or in the street or at Douglas' as we would be less likely to be seen.

The house is on 15th between K and L on the left hand side of the way. Arranged the interview for Wednesday in the street (I think) on Monday of this week when I was there. On Monday, I went in the front door; it was open. Occupied the same room. Undressed myself and he did the same. We went to bed together. Mr. Key has ridden in Mr. Sickles' carriage and has called at his house without Mr. Sickles' knowledge, and after my being told not to invite him to do so and against Mr. Sickles' repeated request. Signed Teresa Bagioli 26 February 1859[1355]

The trial ended on 26 April 1859 when Sickles was found "not guilty." He shook hands with the jury, many of whom cried, and he was carried out of the courtroom on the shoulders of the crowd and driven in his carriage to a friend's house.[1356]

The presses from around the country disagreed with the jury's acquittal. Some thought the President intervened on Sickles' behalf as Sickles and the

President were friends. Many felt the verdict was disgraceful because they felt Sickles' had definitely murdered Key.[1357]

Chapter Forty-one

CONCLUSION

Did the penitentiary system work to deter crime? A high rate of recidivism suggests that it didn't. Matron Marceron felt "as a general thing, their faults do not seem to be the offspring of bad hearts, but owing to ignorance and the little care that has been taken of them in their childhood."[1358] Warden Isaac Clarke felt that the good food served by the prison and the lenient rule was the reason that many prisoners kept coming back to serve one term after another. The Board of Inspectors agreed that "some [prisoners] have been returned to the penitentiary upon a second, and even a third conviction; but they are persons so habitually disposed to evil, that no moral impressions can be made upon them."[1359]

Yet, there were some like convict John P. Millard (1858), for whom the system worked. He, like many others, spent his time reflecting on the bad habits that brought him to the penitentiary, attributing his fall and the fall of his fellow inmates primarily to "bad associations" brought about through drunkenness. He aspired to "regain the regard of [his] fellowmen" upon release.[1360]

Did the penitentiary meet its goals? Though its operation was short-lived and it never became the self-supporting institution originally hoped for, the U.S. Penitentiary did manage to do a good job of reforming many of its inmates. Though some chose to ignore the fact, each prisoner learned that all actions hold consequence. Improper behavior was punished, and good behavior brought reward. An opportunity for betterment was presented to every prisoner. Each was taught a job skill. Each was given the opportunity to learn to read and write. And, each was given religious instruction.

There were problems and there were mistakes made at the U.S. Penitentiary, but overall, the citizens of the District of Columbia agreed with the Board of Inspectors, who in 1837 said, "There is, perhaps, no part of the country where a penitentiary has been of so much service to the community as at this place."[1361]

During the course of its thirty-three year operation, the Penitentiary for the District of Columbia held none who were nationally notorious. In July 1865, however, several years after closing its doors, the penitentiary temporarily housed some who were quite notorious at the time—the eight conspirators in the assassination of President Lincoln. For safekeeping, these prisoners were held under heavy guard in the cells at the old penitentiary. They were tried within its walls, and four--Lewis Powell Payne, George A. Atzerodt, David E. Herold, and Mary Surratt--were executed and buried in its prison yard.

Under heavy guard, about 10:30 p.m. on 29 April 1865, the eight conspirators were transported to the old penitentiary aboard the steamer *Keyport*. Their trials were conducted at the old penitentiary, and the execution of the four who were sentenced to death was performed in the old prison yard.

On the day of the execution, Payne, Atzerodt, Herold, and Surratt were led from their cells to the gallows. As they entered the yard, they could see four coffins lined up and four holes that had been dug beside them. At 1:26 p.m. on 7 July 1865, these four, the most famous of the criminals housed in the cells of the Penitentiary for the District of Columbia, were hung by the neck until dead. Their bodies were placed in the awaiting coffins and buried in the yard, just steps from the gallows.[1362] John Wilkes Booth, Lincoln's assassin, was buried 27 April 1865 beneath one of the old penitentiary's cells. The families later claimed the bodies and moved them elsewhere.[1363]

In 1867, the government wanted to take down the old buildings of the penitentiary. Bids, ranging from $7,500 to $14,000, were accepted from contractors. The lowest bidder, J. T. Stockbridge, was given the contract. He was to start the job on 7 October 1867 and have the work completed within ninety days.

All the walls and buildings of the old penitentiary, except for the houses on the east and west ends, were to be torn down. Materials unable to be used again were to be removed from the site, and salvageable items such as bricks were to be cleaned and stacked so that they might be used elsewhere.

By 14 November 1867, work had halted. Stockbridge could not pay his workers and abandoned the job. On 28 November 1867, he formally forfeited the contract. He had already done about $500 worth of work but was paid nothing. According to the stipulations of the contract, Stockbridge owed the government $14,000 for failing to complete the job according to the terms of the contract.

At a cost of $10,021.77, the government hired another company to do the work, and by June 1868, the job was done.[1364]

A proposal for a new penitentiary was presented to Congress in 1864 with a letter from the judges of the Supreme Court for the District of Columbia justifying the expense. It was "not very credible to the country that, at the capital of this great nation, there is no building in which to confine those who offend against the laws of the land; no house of corrections for the reclamation of juvenile offenders, and a jail little better than the black-hole of Calcutta."[1365] Remarks from the Metropolitan Police affirmed the need for new correctional facilities as being "a very great moral advantage" for the community. Even so, no approval ever came to build another penitentiary in the District of Columbia, and criminals in the nation's capital have continued to be transported elsewhere to serve their time.

NOTES

Chapter One
1. David K. Sullivan, *District of Columbia Penal System, 1825-1875*. Washington, DC: Georgetown University, Thesis 4207, March 1973, ii.
2. "District of Columbia Code of Laws," CIS Vol. 200, (21-1), House Report 269, 3 March 1830.
3. Sullivan, 168.
4. "Report of the Committee on the District of Columbia on the Subject of Prisons in the District," CIS Vol. 122, (18-2), House Report 52.
5. Sullivan, 169.
6. "Report of Bulfinch on the subject of Penitentiaries,"CIS Vol. 152, (19-2), Report 98, 13 February 1827.

Chapter Two
7. "D.C. Penitentiary, 1830 Report of Inspectors," CIS Vol. 196, (21-1), House Doc. 46, 1 February 1830.
8. Sullivan, 212.
9. Sullivan, 268.
10. Sullivan, 291.
11. "Criminal Court Minutes: 1838-1862," RG 21, Entry 43, National Archives, Washington, DC.

Chapter Three
12. "Code of Laws," March 3,1830.
13. "Minutes of the U.S. Circuit Court for the District of Columbia: 1801-1861," Microfilm. M1021, Roll 1, 25 June 1801. Washington, DC: National Archives.
14. "Minutes of U.S. Circuit Court," 27 June 1801.
15. "Minutes of U.S. Circuit Court," August 1802.
16. Sullivan, 21.
17. Sullivan, 334-335.
18. "Code of Laws," 3 March 1830.
19. "Criminal Court Minutes," Vol. 8.
20. "Criminal Court Minutes," Vol. 11.
21. "Criminal Court Minutes," Vol. 9.
22. "Criminal Court Minutes," Vol. 8.

23. "Criminal Court Minutes," Vol. 11.
24. "Criminal Court Minutes," Vol. 14.
25. "Criminal Court Minutes," Vol. 15, 19 December 1853.
26. Ibid.
27. "Criminal Court Minutes," Vol. 18, 24 July 1856.
28. Sullivan, 32.
29. Sullivan, 90.

Chapter Four
30. "Report of Bulfinch," 13 February 1827.
31. "Eighth Annual Report of the Warden of the Penitentiary," CIS Vol. 303, (24-2), Doc. 97, 23 January 1837, 5.
32. "1830 Report of Inspectors,"1 February 1830.
33. "Fourteenth Annual Report of the Warden of the Penitentiary," CIS Vol. 420, (27-3), House Doc. 67, 17 January 1843
34. "1830 Report of Inspectors," 1 February 1830, 10.
35. Sullivan, 347.
36. Ibid.
37. *Evening Star*, Local Affairs, 23 September 1862, Microfilm, Washingtonia Division, DC Main Library.
38. Mary Hostetler Oakley, *Journey From the Gallows: Historical Evolution of the Penal Philosophy and Practices in the Nation's Capital* (Lanham, MD: University Press of America, 1988), 36.

Chapter Six
39. "Minute Book of the Inspectors: U.S. Penitentiary, April 1829 to July 1857," RG 48, Entry 464, 23 February 1832, National Archives II, College Park, MD, 63.
40. Ibid.
41. Ibid.
42. Ibid., 72.
43. Ibid.
44. "Miscellaneous Records relating to the U.S. Penitentiary for the District of Columbia 1826-1865," Entry 470, RG 48, 2 May 1828, National Archives II, College Park, MD.
45. "1830 Report of Inspectors," 1 February 1830, 2.
46. "Penitentiary, District of Columbia: Fourth Annual Report," CIS Vol. 234, (22-2), Doc. 49, 19 January 1833, 6.

47. "Charges against officers of the Penitentiary, District of Columbia." CIS Vol. 404, (27-2), House Doc. 174, 8 April 1842.
48. Ibid.
49. Ibid.
50. Ibid., 5.
51. Sullivan, 348.
52. "Charges against officers of the Penitentiary," 39.
53. Ibid., 42.
54. Ibid., 40.
55. Ibid., 54.
56. "Fifth Annual Report of the Inspectors of the Penitentiary in the District of Columbia," CIS Vol. 255, (23-1), Doc. 70, 28 January 1834.
57. "Seventh Annual Report of the Warden of the Penitentiary," CIS Vol. 288, (24-1), Doc. 81, 28 January 1836.
58. Ibid.
59. "Eleventh Annual Report of the Warden of the Penitentiary," CIS Vol. 365, (26-1), House Doc. 99, 12 February 1840, 2.
60. Ibid.
61. "Twelfth Annual Report of the Warden of the Penitentiary," CIS Vol. 384, (26-2), House Doc. 92, 30 January 1841.
62. "Thirteenth Annual Report of the Warden of the Penitentiary," CIS Vol. 402, (27-2), House Doc. 50, 20 January 1842.
63. Ibid.
64. "Fourteenth Annual Report of the Warden," CIS Vol. 420, (27-3), House Doc. 67, 17 January 1843.
65. "Nineteenth Annual Report of the Inspectors of the Penitentiary of the District of Columbia for the year 1847," CIS Vol. 516, (30-1), Doc. 28, 26 January 1848.
66. "Twentieth Annual Report of the Inspectors of the Penitentiary for the District of Columbia," CIS Vol. 540, (30-2), House Executive Doc. 29, 16 January 1849, 2.
67. Ibid., 4.
68. Ibid., 5.
69. Ibid., 7,8.
70. Ibid., 10.
71. Ibid., 11.
72. "Criminal Court Minutes," Vol. 11, National Archives, Washington, DC.

73. "Annual Report of the Inspectors of the Penitentiary for the District of Columbia," CIS Vol. 576, (31-1), House Executive Doc. 33, 6 Feb 1850, 14.
74. Ibid., 27.
75. "Penitentiary of the District of Columbia," CIS Vol. 545, (30-2), Report 140 to accompany bill H.R. 814, 2 March 1849.
76. "The Annual Report of the Inspectors of the Penitentiary," CIS Vol. 599, (31-2), House Ex. Doc. 43, 3 March 1851.
77. 1850 U.S. Census, District of Columbia, Washington County, 7th Ward, 21 September 1850, M432, Roll 57, 146B. National Archives, Washington, DC.
78. Ibid.
79. "Annual Report of the Inspectors of the Penitentiary," 3 March 1851.
80. Ibid.
81. Ibid., 19.
82. Ibid.
83. Ibid., 20.
84. "Criminal Court Minutes."
85. "Penitentiary for the District of Columbia." CIS Vol. 723, (33-1), Doc. 72, 3 March 1854.
86. Ibid.
87. "Report of the Warden and Board of Inspectors of the U.S. Penitentiary for the District of Columbia." CIS Vol. 942, (35-1), House Ex. Doc. 2, November 1857.
88. "Report of the Warden of the Penitentiary," CIS Vol. 840, (34-1), House Ex. Doc.1, 1 October 1855, 613.
89. Ibid.
90. "Report of the Warden of the Penitentiary," CIS Vol. 893, (34-3), House Ex. Doc.1, 1 October 1856.
91. "Report of the Warden and Board of Inspectors," Vol. 942, November 1857, 750.
92. Ibid.
93. Ibid.
94. "Report of the Warden of the Penitentiary accompanying the 30th Annual Report of the Secretary of the Interior." CIS Vol. 974, (35-2), Senate Ex. Doc. 1, 1 November 1858, 707.
95. Ibid.
96. Ibid.
97. Ibid.

98. Sullivan, 350.
99. 1860 U.S. Census, District of Columbia, Washington County, 7th Ward, 31 July 1860, M653, Roll 104, 938. National Archives, Washington, DC.
100. "Miscellaneous Letters," RG 48, Entry 466. National Archives II, College Park, MD.
101. Ibid., 23 January 1860.
102 "Miscellaneous Records relating to the U.S. Penitentiary for the District of Columbia 1826-1865." RG 48, Entry 470, National Archives II, College Park, MD, 2 March 1861. This record group contains a variety of reports, orders, financial statements, and letters regarding some of the inmates as well as several letters written to various inmates
103. Ibid., 15 October 1861.
104. Sullivan, 31.
105. Ibid., 359.
106. Star, 9 May 1861.
107. "Criminal Court District of Columbia Case Papers, 1838-63," RG 21, Entry 45, 30 June 1861, T152. National Archives, Washington, DC. (**NOTE:"T" stands for "trial number."**)
108. Ibid., 4 August 1861, T136.
109. Ibid., June 1862, T44.
110. Ibid., June 1862, T53.
111. Ibid., June 1862, T54.
112. Oakley, 36.

Chapter Seven
113. "Miscellaneous Records, 1826-1865." National Archives II.
114. Ibid.
115. Ibid.
116. Ibid.
117. Ibid.
118. Ibid.

Chapter Eight
119. "Miscellaneous Records 1826-1865."
120. "List of Convictions 1831-1853." RG 21, Entry 41, T54, National Archives, Washington, DC.
121. Ibid., T73, May 1831.

122. Ibid., T77, May 1831.
123. Ibid., T78, May 1831.
124. Ibid., T79, May 1831.
125. Ibid., T91, May 1831.
126. Ibid., T97, May 1831.
127. Ibid., T102, May 1831.
128. "List of Convictions," T98, May 1831 and "Charges against officers of the Penitentiary," CIS Vol. 404, 8 April 1842.
129. "List of Convictions," T104, May 1831.
130. Ibid., T121, May 1831.
131. "Fourth Annual Report," 19 January 1833.
132. "List of Convictions," T140, May 1831. and "Register of Convicts 1831-1862," RG 48, Entry 474, National Archives II, College Park, MD.
133. "List of Convictions," T116, May 1831.
134. Ibid., T164, May 1831.
135. Ibid., T165, May 1831.
136. Ibid., T166, March 1831.
137. "Register of Convicts," 19 November 1831.
138. Ibid.
139. "List of Convictions," T64, December 1831.
140. Ibid., T65, December 1831.
141. Ibid., T59, December 1831, and Sullivan, 347.

Chapter Nine

142. "List of Convictions," T72, December 1831.
143. "List of Convictions," T77, December 1831, and "Fifth Annual Report of the Inspectors," 28 January 1834.
144. "List of Convictions," T22, May 1832 (2y), and T26, May 1832 (2y).
145. Ibid., T28, May 1832.
146. Ibid., T40, May 1832.
147. Ibid., T43, May 1832 (2y6m) and T45, May 1832.
148. Ibid., T56 May 1832 (2y), T59, May 1832 (2y), T60, May 1832 (2y)
149. Ibid., T61, May 1832.
150. Ibid., T65.
151. Ibid., T25.
152. Ibid., T35.
153. Ibid., T31.

154. Ibid., T84.
155. Ibid., T95.
156. Ibid., T91.
157. "Register of Convicts," 8 November 1832.
158. Ibid.
159. Ibid.
160. "List of Convictions," T32, November 1832.
161. "Register of Convicts,"15 December 1832.
162. Ibid., 18 December 1832.

Chapter Ten
163. "List of Convictions," T133, November 1832.
164. Ibid., T134.
165. Ibid., T91.
166. Ibid., T117.
167. Ibid., T118.
168. Ibid., T65.
169. "Register of Convicts," 25 January 1833.
170. Ibid., 28 January 1833.
171. "List of Convictions," T58, March 1833.
172. Ibid., T13.
173. Ibid., T45.
174. Ibid., T5.
175. Ibid., T75.
176. Ibid., T77.
177. "Minutes of the U.S. Circuit Court," (1833), T107-109.
178. "List of Convictions," T51, March 1833 (2y) and T53, March 1833 (2y).
179. Ibid. T51, September 1833.
180. Ibid., T52.
181. Ibid., T55.
182. Ibid., T69.
183. Ibid., T84.
184. Ibid., T125.
185. Ibid., T47.
186. Ibid., T48 (2y) and T49 (4y).
187. Ibid., T38, 39, 40, 41 (1y).
188. "Pardon papers 1832-1862," RG 48, Entry 476, Pardon #8. National Archives II, College Park, MD.
189. "Register of Convicts,"16 November 1833.

190. Ibid., 18 November 1833.
191. "List of Convictions," T88, November 1833.
192. Ibid., T89.
193. Ibid., T86.

Chapter Eleven

194. "List of Convictions," T102.
195. Ibid., T95.
196. Ibid., T121, March 1834.
197. Ibid., T106.
198. Ibid., T144.
199. Ibid., T124 (2y), 126 (2y) and 130 (1y).
200. "Register of Convicts," 16 May 1834.
201. Ibid.
202. Ibid.
203. Ibid, 16 October 1834.
204. Ibid.
205. Ibid., 7 November 1834.
206. "List of Convictions," T64, November 1834.
207. Ibid., T81.

Chapter Twelve

208. "List of Convictions," T65, November 1834.
209. Ibid., T13.
210. Ibid., T15 (1y), T120 (1y6m).
211. Ibid., T116 (1y), T120 (1y6m).
212. "List of Convictions," T127.
213. Ibid., T160.
214. Ibid., T145.
215. Ibid., T70.
216. Ibid., T162.
217. Ibid., T129, March 1835.
218. Ibid., T118.
219. Ibid., T102.
220. Ibid., T76.
221. Ibid., T55, September 1833.
222. "Minutes of the U.S. Circuit Court," 18 May 1835.
223. "List of Convictions," T176, March 1835.
224. Ibid., T166.
225. Ibid., T160.
226. Ibid., T152.
227. Ibid., T151.

228. Ibid., T126.
229. Ibid., T105.
230. Ibid., T105.
231. Ibid., T105.
232. "List of Convictions," T130, November 1835.
233. "Seventh Annual Report of the Warden," January 1836.
234. "List of Convictions," T74, November 1835.
235. Ibid., T75.
236. Ibid., T112.
237. Ibid., T100.
238. Ibid., T94.
239. Ibid., T139.
240. Ibid., T45 (2y), T136 (3y).
241. "Seventh Annual Report of the Warden," January 1836.
242. "List of Convictions," T91, November 1835.

Chapter Thirteen
243. "List of Convictions," T73, November 1835.
244. Ibid., T89, 18 December 1835.
245. Ibid., T145, November 1835.
246. Ibid., T184, 16 January 1835.
247. Ibid., T93, March 1836.
248. "List of Convictions," T131, March 1836.
249. Ibid., T135, March 1836.
250. Ibid., T64, March 1836.
251. Ibid., T178/184, March 1836.
252. Ibid., T136, March 1836.
253. Ibid., T92 (1y), T122 (1y), March 1836.
254. Ibid., T83, March 1836.
255. "Eighth Annual Report of the Warden," 23 January 1837.
256. Ibid.
257. "List of Convictions," T84, March 1836.
258. Ibid., T162.
259. Ibid., T163.
260. Ibid., T181.
261. Ibid., T177 (1y6m), T185 (1y6m).
262. Ibid., T162.
263. Ibid., T179 (1y6m), T183 (1y6m).
264. Ibid., T91 (1y), T121 (1y).
265. "Eighth Annual Report of the Warden," 23 January 1837.
266. "List of Convictions," T136, March 1836.

267. Ibid., T178/184.
268. "List of Convictions," T97, November 1836.
269. Ibid., T95.
270. Ibid., T98.
271. Ibid., T90.
272. Ibid., T109.
273. Ibid., T106.
274. "Eighth Annual Report of the Warden," 23 January 1837.
275. "List of Convictions," T120, 17 December 1836.
276. Ibid., T109, November 1836.

Chapter Fourteen
277. "List of Convictions," T137, November 1836.
278. Ibid., T171, November 1836.
279. Ibid., T169, November 1836.
280. Ibid., T158, November 1836.
281. Ibid., T59, November 1836.
282. Ibid., T172, November 1836.
283. Ibid., T159, November 1836.
284. Ibid., T182, November 1836.
285. "List of Convictions," T183, November 1836.
286. Ibid., T67, March 1837.
287. Ibid., T88.
288. "Ninth Annual Report of the Inspectors of the Penitentiary of Washington," CIS Vol. 326, (25-2), House Doc. 140, 2 Feb 1838. (13 May 1837).
289. Ibid., 13 May 1837.
290. Ibid.
291. Ibid.
292. "List of Convictions," T116, March 1837.
293. Ibid. T118, November 1837.
294. Ibid., T120.
295. "Ninth Annual Report of the Inspectors," 2 Feb 1838. (14 July 1837).
296. Ibid., 14 October 1837.
297. "List of Convictions," T43, November 1836.
298. Ibid., T58, March 1837.
299. Ibid., T62, November 1837.
300. Ibid., T70.
301. Ibid., T87.
302. Ibid., T116.

303. "List of Convictions," T71, November 1837.
304. Ibid., T75.
305. Ibid., T106.
306. Ibid., T111.
307. Ibid., T112.
308. Ibid., T130 (1y), T131 (1y), T134 (1y).

Chapter Fifteen

309. Ibid., T118 (2y), T120 (2y).
310. Ibid., T119.
311. Ibid., T121.
312. Ibid. T153.
313. Ibid., T171.
314. Ibid., T172.
315. Ibid., T76.
316. Ibid., T119.
317. "Eleventh Annual Report of the Warden," 12 February 1840. (22 January 1828).
318. "List of Convictions," T154 (2y), T155 (2y), T156 (3y), November 1837.
319. Ibid., T80, March 1838.
320. "List of Convictions," T85 (1y), T86 (1y), T87 (1y), T88 (1y), T89 (1y).
321. "Eleventh Annual Report of the Warden," 12 February 1840. (5 June 1838).
322. "List of Convictions," T153/154, March 1838.
323. Ibid., T103.
324. Ibid., T125.
325. Ibid. T140.
326. Ibid., T57, September 1838.
327. Ibid., T87 (2y), 88 (1y), September 1838.
328. Ibid., T92.
329. Ibid., T93.
330. Ibid., T106.
331. Ibid., T110.
332. Ibid., T151.
333. Ibid., T153.
334. Ibid., T160.
335. Ibid., T96, and "Case Papers 1838-63."
336 "Pardon papers 1832-1862."

337. "Eleventh Annual Report of the Warden," 12 February 1840. (12 November 1838)
338. Ibid.
339. Ibid.
340. Ibid.
341. Ibid., 10 December 1838.

Chapter Sixteen

342. "List of Convictions," T81, March 1839 and "Criminal Court Minutes," 19 March 1839.
343. "Case Papers 1838-63," and "List of Convictions," T92/128, March 1839, and "Minutes: 1838-1862," 27 March 1839.
344. "Criminal Court Minutes," 25 March 1839, and "List of Convictions," T100, March 1839, and "Case Papers 1838-63."
345. "Case Papers 1838-63," and "List of Convictions," T130, March 1839.
346. "Criminal Court Minutes," 22 March 1839, and "List of Convictions," T21 March 1839.
347. "Criminal Court Minutes," 19 March 1839, and "List of Convictions," T71, March 1839.
348. "List of Convictions," T76 (3y), T82 (2y), March 1839.
349. "List of Convictions," T105, March 1839, and "Criminal Court Minutes," 25 March 1839, and "Case Papers, 1838-63."
350. "List of Convictions," T36, March 1839, and "Criminal Court Minutes," 13 March 1839, and "Case Papers 1838-63."
351. "Eleventh Annual Report of the Warden," 12 February 1840. (4 April 1839).
352. Ibid.
353. Ibid.
354. Ibid., 15 June 1839.
355. "Criminal Court Minutes," 6 June 1839 and "Case Papers 1838-63." T51, June 1839 term.
356. "Pardon papers 1832-1862."
357. "Eleventh Annual Report of the Warden," 12 February 1840. (19 November 1839).
358. Ibid.
359. Ibid.
360. "List of Convictions," T69, October 1839.
361. Ibid., T90.
362. Ibid., T95.
363. Ibid., T135.

364. Ibid., T113 (1y), T120 (1y).
365. Ibid., T55, December 1839 and "Case Papers," T55, December 1839 term.
366. "List of Convictions," T54, December 1839.

Chapter Seventeen

367. "List of Convictions," T45, March 1840, and "Case Papers, " T45, March 1840 term.
368. "List of Convictions," T45, March 1840 and "Criminal Court Minutes," 14 March 1840.
369. "List of Convictions," T57, March 1840 and "Criminal Court Minutes," 14 March 1840.
370. "List of Convictions," T55, March 1840 and "Criminal Court Minutes," 14 March 1840.
371. "Twelfth Annual Report of the Warden," 30 January 1841. (9 April 1840).
372. Ibid.
373. Ibid.
374. "List of convictions," T92, June 1840.
375. Ibid., T71.
376. Ibid., T18.
377. Ibid., T60, October 1840 and "Criminal Court Minutes," 28 October 1840.
378. "Twelfth Annual Report of the Warden," 30 January 1841. (6 November 1840).
379. "List of convictions," T112, October 1840.
380. Ibid., T89 and "Criminal Court Minutes," 23 November 1840 and "Case Papers," Oct.-Dec.1840, A89. (**Note: "A" stands for "appearance number"**).
381. "List of Convictions," T95, October 1840 and "Case Papers," Oct.-Dec. 1840, A89.
382. "List of convictions," T83, October 1840, and "Criminal Court Minutes," 17 November 1840, and "Case Papers," Oct.-Dec. 1840, T95.
383. "List of convictions," T87, October 1840, and "Criminal Court Minutes," 25 November 1840, and "Case Papers," Oct.-Dec. 1840. A87.
384. "List of Convictions," T114, October 1840.

Chapter Eighteen

385. "List of convictions," T99, December 1840, and "Criminal Court Minutes," 5 January 1841, and "Case Papers," Oct.-Dec. 1840, A99.

386. "List of convictions," T103, December 1840 and "Case Papers," Oct.-Dec.1840, T105.

387. "List of convictions," T90, December 1840, and "Criminal Court Minutes," 4 January 1841, and "Case Papers," Oct.-Dec. 1840, A90.

388. "List of convictions," T105, March 1841.

389. "List of convictions," T113, March 1841, and "Criminal Court Minutes," 13 March 1841, and "Case Papers," March 1841, A113.

390. "List of convictions," T90, 91, and 92, March 1841; T88, December 1841, and "Criminal Court Minutes," 9 March 1841, and "Case Papers," March 1841, T90, A91, 92.

391. "List of convictions," T110, March 1841, and "Criminal Court Minutes," 12 March 1841, and "Case Papers," March 1841, A116.

392. "List of convictions," T137, March 1841, and "Criminal Court Minutes," 16 March 1841, and "Case Papers," March 1841, A132.

393. "List of convictions," T106, March 1841, and "Criminal Court Minutes," 13 March 1841, and "Case Papers," March 1841, A106.

394. "List of convictions," T110, March 1841, and "Criminal Court Minutes," 12 March 1841, and "Case Papers," March 1841, A110.

395. "List of convictions," T131, March 1841, and "Criminal Court Minutes," 16 March 1841, and "Case Papers," March 1841, A131.

396. "Thirteenth Annual Report of the Warden," 20 January 1842. (10 April 1841).

397. "Criminal Court Minutes," 13 March 1841 and "Case Papers," March 1841, A107/108.

398. "Thirteenth Annual Report of the Warden," 20 January 1842. (9 June 1841).

399. "List of convictions," T109, June 1841, and "Criminal Court Minutes," 12 June 1841, and "Case Papers," March 1841, A109.

400. "List of convictions," T110, June 1841, and "Criminal Court Minutes," 12 June 1841, and "Case Papers," March 1841, A110.
401. "List of convictions," T112, June 1841, and "Criminal Court Minutes," 12 June 1841, and "Case Papers," March 1841, A112.
402. "List of convictions," T116, June 1841 and "Case Papers," March 1841, T116.
403. "List of convictions," T130, June 1841, and "Criminal Court Minutes," 17 June 1841, and "Case Papers," March 1841, A130.
404. "List of convictions," T136, June 1841, and "Criminal Court Minutes," 15 June 1841, and "Case Papers," March 1841, A136.
405. "List of convictions," T139, June 1841, and "Criminal Court Minutes," 17 June 1841, and "Case Papers," March 1841, A139.
406. "List of convictions," T157, June 1841 and "Case Papers," March 1841, A157.
407. "Pardon papers 1832-1862," pardon 19.
408. "List of convictions," T138, October 1841.
409. "List of convictions," T153, October 1841 and "Case Papers," March 1841, A153.
410. "List of convictions," T179, October 1841, and "Criminal Court Minutes," 11 November 1841, and "Case Papers," March 1841, A179.
411. "List of convictions," T180, October 1841, and "Criminal Court Minutes," 11 November 1841, and "Case Papers," March 1841, A180.
412. "List of convictions," T155, November 1841, and "Criminal Court Minutes," 9 November 1841, and "Case Papers," March 1841, A155.
413. "List of convictions," T132, October 1841.

Chapter Nineteen

414. "List of convictions," T177, December 1841 and "Case Papers," March 1841, A177.
415. "List of convictions," T139, December 1841, and "Criminal Court Minutes," 7 March 1842, and "Case Papers," December 1841, A139.

416. "List of convictions," T168, December 1841, and "Criminal Court Minutes," 7 March 1842, and "Case Papers," December 1841, T168.

417. "List of convictions," T160, December 1841, and "Criminal Court Minutes," 12 March 1842, and "Case Papers," December 1841, T160.

418. "List of convictions," T161, December 1841, and "Criminal Court Minutes," 7 March 1842, and "Case Papers," December 1841, A161.

419. "List of convictions," T153, December 1841, and "Criminal Court Minutes," 8 March 1842, and "Case Papers," December 1841, A153.

420. "Fourteenth Annual Report of the Warden," 17 January 1843.

421. "List of convictions," T34, March 1842 and "Criminal Court Minutes," March 1842 and "Case Papers," December 1841, T34.

422. "List of convictions," T120, March 1842.

423. "List of convictions," T139 (1y)/140, March 1842.

424. "List of convictions," T30, March 1842.

425. "Pardon papers 1832-1862," 15 January 1847.

426. "Fourteenth Annual Report of the Warden," 17 January 1843.

427. Ibid.

428. Ibid.

429. "List of convictions," T154, October 1841.

430. "List of convictions," T145, June 1842 and "Case Papers," December term 1841, T15.

431. "List of convictions," T141, June 1842.

432. "Criminal Court Minutes," June 1842, T166/168.

433. "List of convictions," T156(1y), T157 (2y) T198 (1y), June 1842.

434. "List of convictions," T130, October 1842.

435. "List of convictions," T140, October 1842.

436. "List of convictions," T150, October 1842.

437. "Fourteenth Annual Report of the Warden," 17 January 1843.

438. Ibid.

Chapter Twenty

439. "List of convictions," T146, October 1842.
440. "List of convictions," T153, October 1842.
441. "List of convictions," T139, December 1842.
442. "List of convictions," T144, December 1842.
443. "List of convictions," T129, March 1843.
444. "List of convictions," T146, March 1843.
445. "List of convictions," T139, March 1843.
446. "List of convictions," T141, March 1843.
447. "List of convictions," T150, March 1843.
448. "List of convictions," T154, March 1843.
449. "List of convictions," T143-145 (1y each count), March 1843.
450. "Fifteenth Annual Report of the Inspectors of the Penitentiary of the District of Columbia for the year 1843," Vol. 442, (28-1), House Doc 75, 23 January 1844.
451. Ibid.
452. Ibid.
453. Ibid.
454. Ibid.
455. "List of convictions," T156, June 1843 and "Case Papers," December 1842 term, T156.
456. "List of convictions," T175, June 1843 and "Case Papers," December 1842 term, A175 and "Criminal Court Minutes," June 1843.
457. "List of convictions," T149, March 1843.
458. "List of convictions," T17, October 1843 and "Case Papers," October 1843 term, A17.
459. "List of convictions," T141, October 1843.
460. "List of convictions," T166, October 1843.
461. "List of convictions," T177, October 1843.
462. "List of convictions," T202, October 1843.
463. "List of convictions," T224, October 1843.
464. "List of convictions," T205, October 1843.
465. "Twentieth Annual Report of the Inspectors," 16 January 1849, 10.
466. "Fifteenth Annual Report of the Inspectors," 23 January 1844.
467. Ibid.
468. Ibid.
469. Ibid.

Chapter Twenty-One
470. "List of convictions," T149, December 1843.
471. "List of convictions," T150, December 1843.
472. "List of convictions," T120, December 1843
473. "Annual Report of the Inspectors of the Penitentiary," Vol. 465, (28-2), House Doc. 115, 12 February 1845.
474. "List of convictions," T47/49, March 1844 and "Case Papers," October 1843 term, T47.
475. "List of convictions," T19, March 1844 and "Case Papers," October 1843 term, T19, 11 March 1844.
476. "Criminal Court Minutes," 1 March 1844, T18.
477. "Sixteenth Annual Report of the Inspectors of the Penitentiary," Vol. 465, (28-2), House Doc. 115, 12 February 1845.
478." Criminal Court Minutes," 4 February 1853.
479. "Sixteenth Annual Report of the Inspectors," 12 February 1845.
480. "Pardon papers 1832-1862," 2 June 1848.
481. "Sixteenth Annual Report of the Inspectors," 12 February 1845.
482. "List of convictions," T146, June 1844.
483. "List of convictions," T147, June 1844.
484. "Sixteenth Annual Report of the Inspectors," 12 February 1845.
485. Ibid.
486. Ibid.
487. "List of convictions," T112, October 1844.
488. "List of convictions," T145, October 1844.
489. "List of convictions," T166/167, October 1844 and "Criminal Court Minutes," 11 June 1844.
490. "List of convictions," T168, October 1844 and "Criminal Court Minutes," 11 June 1844.
491. "List of convictions," T169, October 1844 and "Criminal Court Minutes," 11 June 1844.
492. "List of convictions," T209, October 1844.
493. "Case Papers," October 1843 term, T44
494. "Sixteenth Annual Report of the Inspectors," 12 February 1845 and "Nineteenth Annual Report of the Inspectors," 26 January 1848.

Chapter Twenty-two

495. "List of convictions," T29/38, June 1844 and "Case Papers," June 1844 term, T29.

496. "Pardon papers," 4 August 1845.

497. "List of convictions," T34, March 1845 and "Case Papers," June 1844 term, T34.

498. "List of convictions," T124, March 1845 and "Criminal Court Minutes," 14 March 1845.

499. "List of convictions," T130, March 1845 and "Criminal Court Minutes," 13 March 1845.

500. "List of convictions," T139, March 1845.

501. "List of convictions," T149, March 1845 and "Criminal Court Minutes," 19 March 1845.

502. "List of convictions," T154, March 1845 and "Criminal Court Minutes," 15 March 1845.

503. "List of convictions," T127, March 1845 and "Criminal Court Minutes," 12 March 1845.

504. "List of convictions," T141, March 1845.

505. "List of convictions," T22, March 1845.

506. "List of convictions," T134, March 1845.

507. "Criminal Court Minutes," 23 June 1845, T37.

508. "Nineteenth Annual Report of the Inspectors," 26 January 1848.

509. "List of convictions," T174, June 1845.

510. "List of convictions," T143(?), March 1845.

511. "List of convictions," T131, December 1845 and "Criminal Court Minutes," 8 December 1845, A131.

512. "List of convictions," T139, December 1845 and "Criminal Court Minutes," 8 December 1845, A139.

513. "List of convictions," T163, December 1845 and "Criminal Court Minutes," 11 December 1845, A163.

514. "List of convictions," T164, December 1845 and "Criminal Court Minutes," 11 December 1845, A164.

515. "List of convictions," T169, December 1845 and "Criminal Court Minutes," 10 December 1845, A169.

516. "List of convictions," T65, December 1845 and "Criminal Court Minutes," 16 December 1845, T65.

517. "List of convictions," T160, December 1845.

518. "List of convictions," T142, December 1845.

519. "List of convictions," T145, December 1845.

520. "List of convictions," T179, December 1845.

521. "List of convictions," T159, December 1845 and "Criminal Court Minutes," 26 December 1845, A159.

522. "List of convictions," T222 (1y), 225 (3y), 227 (4y6m), December 1845 and "Criminal Court Minutes," 27 December 1845, A226.

523. "Criminal Court Minutes," December 1845, A154.

Chapter Twenty-three

524." Criminal Court Minutes," 5 January 1846, A157.

525."List of convictions," T238, December 1845, and "Criminal Court Minutes," 6 January 1846, A238.

526. "List of convictions," T171 (2y), 263 (2y), December 1845 and "Criminal Court Minutes," 12 January 1846, A171/263.

527. "List of convictions," T62, December 1845 and "Case Papers," June 1844, T62.

528. "Criminal Court Minutes," 2 January 1846, T63.

529. "List of convictions," T139, March 1846 and" Case Papers," March 1846, T39 and "Criminal Court Minutes," 6 March 1846, A139.

530. "List of convictions," T141, March 1846 and "Criminal Court Minutes," 6 March 1846, A141.

531. "List of convictions," T146, March 1846, and "Case Papers," March 1846, T140, and "Criminal Court Minutes," March 1846, A140.

532. "Case Papers," March 1846, T149.

533. "List of convictions," T107, December 1846, and "Case Papers," December 1846, T107, and "Criminal Court Minutes," 14 December 1846, A107.

534. "List of convictions," T78, March 1847, and "Case Papers," December 1846, T78, and "Criminal Court Minutes," 5 March 1847, A78.

535. "List of convictions," T64, March 1847 and "Criminal Court Minutes," 4 March 1847, A47.

536. "List of convictions," T135 (3y), December 1846, T35 (3y), March 1847 and "Case Papers," December 1846, T135.

537. "List of convictions," T175, December 1846 and "Case Papers," December 1846, T24.

538. "List of convictions," T125, March 1847, and "Case Papers," December 1846, A125, and "Criminal Court Minutes," 23 March 1847, A78.

539. "List of convictions," T79 (1y), 101 (1y), 109 (2y), 112 (2y), 113 (2y), March 1847, and "Case Papers," December 1846, A79/100-106/108-115, and "Criminal Court Minutes," 20 March 1847, A79/101.

540. "Nineteenth Annual Report of the Inspectors," 26 January 1848.

541. "Pardon papers," 3 February 1851.

542. "List of convictions," T57, June 1847, and "Case Papers," June 1847, A57, and "Criminal Court Minutes," 24 June 1847, A57.

Chapter Twenty-four

543. "List of convictions," T61, June 1847 and "Case Papers," June 1847, T61.

544. "List of convictions," T64, March 1847.

545. "List of convictions," T135 (3y), December 1846, and T35 (3y), March 1847 and "Case Papers," December 1846, T135.

546. "List of convictions," T160 (1y), 161 (1y), 162 (3y), 163 (1y), 164 (1y), 173(1y), 174 (1y), 175 (1y), December 1846 and "Case Papers," December 1846, T32, A21, 22, 23, 29, 30, 31.

547. "List of convictions," T125, March 1847, and "Criminal Court Minutes," 20 March 1847, 23 March 1847, and "Case Papers," December 1846 term, A79, 100-106, 108-115, 125.

548. "List of convictions," T79 (1y), 101 (1y), 109 (2y), 112 (2y), 113 (2y), March 1847.

549. "Nineteenth Annual Report of the Inspectors," 26 January 1848.

550. "Pardon papers," 3 February 1851.

551. "Case Papers," June 1847 term, T57 and T65.

552. Ibid., T61

553. "Nineteenth Annual Report of the Inspectors," 26 January 1848.

554. "Case Papers," December1847 term, T49, and "List of convictions," December 1847, T47, and "Criminal Court Minutes," 9 December 1847, A47.

555. "Case Papers," December 1847 term, T43 and "List of convictions," December 1847, T43 and "Criminal Court Minutes," 11 December 1847, A43.

556. "Case Papers," December 1847 term, T60, and "List of convictions," December 1847, T60, and "Criminal Court Minutes," 11 December 1847, A60.

557. "Case Papers," December 1847 term, T639, and "List of convictions," December 1847, T63, and "Criminal Court Minutes," 11 December 1847, A63.

558. "Case Papers," December 1847 term, T59, and "List of convictions," December 1847, T59, and "Criminal Court Minutes," 11 December 1847, A59.

559. "List of convictions," December 1847, T72. "Criminal Court Minutes," 11 December 1847, A72.

Chapter Twenty-five

560. "List of convictions," December 1847, T115. "Criminal Court Minutes," 30 December 1847, A115.

561. "Criminal Court Minutes," 10 March 1848, A27.

562. "Criminal Court Minutes," 9 March 1848, A30. "List of convictions," March 1848, T30.

563. "Criminal Court Minutes," 9 March 1848, A29. "List of convictions," March 1848, T29.

564. "Criminal Court Minutes," 21 March 1848, A64.

565. "List of convictions," June 1847, T77, and. "Case Papers," June 1847, T77.

566. "Miscellaneous Records, 1826-1865," "Journal of Convicts."

567. "List of convictions," June 1848, T15, and "Criminal Court Minutes," 20 June 1848, A15, and "Case Papers," June 1848, T15.

568. "List of convictions," June 1848, T78, and "Criminal Court Minutes," 1 July 1848, A78, and "Case Papers," June 1848, T78.

569. "List of convictions," June 1848, T12, and "Criminal Court Minutes," 13 July 1848, A12, and "Case Papers," June 1848, T12.

570. "List of convictions," June 1848, T479, and "Criminal Court Minutes," 21 August 1848, A479, and "Case Papers," June 1848, T479.

571. Miscellaneous Records, 1826-1865, "Journal of Convicts."

572. "List of convictions," December 1848, T45 and "Case Papers," June 1848, T45.

573. "List of convictions," December 1848, T118, and "Criminal Court Minutes," 27 December 1848, A118, and "Case Papers," December 1848, T118.

574. "List of convictions," December 1848, T117, and "Criminal Court Minutes," 27 December 1848, A117, and "Case Papers," December 1848, T117.

Chapter Twenty-six

575. "List of convictions," June 1848, T453.

576. "List of convictions," March 1849, T137, and "Criminal Court Minutes," 10 March 1849, A137, and "Case Papers," March 1849, T137.

577. "List of convictions," March 1849, T223.

578. 1850 U.S. Census, M432, 146B.

579. "List of convictions," March 1849, T238, and "Criminal Court Minutes," 16 April 1849, A238, and "Miscellaneous Records 1826-1865," 25 November 1849.

580. "List of convictions," March 1849, T205.

581. "List of convictions," June 1849, T46, and "Criminal Court Minutes," 22 June 1849, A46, and "Case Papers," June1849, T46.

582. "List of convictions," June 1849, T77 and "Case Papers," June1849, T77.

583. "List of convictions," June 1849, T103, and "Criminal Court Minutes," 11 July 1849, A103, and "Case Papers," June term 1849, T103.

584. "Pardon papers."

585. "List of convictions," December 1849, T50, and "Criminal Court Minutes," 4 December 1849, A50, and "Case Papers," December term 1849, T50.

586. "Criminal Court Minutes," 6 December 1849, A51.

587. "List of convictions," December 1849, T57, and "Criminal Court Minutes," 6 December 1849, A57, and "Case Papers," December term 1849, T57.

588. "List of convictions," December1849, T10.

589. "List of convictions," December 1849, T99, and "Criminal Court Minutes," 11 December 1849, A99, and "Case Papers," December term 1849, T99.

590. "List of convictions," December 1849, T90 and "Criminal Court Minutes," 11 December 1849, A90.

591. "List of convictions," December 1849, T88, and "Criminal Court Minutes," 11 December 1849, A88, and "Case Papers," December term 1849, T88.

592. "List of convictions," December 1849, T56 (1y0, 62 (1y) and "Case Papers," December term 1849, T56/62.

593. "List of convictions," March 1849, T104, and "Criminal Court Minutes," 13 December 1849, A104, and "Case Papers," December term 1849, T104.

594. "List of convictions," December 1849, T92, and "Criminal Court Minutes," 8 December 1849, A92, and "Case Papers," December term 1849, T92.

595. "List of convictions," December 1849, T159, and "Criminal Court Minutes," 22 December 1849, A159, and "Case Papers," December term 1849, T159.

596. "List of convictions," December 1849, T157, and "Criminal Court Minutes," 24 December 1849, A157, and "Case Papers," December term 1849, T157.

597. "List of convictions," December 1849, T158, and "Criminal Court Minutes," 24 December 1849, A158, and "Case Papers," December term 1849, T158.

598. "List of convictions," December 1849, T142, and "Criminal Court Minutes," 26 December 1849, A142, and "Case Papers," December term 1849, T142.

599. "List of convictions," March 1849, T166and "Criminal Court Minutes," 26 December 1849, A166, and "Case Papers," December term 1849, T166.

600. 1850 U.S. Census, M432, 146B.

Chapter Twenty-seven

601. "List of convictions," December 1849, T185, and "Criminal Court Minutes," 29 December 1849, A185, and "Case Papers," December term 1849, T185.

602. "List of convictions," December 1849, T257, and "Criminal Court Minutes," 5 January 1850, A257, and "Case Papers," December term 1849, T257.

603. "List of convictions," December 1849, T275, and "Criminal Court Minutes," 10 January 1850, A275, and "Case Papers," December term 1849, T275.

604. "List of convictions," March 1850, T85, and "Criminal Court Minutes," 15 March 1850, A85, and "Case Papers," March 1850, T85.

605. "List of convictions," March 1850, T86, and "Criminal Court Minutes," 15 March 1850, A86, and "Case Papers," March 1850, T86.

606. "List of convictions," March 1850, T94, and "Criminal Court Minutes," 15 March 1850, A94, and "Case Papers," March 1850, T94.

607. "List of convictions," March 1850, T103, and "Criminal Court Minutes," 16 March 1850, A103, and "Case Papers," March 1850, T103.

608. "List of convictions," March 1850, T77 (1y), 78 (1y), 96 (2y), and "Criminal Court Minutes," 19 March 1850, A77/78/96, and "Case Papers," March 1850, T77/78/96.

609. "List of convictions," March 1850, T95, and "Criminal Court Minutes," 18 March 1850, A95, and "Miscellaneous Records 1826-1865," 20 September 1850, National Archives II, College Park, MD

610. "Annual Report of the Inspectors of the Penitentiary," 3 Mar 1851.

611. 1850 U.S. Census, M432, 146B.

612. "Miscellaneous Records 1826-1865," 20 September 1850, and "List of convictions," June 1850, T106, and "Criminal Court Minutes," 28 June 1850, A106.

613. "List of convictions," June 1850, T113 and "Criminal Court Minutes," 1 July 1850, A114.

614. "Criminal Court Minutes," 2 July 1850, A110.

615. "Criminal Court Minutes," 5 July 1850, A137, and "Miscellaneous Records, 1826-1865," 20 September 1850.

616. "List of convictions," June 1850, T146 and "Criminal Court Minutes," 17 July 1850, A146.

617. "List of convictions," June 1850, T162.

618. "List of convictions," March 1850, T15 and "Criminal Court Minutes," 20 July 1850, A145.

619. "List of convictions," June 1850, T99.

620. Ibid, T90.

621. Ibid., T14 (1y), T15 (1y).

622. "List of convictions," December 1850, T88 and "Criminal Court Minutes," 11 December 1850, A88.

623. "Criminal Court Minutes," 11 December 1850, A92.

624. "List of convictions," December 1850, T121 (3y), T122 (3y).

625. "Pardon papers," 23 January 1851.

626. "Miscellaneous Records 1826-1865," 21 July 1851, and "Criminal Court Minutes," 30 December 1850, A152, and "List of Convictions," December 1850, T129 (1y), T130 (1y), T152 (1y)

627. "List of Convictions," December 1850, T148 and "Criminal Court Minutes," 30 December 1850, A148.

Chapter Twenty-eight

628. "List of Convictions," December 1850, T146.
629. "List of Convictions," December 1850, T132 and "Criminal Court Minutes," 31 December 1850, A141.
630. "List of Convictions," December 1850, T52 (1y), T93 (1y), T71 (1y) and "Criminal Court Minutes," 4 January 1851, A147.
631. "Criminal Court Minutes," 6 January 1851, A221.
632. "Miscellaneous Records 1826-1865," 9 December 1856, and "List of Convictions," December 1850, T157, and "Criminal Court Minutes," 31 December 1850, A157.
633. "List of Convictions," March 1850, T163 (1y), 165 (1y) and "Criminal Court Minutes," 31 December 1850, A163/165.
634. "List of Convictions," December 1850, T79 and "Criminal Court Minutes," 8 January 1851, A179.
635. "List of Convictions," December 1850, T254 and. "Criminal Court Minutes," 11 January 1851, A254.
636. "List of Convictions," December 1850, T223 (1y), 224 (1y) and "Criminal Court Minutes," 6 January 1851, A224.
637. "List of Convictions," June 1850, T253 and "Criminal Court Minutes," 11 January 1851, A253.
638. "List of Convictions," December 1850, T267 and "Criminal Court Minutes," 30 January 1851, A267.
639. "Miscellaneous Records, 1826-1865," 2 June 1854.
640. "List of Convictions," December 1850, T211 (2y), T213 (2y), T215 (2y), T217 (2y), T219 (2y).
641. "List of Convictions," December 1850, T212 (2y), T214 (2y), T216 (2y), T218 (2y), T220 (2y).
642. "Miscellaneous Records, 1826-1865," 3 June 1855.
643. "List of Convictions," December 1850, T77 and *Star*, 8 June 1854.
644. "The Report of the Inspectors of the Penitentiary in the District of Columbia, Vol. 644, (32-1), Doc 97, 3 May 1852.
645. "List of Convictions," December 1850, T264.
646. "List of Convictions," March 1851, T175 and "Criminal Court Minutes," 5 March 1851, A175.
647. "List of Convictions," March 1851, T5 and "Criminal Court Minutes," 6 March 1851, A5.

648. "List of Convictions," March 1851, T199 and "Criminal Court Minutes," 17 March 1851, A199.
649. "List of Convictions," March 1851, T192 and "Criminal Court Minutes," 17 March 1851, A192.
650. "List of Convictions," March 1851, T25 (3y), 26 (3y) and "Criminal Court Minutes," 14 March 1851, A25/26.
651. "List of Convictions," March 1851, T126 and "Criminal Court Minutes," 19 March 1851, A126.
652. "List of Convictions," March 1851, T125 and "Criminal Court Minutes," 22 March 1851, A125.
653. "List of Convictions," March 1851, T17 (2y), 120 (2y) and "Criminal Court Minutes," 3 March 1851, A17.
654. "List of Convictions," June 1851, T143 and "Criminal Court Minutes," 20 June 1851, A143.
655. "List of Convictions," June 1851, T144 and "Criminal Court Minutes," 18 June 1851, A144.
656. "List of Convictions," March 1851, T124, June 1851, T142 and "Criminal Court Minutes," 26 June 1851, A142.
657. "List of Convictions," June 1851, T190 and "Criminal Court Minutes," 3 July 1851, A190.
658. "List of Convictions," June 1851, T174 and "Criminal Court Minutes," 3 July 1851, A174.
659. "List of Convictions," June 1851, T167 and "Criminal Court Minutes," 15 July 1851, A167.
660. "List of Convictions," June 1851, T238 and "Criminal Court Minutes," 17 July 1851, A238.
661. "List of Convictions," December 1850, T262 and "Criminal Court Minutes," 5 August 1851, A262.
662. "List of Convictions," June 1851, T176.
663. "List of Convictions," December 1851, T121 and "Criminal Court Minutes," 4 December 1851, A121.
664. "List of Convictions," December 1851, T24 and "Criminal Court Minutes," 10 December 1851, A24.
665 "List of Convictions," December 1851, T166 and "Criminal Court Minutes," 17 December 1851, A166.
666. "List of Convictions," December 1851, T162 and "Criminal Court Minutes," 18 December 1851, A161.
667. "List of Convictions," December 1851, T145 and "Criminal Court Minutes," 20 December 1851, A145.

Chapter Twenty-nine

668. "List of Convictions," December 1851, T210 (3y), 227 (3y) and "Criminal Court Minutes," 9 January 1852, A210.

669. "List of Convictions," December 1851, T259 and "Criminal Court Minutes," 14 January 1852, A259.

670. "List of Convictions," December 1851, T149 (1y), 179 (1y).

671. "List of Convictions," December 1851, T209 and "Criminal Court Minutes," January 1852, A283.

672. "List of Convictions," March 1852, T128 (1y), 129 (1y) and "Criminal Court Minutes," 10 March 1852, A128/129.

673. "List of Convictions," March 1852, T118 and "Criminal Court Minutes," 12 March 1852, A118.

674. "List of Convictions," March 1852, T132 and "Criminal Court Minutes," 15 March 1852, A132.

675. "List of Convictions," March 1852, T2 and "Criminal Court Minutes," 16 March 1852, T2.

676. "List of Convictions," March 1852, T130 and "Criminal Court Minutes," 26 March 1852, A130.

677. "List of Convictions," March 1852, T178 and "Criminal Court Minutes," 31 March 1852, T178.

678. "List of Convictions," March 1852, T185 and "Criminal Court Minutes," 6 April 1852, T185.

679. "List of Convictions," December 1851, T134 and "Criminal Court Minutes," 29 January 1852, A134.

680. "List of Convictions," March 1852, T18 and "Criminal Court Minutes," 8 April 1852, T18.

681. "List of Convictions," December 1851, T141.

682. "Penitentiary District of Columbia: Report of Inspectors," Vol. 677, (32-2), Doc. 41, 12 Feb 1853.

683. "Pardon papers."

684. "List of Convictions," June 1852, T120 and "Criminal Court Minutes," 26 June 1852, T120.

685. "List of Convictions," June 1852, T37 and "Criminal Court Minutes," 6 July 1852, T37.

686. "List of Convictions," June 1852, T135.

687. "List of Convictions," June 1852, T148 (1y), 157 (1y), 174 (3y), and "Criminal Court Minutes," 23 July 1852, A174 and "Miscellaneous Records 1826-1865," 24 September 1855.

688. "List of Convictions," June 1852, T131 and "Criminal Court Minutes," 2 August 1852, A131.

689. "List of Convictions," June 1852, T108.
690. "List of Convictions," June 1852, T153 and "Criminal Court Minutes," 22 July 1852, A153.
691. "List of Convictions," June 1851, T122.
692. "List of Convictions," June 1852, T260 and "Criminal Court Minutes," 4 August 1852, A260.
693. "List of Convictions," June 1852, T137 (1y), 138 (1y).
694. "List of Convictions," June 1852, T257 (2y), 258 (2y) and " Criminal Court Minutes," 4 August 1852, A258.
695. "List of Convictions," June 1852, T290.
696. "List of Convictions," June 1852, T294 (2y), 280 (18m) and "Criminal Court Minutes," 14 August 1852, A294.
697. "List of Convictions," June 1852, T230 (18m), 241 (3y), 243 (18m) 244 (18m) and "Criminal Court Minutes," 4 August 1852, A241/243/244.
698. " List of Convictions," June 1852, T272 and "Criminal Court Minutes," 12 August 1852, A272.
699. "List of Convictions," June 1852, T165 and "Criminal Court Minutes," 17 August 1852, A165.
700. 1860 U.S. Census, M653, 938.
701. "Report of Inspectors," Vol. 677, 12 Feb 1853.
702."Criminal Court Minutes," 9 December 1852, A142.
703. "List of Convictions," December 1852, T149 and "Criminal Court Minutes," 20 December 1852, A149.
704. "List of Convictions," December 1852, T139 and "Criminal Court Minutes," 17 December 1852, A139.
705. "List of Convictions," December 1852, T186 and "Criminal Court Minutes," 24 December 1852, A186.
706. "List of Convictions," December 1852, T170 and "Criminal Court Minutes," 24 December 1852, A170.
707. "List of Convictions," December 1852, T198 and "Criminal Court Minutes," 28 December 1852, A198.

Chapter Thirty

708. *Star*, 31 December 1852 and "List of Convictions," December 1852, T182.
709. "List of Convictions," December 1852, T233 and "Criminal Court Minutes," 7 January 1853, A233.
710. "List of Convictions," December 1852, T143 and "Criminal Court Minutes," 12 January 1853, A143.

711. "List of Convictions," December 1852, T223 and "Criminal Court Minutes," 12 January 1853, A223.
712. "List of Convictions," December 1852, T158 and "Criminal Court Minutes," 14 January 1853, A158.
713. "List of Convictions," June 1852, T204.
714. "List of Convictions," June 1852, T175.
715. "List of Convictions," 28 December 1851, T28.
716. "Penitentiary for the District of Columbia." Vol. 723, 3 Mar 1854.
717. "List of Convictions," December 1852, T29 (3y), 172 (3y) and "Criminal Court Minutes," 1 February 1853, A172.
718. *Star*, 27 January 1853 and "List of Convictions," December 1852, T148.
719. *Star*, 2 January 1853, and "List of Convictions," December 1852, T249, and "Criminal Court Minutes," 24 January 1853, A249.
720. "List of Convictions," December 1852, T345 and "Criminal Court Minutes," 12 February 1853, A345.
721. "Criminal Court Minutes," 15 February 1853, A351.
722. "List of Convictions," December 1852, T328.
723. "List of Convictions," December 1852, T184.
724. "List of Convictions," December 1852, T335 (2y), 336 (2y) and *Star*, 28 February 1853.
725. "List of Convictions," December 1852, T333 (2y), 334 (2y) and "Criminal Court Minutes," 12 February 1853, A333/334.
726. "List of Convictions," June 1852, T268.
727. "List of Convictions," December 1852, T187.
728. "List of Convictions," December 1852, T221 and "Case Papers," June 1853 term, T24.
729. "List of Convictions," December 1852, T384 (1y), T385 (2y), T386 (2y) and *Star*, 28 February 1853.
730. "List of Convictions," June 1853, T73.
731. "List of Convictions," December 1852, T197.
732. "List of Convictions," June 1853, T153.
733. "List of Convictions," June 1853, T154 and "Criminal Court Minutes," 6 July 1853, A154.
734. "List of Convictions," June 1853, T139 and "Criminal Court Minutes," 7 July 1853, A139.
735. "Criminal Court Minutes," 12 July 1853, A194.
736. "List of Convictions," June 1853, T148 and "Criminal Court Minutes," 14 July 1853, A148.

737. "List of Convictions," December 1852, T205 and *Star*, 27 January 1853.
738. "List of Convictions," June 1853, T167 (6y), 170 (6y) and *Star*, 1 August 1853.
739. "List of Convictions," June 1853, T163 (6y), 165 (6y).
740. "Criminal Court Minutes," 11 August 1853, A269 and *Star*, 12 August 1853.
741. "Criminal Court Minutes," 7 December 1853, T10 and *Star*, 7 December 1853.

Chapter Thirty-one
742. *Star*, 7 March 1854.
743. "Criminal Court Minutes," 8 March 1854, T195.
744. "Criminal Court Minutes," 8 March 1854, T67 and "Miscellaneous Records1826-1865," 23 August 1854.
745. "Criminal Court Minutes," 9 March 1854, T77.
746. "Criminal Court Minutes," 17 March 1854, T79.
747. "Pardon papers."
748. Ibid.
749. Ibid.
750. "Criminal Court Minutes," 17 March 1854, T96.
751. "Report of the Warden of the Penitentiary." Vol. 777, (33-2), House Ex. Doc.1, 1 October 1854, 609.
752. "Pardon papers."
753. *Star*, 5 May 1854.
754. "Miscellaneous Records 1826-1865," 8 December 1853.
755. "Criminal Court Minutes," 2 July 1854, A146.
756. *Star*, 21 June 1854.
757. "Miscellaneous Records 1826-1865," 3 February 1856 and "Criminal Court Minutes," 27 June 1854, T55.
758. "Penitentiary for the District of Columbia." Vol. 723, 3 Mar 1854.
759. "Criminal Court Minutes," 8 July 1854, A209.
760. "Criminal Court Minutes," 28 June 1854, A156.
761. "Criminal Court Minutes," 5 July 1854, A179.
762. "Criminal Court Minutes," 21 July 1854, A227.
763. "Criminal Court Minutes," 21 July 1854, A226.
764. "Criminal Court Minutes," 21 July 1854, A225.
765. *Star*, 21 July 1854.
766. "Criminal Court Minutes," 12 July 1854, A188.

767. "Criminal Court Minutes," 17 July 1854, T2, and *Star*, 21 July 1854.
768. "Criminal Court Minutes," 19 July 1854, T39.
769. "Criminal Court Minutes," 18 July 1854, A246 and "Miscellaneous Records 1826-1865," 8 April 1856.
770. "Report of the Warden of the Penitentiary." Vol.777, 1 October 1854.
771. "Criminal Court Minutes," 12 December 1854, A150.

Chapter Thirty-two

772. "Criminal Court Minutes," 22 December 1854, A256.
773. "Criminal Court Minutes," 15 January 1855, A371
774. "Pardon papers."
775. "Report of the Warden of the Penitentiary," Vol. 840, 1 October 1855, 613.
776. Ibid.
777. "Pardon papers."
778. "Criminal Court Minutes," 23 June 1855, A118.
779. Ibid., 29 June 1855, A135.
780. Ibid., A134.
781. "Criminal Court Minutes," 29 June 1855, A133.
782. "Report of the Warden," Vol. 840, October 1855, 613.
783. "Criminal Court Minutes," 3 July 1855, A66.
784. "Report of the Warden," Vol. 840, 1 October 1855, 613.
785. "Criminal Court Minutes," 16 July 1855, A108.
786. *Star*, 20 July 1855.
787. *Star*, 21 July 1855 and "Criminal Court Minutes," 21 July 1855, T249.
788. 1860 U.S. Census, M653, 938.
789. "Pardon papers."
790. "Criminal Court Minutes," 7 December 1855, A75.
791. "Criminal Court Minutes," 17 December 1855, A85.
792. "Criminal Court Minutes," 19 December 1855, A130 and A144.
793. "Criminal Court Minutes," 18 December 1855, A129.
794. "Criminal Court Minutes," 21 December 1855, A150.
795. "Criminal Court Minutes," 22 December 1855, A167.
796. "Criminal Court Minutes," 21 December 1855, A149.
797. "Criminal Court Minutes," 9 December 1855, A194.
798. "Criminal Court Minutes," 29 December 1855, A200.

799. "Criminal Court Minutes," 28 December 1855, A168 and A202.

800. 1860 U.S. Census, M653, 938.

Chapter Thirty-three

801. "Pardon papers."

802. "Criminal Court Minutes," 4 January 1856, A225.

803. "Criminal Court Minutes," 8 January 1856, A233.

804. "Criminal Court Minutes," 7 January 1856, T49.

805. "Criminal Court Minutes," 24 January 1856, A238.

806. "Criminal Court Minutes," 11 March 1856, A89, and *Star*, 12 March 1856.

807. "Criminal Court Minutes," 12 March 1856, A79, and *Star*, 13 March 1856.

808. "Criminal Court Minutes," 15 March 1856, A109.

809. "Criminal Court Minutes," 24 March 1856, A144 and *Star*, 25 March 1856.

810. "Criminal Court Minutes," 3 March 1856, T46 and *Star*, 15 March 1856 and "Miscellaneous Letters," Entry 466. 21 October 1857.

811. *Star*, 25 March 1856.

812. "Criminal Court Minutes," 24 June 1856, A92/94 and "Miscellaneous Letters," 21 October 1857.

813. "Criminal Court Minutes," 26 June 1856, A100 and *Star*, 27 June 1856.

814. "Report of the Warden," Vol. 893, 1 October 1856.

815. "Criminal Court Minutes," 28 June 1856, A122.

816. "Criminal Court Minutes," 26 June 1856, A101.

817. "Report of the Warden," Vol. 893, 1 October 1856.

818. "Criminal Court Minutes," 30 July 1856, A281, and *Star*, 28 April 1859, and "Miscellaneous Records 1826-1865."

819. "Criminal Court Minutes," 31 July 1856, A79 and *Star*, 31 July 1856.

820. "Criminal Court Minutes," 6 August 1856, A157.

821. *Star*, 5 July 1859.

822. "Criminal Court Minutes," 6 August 1856, A156/176 and "Miscellaneous Letters," 21 October 1857.

823. 1860 U.S. Census, M653, 938.

824. "Report of the Warden," Vol. 893, 1 October 1856.

825. "Criminal Court Minutes," 5 December 1856, A152, and *Star*, 6 December 1856.

826. "Criminal Court Minutes," 8 December 1856, A157, and *Star*, 9 December 1856.
827. "Criminal Court Minutes," 8 December 1856, A163, and *Star*, 9 December 1856.
828. "Criminal Court Minutes," 18 December 1856, A201, and *Star*, 19 December 1856.
829. "Report of the Warden and Board of Inspectors," Vol.942, November 1857.
830. "Criminal Court Minutes," 19 December 1856, A199.
831. *Star*, 17/18 December 1856.
832. Ibid.
833. "Criminal Court Minutes," 18 December 1856, A196.
834. "Criminal Court Minutes," 18 December 1856, A197, and *Star*, 30 December 1856.
835. "Criminal Court Minutes," 18 December 1856, A198, and *Star*, 30 December 1856.

Chapter Thirty-four

836. "Criminal Court Minutes," 2 January 1857, A254 and *Star*, 3 January 1857.
837. *Star*, 18 December 1856.
838. *Star*, 7 January 1857.
839. "Criminal Court Minutes," 12 March 1857, A99/100 and *Star*, 12 March 1857.
840. "Criminal Court Minutes," 13 March 1857, A102 and *Star,* 13 March 1857.
841. "Criminal Court Minutes " 13 March 1857, A121.
842. "Criminal Court Minutes," 12 March 1857, A97 and *Star*, 13 March 1857.
843. "Miscellaneous Letters," 7 November 1860 and *Star,* 19 March 1857.
844. "Report of the Warden and Board of Inspectors," Vol. 942, November 1857.
845. "Miscellaneous Letters," 21 October 1857 and "Criminal Court Minutes," 31 March 1857, A206.
846. "Criminal Court Minutes," 31 March 1857, A198.
847. "Miscellaneous Letters," November 1860 and *Star,* 6 December 1856.
848. *Star,* 6 December 1856.
849. "Criminal Court Minutes," 17 June 1857, A102 and *Star*, 18 June 1857.

850. "Criminal Court Minutes," 20 June 1857, A109 and *Star*, 22 June 1857.
851. "Criminal Court Minutes," 20 June 1857, A121.
852. "Criminal Court Minutes," 26 June 1857, A133 and *Star*, 2 June 1857.
853. "Criminal Court Minutes," 8 July 1857, A221 and *Star*, 18 July 1857.
854. *Star* 2/3 July 1857, 4 June 1859, and 27 June 1861.
855. *Star* 6 March 1861.
856. *Star* 11 December 1857.
857. *Star* 12 December 1857.
858. "Report of the Warden of the Penitentiary accompanying the 30th Annual Report of the Secretary of the Interior," Vol. 974, (35-2), Senate Ex. Doc.1, 1 November 1858, 707.
859. *Star*, 17 December 1857 and "Criminal Court Minutes," 16 December 1857, A120.
860. *Star*, 16 July 1857.
861. *Star*, 21 December 1857, and "Criminal Court Minutes," 21 December 1857, A149.
862. *Star*, 22 December 1857, and "Criminal Court Minutes," 21 December 1857, A152.
863. *Star*, 22 December 1857, and "Criminal Court Minutes," 21 December 1857, A153.
864. *Star*, 23 December 1857.
865. *Star*, 22 December 1857, and "Criminal Court Minutes," 22 December 1857, A136.

Chapter Thirty-five

866. *Star*, 28 April 1859 and "Criminal Court Minutes," 29 December 1857, A75/79.
867. *Star*, 20 June 1862 and "Criminal Court Minutes," 5 January 1858, A181.
868. "Criminal Court Minutes," 5 January 1858, A190.
869. "Criminal Court Minutes," 6 January 1858, A163.
870. "Criminal Court Minutes," 5 January 1858, A186 and *Star*, 5 January 1858.
871. "Criminal Court Minutes," 6 January 1858, A198 and *Star*, 7 January 1858.
872. *Star*, 26 August 1861.
873. "Criminal Court Minutes," 6 January 1858, A196 and *Star*, 7 January 1858.

874. "Criminal Court Minutes," 4 January 1858, A165 and *Star*, 5 January 1858.
875. "Criminal Court Minutes," 7 January 1858, A204.
876. "Criminal Court Minutes," 7 January 1858, A202 and *Star*, 8 January 1858.
877. *Star*, 8 January 1858, 6 March 1861.
878. "Criminal Court Minutes," 27 January 1858, A119 and *Star*, 28 January 1858.
879. *Star*, 11 January 1858.
880. "Criminal Court Minutes," 15 January 1858, A197 and *Star*, 16 January 1858.
881. "Criminal Court Minutes," 30 December 1857, A184.
882. 1860 U.S. Census, M653, 938. National Archives, Washington, DC.
883. "Criminal Court Minutes," 26 January 1858, A241 and *Star*, 27 January 1858.
884. "Criminal Court Minutes," 8 January 1858, A208.
885. "Criminal Court Minutes," 29 January 1858, A258 and *Star*, 30 January 1858.
886. "Criminal Court Minutes," 30 January 1858, A271 and *Star*, 1 February 1858.
887. "Criminal Court Minutes," 2 February 1858, A275 and *Star*, 2 February 1858.
888. *Star*, 8 February 1858.
889. "Report of the Warden," Vol. 974, 1 November 1858, 707.
890. *Star*, 30 January 1858.
891. "Miscellaneous Records 1826-1865."
892. *Star*, 10 March 1858.
893. *Star*, 6 March 1858.
894. *Star*, 5 March 1858.
895. "Criminal Court Minutes," 7 April 1858, A187 and *Star*, 7 April 1858.
896. "Report of the Warden," Vol. 974, 1 November 1858, 707.
897. "Criminal Court Minutes," 9 April 1858, A194.
898. *Star*, 6 March 1858.
899. "Miscellaneous Records 1826-1865," ("Improper Letters to and from Convicts," 8 September 1858) and "Criminal Court Minutes," 24 April 1858, A192.

900. "Criminal Court Minutes," 29 April 1858, A36 and *Star*, 28 April 1858.
901. "Criminal Court Minutes," 4 May 1858, A227 and *Star*, 4 May 1858.
902. "Criminal Court Minutes," 4 May 1858, A225 and *Star*, 4 May 1858.
903. "Criminal Court Minutes," 4 May 1858, A226 and *Star*, 4 May 1858.
904. "Criminal Court Minutes," 4 May 1858, A228 and *Star*, 4 May 1858.
905. "Criminal Court Minutes," 4 May 1858, A229 and *Star*, 4 May 1858.
906. "Criminal Court Minutes," 5 May 1858, A220 and *Star*, 6 May 1858.
907. *Star*, 8 May 1858.
908. "Report of the Warden," Vol. 974, 1 November 1858, 707.
909. "Criminal Court Minutes," 10 May 1858, A123 and *Star*, 11 May 1858.
910. 1860 U.S. Census, M653, 938.
911. *Star*, 26 June 1858.
912. "Report of the Warden," Vol. 974, 1 November 1858, 707.
913. "Criminal Court Minutes," 8 July 1858, A104 and *Star*, 9 July 1858.
914. "Criminal Court Minutes," 8 July 1858, A140 and *Star*, 9 July 1858.
915. "Criminal Court Minutes," 8 July 1858, A139 and *Star*, 9 July 1858.
916. *Star*, 1 July 1858.
917. Ibid.
918. " Criminal Court Minutes," 5 August 1858, T28 and *Star*, 5 April 1858, 21 July 1858, and 5 August 1858.
919. "Miscellaneous Letters." Entry 466. "Criminal Court Minutes," 5 August 1858, T29, and *Star*, 6 August 1858.
920. "Criminal Court Minutes," 13 July 1858, A130 and *Star*, 16 July 1858, 6 August 1858, and 12 January 1860.
921. "Criminal Court Minutes," 5 August 1858, A152 and *Star*, 7 August 1858, 5 March 1861.
922. Ibid.

923. "Report of the Warden," Vol. 1023, (36-1), Senate Ex. Doc. 2, 1859, 859.
924. "Miscellaneous Records 1826-1865," Entry 470, 23 October 1859.
925. "Report of the Warden, 1859," Vol. 1023, 859.
926. Ibid.
927. Ibid.
928. "Criminal Court Minutes," 16 December 1858, A146.
929. "Criminal Court Minutes," 18 December 1858, A133 and *Star*, 20 December 1858.
930. "Criminal Court Minutes," 18 December 1858, A143.
931. "Criminal Court Minutes," 22 December 1858, A169.
932. "Criminal Court Minutes," 22 December 1858, A17 and *Star*, 22 December 1858.
933. "Criminal Court Minutes," 23 December 1858, A177 and *Star*, 22 December 1858.
934. "Report of the Warden, 1859," Vol. 1023, 859.
935. *Star*, 24 December 1858.
936. "Report of the Warden, 1859," Vol. 1023, 859.

Chapter Thirty-six

937. "Criminal Court Minutes," 6 January 1859, A199 and *Star*, 10 January 1859.
938. "Criminal Court Minutes," 7 January 1859, A172 and *Star*, 7 January 1859.
939. "Criminal Court Minutes," 7 January 1859, A212-215 and *Star*, 8 January 1859.
940. "Criminal Court Minutes," 12 January 1859, A235 and *Star*, 18 January 1859.
941. "Criminal Court Minutes," 11 January 1859, A234 and *Star*, 18 January 1859.
942. "Criminal Court Minutes," 12 January 1859, A236 and *Star*, 18 January 1859.
943. "Criminal Court Minutes," 3 January 1859, A188 and *Star*, 18 January 1859.
944. "Criminal Court Minutes," 4 January 1859, A196 and *Star*, 22 December 1858.
945. "Criminal Court Minutes," 22 January 1859, A274 and *Star*, 24 January 1859.
946. "Criminal Court Minutes," 20 January 1859, A168 and *Star*, 20 January 1859, 11 July 1862.

947. "Criminal Court Minutes," 11 March 1859, A94.
948. "Criminal Court Minutes," 14 March 1859, A104.
949. "Report of the Warden, 1859," Vol. 1023, 859.
950. "Criminal Court Minutes," 20 December 1858, A157/158 and *Star*, 21 December 1858.
951. 1860 U.S. Census, M653, 938.
952. "Criminal Court Minutes," 16 May 1859, A192 and *Star*, 17 May 1859.
953. "Criminal Court Minutes," 21-22 June 1859, A11/13/15 and *Star*, 23 June 1859.
954. "Criminal Court Minutes," 24 June 1859, A74 and *Star*, 25 June 1859.
955. "Miscellaneous Records 1826-1865," Entry 470, 1 May 1861.
956. 1860 U. S. Census, M653, 938.
957. "Miscellaneous Letters," Entry 466, 7 November 1860 and "Miscellaneous Records 1826-1865," Entry 470, 6 September 1860.
958. "Criminal Court Minutes," 25 June 1859, A86.
959. "Criminal Court Minutes," 25 June 1859, A84.
960. *Star*, 9 May 1859.
961. *Star*, 6 July 1859.
962. "Criminal Court Minutes," 5 July 1859, A94.
963. *Star*, 11 July 1859.
964. "Criminal Court Minutes," 11 July 1859, A168.
965. 1860 U.S. Census, M653, 938.
966. "Criminal Court Minutes," 15 July 1859, A183 and *Star*, 19 July 1859.
967. "Criminal Court Minutes," 16 July 1859, A189.
968. "Criminal Court Minutes," 18 July 1859, A198 and *Star,* 19 July 1859.
969. "Criminal Court Minutes," 16 July 1859, A188 and *Star*, 19 July 1859.
970. "Criminal Court Minutes," 20 July 1859, A211.
971. "Criminal Court Minutes," 21 July 1859, A218.
972. "Criminal Court Minutes " 30 July 1859, A224 and *Star*, 1 August 1859.
973. *Star*, 27 August 1859.
974. Ibid.
975. Ibid.
976. Ibid.

977. Ibid.
978. *Star*, 26 August 1859 and "Miscellaneous Records 1826-1865," Entry 470.
979. "Report of the Warden," Vol. 1078. (36-2), Senate Ex. Doc.1, November 1860, 505.
980. 1860 U.S. Census, M653, 938.
981. Ibid.
982. "Criminal Court Minutes," 9 December 1859, A111.
983. 1860 U.S. Census, M653, 938.
984. Ibid.
985. Ibid.
986. *Star*, 16 December 1859.
987. *Star*, 17 December 1859.
988. 1860 U.S. Census, M653, 938.
989. "Criminal Court Minutes," 19 December 1859, A155.
990. "Criminal Court Minutes," 17 December 1859, A139.
991. "Criminal Court Minutes," 19 December 1859, A143.
992. "Criminal Court Minutes," 22 December 1859, A197 and *Star*, 23 December 1859.
993. "Criminal Court Minutes," 24 December 1859, A208.
994. "Criminal Court Minutes," 23 December 1859, A206 and *Star*, 2 September 1861.
995. "Criminal Court Minutes," 24 December 1859, A210, and *Star*, 31 December 1859.
996. 1860 U.S. Census, M653, 938.
997. Ibid.
998. Ibid.

Chapter Thirty-seven

999. "Criminal Court Minutes," 12 December 1859, A123 and *Star*, 23 June 1859, 20 June 1862.
1000. "Criminal Court Minutes," 4 January 1860, A250 and *Star,* 10 December 1856.
1001. *Star,* 4 January 1860.
1002. Ibid.
1003. "Criminal Court Minutes," 29 December 1859, A174-176.
1004. 1860 U.S. Census, M653, 938.
1005. 1860 U.S. Census, M653, 938.
1006. "Criminal Court Minutes," 7 January 1860, A276-277 and *Star*, 9 January 1860.

1007. "Criminal Court Minutes," 10 January 1860, A246 and *Star*, 10 January 1860.

1008. "Criminal Court Minutes," 6 January 1860, A136 and *Star*, 6 January 1860.

1009. "Criminal Court Minutes," 18 January 1860, A297.

1010. "Miscellaneous Letters," Entry 466, 23 January 1860, and "Criminal Court Minutes," 18 January 1860, A242, and *Star* 19 January 1860.

1011. "Criminal Court Minutes," 18 January 1860, A173.

1012. "Criminal Court Minutes," 20 December 1859, A181, 186, 187 and *Star*, 28 January 1860.

1013. "Criminal Court Minutes," 24 January 1860, A184 and *Star*, 24 January 1860.

1014. 1860 U.S. Census, M653, 938.

1015. "Criminal Court Minutes," 13 January 1860, A180/192 and *Star*, 14 January 1860.

1016. "Criminal Court Minutes," 6 March 1860, A56 and *Star*, 7 March 1860.

1017. "Criminal Court Minutes," 6 March 1860, A58 and *Star*, 7 March 1860.

1018. "Criminal Court Minutes," 6 March 1860, appearance 57 and *Star*, 7 March 1860.

1019. "Criminal Court Minutes," 8 March 1860, A69 and *Star*, 8 March 1860.

1020. "Criminal Court Minutes," 8 March 1860, A64 and *Star*, 8 March 1860.

1021. "Criminal Court Minutes," 8 March 1860, A70 and *Star*, 10 March 1860.

1022. "Criminal Court Minutes," 9 March 1860, A85 and *Star*, 10 March 1860.

1023. "Criminal Court Minutes," 9 March 1860, A88 and *Star*, 10 March 1860.

1024. "Criminal Court Minutes," 9 March 1860, A86 and *Star*, 10 March 1860.

1025. "Criminal Court Minutes," 12 March 1860, A52/65 and *Star*, 12 March 1860.

1026. 1860 U.S. Census. M653, 938

1027. "Criminal Court Minutes," 7 March 1860, A60 and *Star*, 7 March 1860, 10 November 1862.

1028. "Criminal Court Minutes," 5 March 1860, T69 and *Star*, 10 March 1860.

1029. "Criminal Court Minutes," 12 March 1860, A108 and *Star*, 13 March 1860.

1030. "Criminal Court Minutes," 13 March 1860, A75 and *Star*, 14 March 1860 and "Miscellaneous Records 1826-1865," Entry 470, 8 June 1862.

1031. "Criminal Court Minutes," 13 March 1860, A73.

1032. "Criminal Court Minutes," 13 March 1860, A74.

1033. "Criminal Court Minutes," 13 March 1860, A136 and *Star*, 19 March 1860.

1034. "Criminal Court Minutes," 17 March 1860, A139 and *Star*, 19 March 1860.

1035. "Criminal Court Minutes," 16 March 1860, A62 and *Star*, 16-17 March 1860.

1036. "Criminal Court Minutes," 7 March 1860, A50/51 and *Star*, 8 March 1860.

1037. "Criminal Court Minutes," 13 March 1860, A90-92/113, and *Star*, 19 March 1860, and "Miscellaneous Records 1826-1865," Entry 470, 8 June 1862.

1038. "Pardon papers," and 1860 U.S. Census, M653, 938.

1039. "Criminal Court Minutes," 25 April 1860, A163/164, and *Star*, 25 April 1860, and "Miscellaneous Letters." Entry 466, 28 November 1860.

1040. "Criminal Court Minutes," 24 April 1860, A150 and *Star*, 25 April 1860.

1041. "Criminal Court Minutes," 25 April 1860, A155 and *Star*, 26 April 1860.

1042. 1860 U.S. Census, M653, 938.

1043. "Criminal Court Minutes," 28 April 1860, A165 and *Star*, 28 April 1860.

1044. 1860 U.S. Census, M653, 938.

1045. Ibid.

1046. 1860 U.S. Census, M653, 938.

1047. "Criminal Court Minutes," 15 March 1860, A76 and *Star*, 15,16 April 1860.

1048. "Criminal Court Minutes," 18 June 1860, T99 and S*tar*, 18 June 1860.

1049. "Criminal Court Minutes," 18 June 1860, T75 and *Star*, 19 June 1860, 8 March 1861.

1050. "Criminal Court Minutes," 22 June 1860, A83.

1051. "Report of the Warden," Vol. 1117, (37-2), Senate Ex. Doc.1, 21 October 1861, 858.

1052. "Criminal Court Minutes," 19 June 1860, A32.
1053. "Criminal Court Minutes," 29 June 1860, A84.
1054. "Criminal Court Minutes," 30 June 1860, A88/89 and *Star*, 15/18 April 1861.
1055. "Report of the Warden," Vol. 1117, 21 October 1861, 858.
1056. Ibid.
1057. "Criminal Court Minutes," 20 June 1860, A87, 27 June 1860, A79.
1058. "Criminal Court Minutes," 28 June 1860, A80.
1059. "Criminal Court Minutes," 12 July 1860, A138 and *Star*, 13 July 1860.
1060. "Criminal Court Minutes," 12 July 1860, A130 and *Star*, 13 July 1860.
1061. "Criminal Court Minutes," 17 July 1860, A161 and *Star*, 18 July 1860.
1062. "Miscellaneous Records 1826-1865," Entry 470, 20 July 1860.
1063. Ibid.
1064. Ibid.
1065. "Criminal Court Minutes," 16 July 1860, A139.
1066. "Criminal Court Minutes," 12 July 1860, A142.
1067. "Criminal Court Minutes," 26 July 1860, A174 and *Star*, 27 July 1860.
1068. "Criminal Court Minutes," 26 July 1860, A175 and *Star*, 27 July 1860.
1069. "Criminal Court Minutes," 26 July 1860, A165, and *Star*, 27 July 1860, and "Miscellaneous Letters," Entry 466 (Letter from Marceron), 17 November 1860.
1070. "Report of the Warden," Vol. 1117, 21 October 1861.
1071. Ibid.
1072. Ibid.
1073. Ibid.
1074. Ibid.
1075. "Criminal Court Minutes," 4 December 1860, A72 and *Star*, 4 December 1860.
1076. "Criminal Court Minutes," 6 December 1860, A73 and *Star*, 8 December 1860.
1077. "Criminal Court Minutes," 6 December 1860, A75.
1078. "Criminal Court Minutes," 7 December 1860, A77/78 and *Star*, 8 December 1860.

1079. "Criminal Court Minutes," 8 December 1860, A80 and *Star*, 10 December 1860.
1080. "Criminal Court Minutes," 8 December 1860, A90 and *Star*, 8 December 1860.
1081. "Criminal Court Minutes," 10 December 1860, A95 and *Star*, 10 December 1860.
1082. "Criminal Court Minutes," 12 December 1860, A99 and *Star*, 13 December 1860.
1083. "Criminal Court Minutes," 10 December 1860, A94 and *Star*, 10 December 1860.
1084. "Criminal Court Minutes," 13 December 1860, A104 and *Star*, 13 December 1860.
1085. "Criminal Court Minutes," 18 December 1860, A122, and *Star*, 19 December 1860.
1086. "Criminal Court Minutes," 19 December 1860, A126 and *Star*, 19 December 1860.
1087. "Criminal Court Minutes," 19 December 1860, A127 and A128 and *Star*, 20 December 1860.
1088. "Criminal Court Minutes," 20 December 1860, A136 and *Star*, 20 December 1860.
1089. "Criminal Court Minutes," 21 December 1860, A142 and *Star*, 22 December 1860.
1090. "Criminal Court Minutes," 21 December 1860, A40 and *Star*, 21 December 1860.
1091. "Criminal Court Minutes," 13 December 1860, A124 and *Star*, 18 December 1860.
1092. "Criminal Court Minutes," 22 December 1860, A148 and *Star*, 26 December 1860.
1093. "Criminal Court Minutes," 29 December 1860, A156 and *Star*, 31 December 1860.

Chapter Thirty-eight

1094. *Star*, 13 December 1860.
1095. "Criminal Court Minutes," 18 January 1861, A205.
1096. "Criminal Court Minutes," 18 January 1861, A207 and *Star*, 18 January 1861.
1097. "Criminal Court Minutes," 21 January 1861, A202 and *Star*, 21 January 1861.
1098. "Criminal Court Minutes," 31 January 1861, A226 and *Star*, 31 January 1861.

1099. "Criminal Court Minutes," 1 February 1861, A245 and *Star*, 1 February 1861.
1100. "Criminal Court Minutes," 2 February 1861, A263 and *Star*, 4 February 1861.
1101. "Criminal Court Minutes," 4 February 1861, A253.
1102. "Report of the Warden," Vol. 1117, 21 October 1861.
1103. Ibid.
1104. Ibid.
1105. Ibid.
1106. Ibid.
1107. Ibid.
1108. "Criminal Court Minutes," 13 March 1861, A76 and *Star*, 13 March 1861.
1109. "Criminal Court Minutes," 13 March 1861, A77.
1110. Ibid., A86 and *Star*, 15 March 1861.
1111. "Criminal Court Minutes," 13 March 1861, A82 and *Star*, 13 March 1861.
1112. "Criminal Court Minutes," 15 March 1861, A91 and *Star*, 16 March 1861.
1113. "Criminal Court Minutes," 15 March 1861, A88 and *Star*, 16 March 1861.
1114. *Star*, 20 March 1861.
1115. "Criminal Court Minutes," 19 March 1861, A95 and *Star*, 19, 20, 22 March 1861.
1116. "Criminal Court Minutes," 22 March 1861, A125 and *Star*, 23 March 1861.
1117. "Criminal Court Minutes," 25 March 1861, A221 and *Star*, 25 March 1861.
1118. *Star*, 20 February 1861, 3 April 1861, and 31 October 1861.
1119. *Star*, 28 February 1861.
1120. "Criminal Court Minutes," March 1861, A92, and "Miscellaneous Records 1826-1865," Entry 470, 8 June 1862.
1121. "Criminal Court Minutes," 21 June 1861, A69 and *Star*, 22 June 1861.
1122. "Criminal Court Minutes," 21 June 1861, A64 and *Star*, 22 June 1861.
1123. "Criminal Court Minutes," 21 June 1861, A65 and *Star*, 22 June 1861.
1124. "Criminal Court Minutes," 22 June 1861, A70.

1125. "Criminal Court Minutes," 22 June 1861, A72 and *Star*, 24 June 1861.
1126. "Criminal Court Minutes," 22 June 1861, A71 and *Star*, 24 June 1861.
1127. "Miscellaneous Records 1826-1865," Entry 470, 8 June 1862 and "Criminal Court Minutes," 29 June 1861, A110.
1128. Ibid., and "Criminal Court Minutes," 1 July 1861, A112.
1129. "Criminal Court Minutes," 28 June 1861, A107.
1130. "Criminal Court Minutes," 5 July 1861, A133.
1131. "Criminal Court Minutes," 24 June 1861, A79/80 and *Star*, 25 June 1861.
1132. "Report of the Warden," Vol. 1117, 21 October 1861.
1133. Ibid.
1134. Ibid.
1135. Ibid.
1136. "Criminal Court Minutes," 9 July 1861, A158 and *Star*, 10 July 1861.
1137. "Criminal Court Minutes," 1 July 1861, A108.
1138. "Criminal Court Minutes," 12 July 1861, A167 and *Star*, 13 July 1861.
1139. "Report of the Warden," Vol. 1117, 21 October 1861.
1140. Ibid.
1141. "Miscellaneous Records 1826-1865." Entry 470, and "Criminal Court Minutes," 18 July 1861, A185 and *Star*, 18 July 1861.
1142. Ibid, and "Criminal Court Minutes," 19 July 1861, A184 and *Star*, 20 July 1861.
1143. "Criminal Court Minutes," 15 July 1861, A174 and *Star*, 16 July 1861.
1144. *Star*, 28 August 1861, 1 October 1861.
1145. Report of the Warden, Vol. 1117, 21 October 1861.
1146. *Star*, 4 September 1861.
1147. *Star*, 19 March 1861 and "Criminal Court Minutes," 18 March 1861, A24, 25.
1148. RG 153, I I 487.
1149. Ibid., I I488.
1150. "Report of the Warden," Vol. 1117, 21 October 1861.
1151. Ibid.
1152. "Criminal Court Minutes," 7 December 1861, A77 and *Star*, 9 November 1861.

1153. "Criminal Court Minutes," 7 December 1861, A74 and *Star*, 9 November 1861.
1154. "Criminal Court Minutes," 12 December 1861, A105 and *Star*, 13 December 1861.
1155. "Criminal Court Minutes," 13 December 1861, A113 and *Star*, 13 December 1861.
1156. "Criminal Court Minutes," 13 December 1861, A114 and *Star*, 14 December 1861.
1157. "Criminal Court Minutes," 14 December 1861, A115 *Star*, 15 December 1861.
1158. "Report of the Warden of the Penitentiary," Vol. 1157, House Ex. Doc.1, (37-3), 1 November 1862, 661.
1159. "Miscellaneous Records 1826-1865," Entry 470, and "Criminal Court Minutes," 10 December 1861, A92, 96, 97 and *Star*, 11 December 1861.
1160. Ibid., and "Criminal Court Minutes," 23 December 1861, A150 and *Star*, 24 December 1861.
1161. Ibid., and "Criminal Court Minutes," 16 December 1861, A127 and *Star*, 16 December 1861.

Chapter Thirty-nine

1162. Ibid., and "Criminal Court Minutes," 2 January 1862, A161 and *Star*, 3 January 1862.
1163. "Criminal Court Minutes," 19 December 1861, A144 and *Star*, 21 December 1861.
1164. "Miscellaneous Records 1826-1865," Entry 470, 8 June 1862 and "Criminal Court Minutes," 3 January 1862, A173.
1165. "Criminal Court Minutes," 26 December 1861, A20 and *Star*, 1 January 1862, 23 September 1862.
1166. "Criminal Court Minutes," 6 January 1862, A188 and *Star*, 7 January 1862.
1167. "Criminal Court Minutes," 6 January 1862, A186/187 and *Star*, 7 January 1862.
1168. "Criminal Court Minutes," 3 January 1862, A171 and *Star*, 4 January 1862.
1169. "Criminal Court Minutes," 7 January 1862, A195 and *Star*, 8 January 1862.
1170. "Pardon papers," Entry 476.
1171. Ibid.
1172. RG 153, I I 539.
1173. Ibid.

1174. RG 153, I I 539.
1175. "Miscellaneous Records 1826-1865," Entry 470, 8 June 1862, and. "Criminal Court Minutes," 6 March 1862, A107, and *Star,* 7 March 1862.
1176. RG 153, I I 786.
1177. "Criminal Court Minutes," 15 March 1862, A208 and *Star,* 16 March 1862.
1178. "Criminal Court Minutes," 16 January 1862, A221 and *Star,* 17 January 1862, 28 May 1862.
1179. "Criminal Court Minutes," 16 January 1862, A220 and *Star,* 17 January 1862.
1180. "Criminal Court Minutes," 10 December 1861, A89 and *Star,* 11 December 1861.
1181. "Criminal Court Minutes," 18 January 1862, A225.
1182. "Report of the Warden," 1 November 1862, 661.
1183. "Criminal Court Minutes," 18 January 1861, A226.
1184. RG 153, I I 606.
1185. Ibid., I I 554.
1186. Ibid., I I 766.
1187. "Report of the Warden," 1 November 1862, 661.
1188. "Criminal Court Minutes," 27 January 1862, A230 and *Star,* 28 January 1862.
1189. RG 153, I I 632.
1190. Ibid.
1191. "Letter from the Secretary of Interior: List of prisoners in Penitentiary of District of Columbia by sentence of Courts-martial," Vol. 1138, (37-2), House Ex. Doc. 127.
1192. "Miscellaneous Records 1826-1865," Entry 470 and "Criminal Court Minutes," 4 February 1862, A270.
1193. "Criminal Court Minutes," 5 February 1862, A280 and *Star,* 6 February 1862.
1194. "Report of the Warden," 1 November 1862, 661.
1195. "Criminal Court Minutes," 5 February 1862, A177/196 and *Star,* 15 January 1862, 6 February 1862.
1196. "Criminal Court Minutes," 28 January 1862, A192 and *Star,* 1 February 1862.
1197. "Miscellaneous Records 1826-1865," Entry 470, 8 June 1862, and "Criminal Court Minutes," 4 February 1862, A256.
1198. "Criminal Court Minutes," 8 February 1862, A300 and *Star,* 10 February 1862.
1199. "Report of the Warden," 1 November 1862, 661.

1200. RG 153, I I 614.
1201. "Report of the Warden," 1 November 1862, 661.
1202. RG 153, I I 620.
1203. Ibid., I I 639.
1204. Ibid. I I 593.
1205. Ibid., I I 620
1206. Ibid., I I 615
1207. "Report of the Warden," 1 November 1862, 661.
1208. Ibid.
1209. "Criminal Court Minutes," 12 February 1862, A108 and *Star,* 13 February 1862.
1210. "Report of the Warden," 1 November 1862, 661.
1211. RG 153, I I 655.
1212. Ibid., I I 781-1.
1213. "Report of the Warden," 1 November 1862, 661.
1214. RG 153, I I 677.
1215. Ibid., I I 677.
1216. "Report of the Warden," 1 November 1862, 661.
1217. RG 153, I I 655.
1218. "Report of the Warden," 1 November 1862, 661, and *Adjutant General's Report Indiana, 1861-1865,* Vol. 4. Indianapolis, IN: Samuel M. Douglass State Printer, 1866, 408-409.
1219. Ibid.
1220. "Report of the Warden," 1 November 1862, 661.
1221. RG 153, I I 643.
1222. Ibid., I I 781-2.
1223. Ibid., I I 618.
1224. "Report of the Warden," 1 November 1862, 661.
1225. RG153, I I 633.
1226. "Report of the Warden," 1 November 1862, 661.
1227. Ibid.
1228. Ibid., and *Adjutant General's Report Indiana, 1861-1865,* 408-409.
1229. "Criminal Court Minutes," 3 March 1862, T35 and, *Star,* 4/6 March 1862, and "Case Papers," March 1862 term, A35, 36.
1230. *Star,* 6 Mar 62.
1231. "Miscellaneous Records, 1826-1865," Entry 470, 8 June 1862 and "Criminal Court Minutes," 5 March 1862, A103.
1232. "Miscellaneous Records, 1826-1865," Entry 470, 8 June 1862.

1233. "Criminal Court Minutes," 5 March 1862, A104 and *Star,* 6 March 1862.
1234. RG153, I I 786.
1235. Ibid.
1236. "Report of the Warden," 1 November 1862, 661.
1237. RG153, II 652.
1238. Ibid.
1239. Ibid.
1240. Ibid.
1241. RG153, KK 404.
1242. "Report of the Warden," 1 November 1862, 661.
1243. RG153, KK 404.
1244. Ibid.
1245. "Report of the Warden," 1 November 1862, 661.
1246. RG153, II 718.
1247. Ibid., II 677.
1248. Ibid., II 615.
1249. Ibid., II 618.
1250. Ibid., II 801.
1251. Ibid.
1252. Ibid., II 652.
1253. "Report of the Warden," 1 November 1862, 661.
1254. RG153, II652.
1255. Ibid.
1256. Ibid., II 803.
1257. Ibid.
1258. Ibid.
1259. Ibid.
1260. "Report of the Warden," 1 November 1862, 661.
1261. Ibid.
1262. RG153, II 807.
1263. "Criminal Court Minutes," 31 March 1862, A22.
1264. "Criminal Court Minutes," 29 March 1862, A149 and "Miscellaneous Records 1826-1865," Entry 470.
1265. "Criminal Court Minutes," 28 March 1862, A148 and "Miscellaneous Records 1826-1865," Entry 470.
1266. "Criminal Court Minutes," 29 March 1862, A156 and *Star,* 29 March 1862.
1267. "Criminal Court Minutes," 4 April 1862, A174 and *Star,* 5 April 1862.
1268. "Report of the Warden," 1 November 1862, 661.

1269. Ibid.
1270. Ibid.
1271. Ibid.
1272. *Star,* 29 March 1862, 10 November 1862.
1273. "Report of the Warden," 1 November 1862, 661.
1274. Ibid.
1275. Ibid.
1276. RG153, II 870.
1277. Ibid., II 908.
1278. *Star,* 29 February 1862.
1279. *Star,* 13 August 1862.
1280. RG153, II 871.
1281. Ibid., II 875.
1282. Ibid., II 782.
1283. Ibid., II 845.
1284. "Report of the Warden," 1 November 1862, 661.
1285. RG153, II 873.
1286. Ibid.
1287. Ibid.
1288. Ibid., II 908.
1289. Ibid.
1290. Ibid.
1291. Ibid.
1292. Ibid.
1293. "Report of the Warden," 1 November 1862, 661.
1294. Ibid.
1295. RG153, II 908.
1296. Ibid., II 911A.
1297. "Pardon papers," Entry 476.
1298. "Report of the Warden," 1 November 1862, 661.
1299. Ibid.
1300. Ibid.
1301. "Report of the Warden," 1 November 1862, 661.
1302. Ibid.
1303. "Criminal Court Minutes," 20 June 1862, A79 and *Star,* 21 June 1862.
1304. "Criminal Court Minutes," 21 June 1862, T50.
1305. "Criminal Court Minutes," 30 June 1862, A82 and *Star,* 30 June 1862.
1306. "Criminal Court Minutes," 1 July 1862, A94 and *Star,* 2 July 1862.

1307. "Criminal Court Minutes," 2 July 1862, A95 and *Star*, 2 July 1862.
1308. *Star*, 24 June 1862.
1309. "Criminal Court Minutes," 15 July 1862, A108.
1310. "Criminal Court Minutes," 15 July 1862, A131 and *Star*, 15 July 1862.
1311. "Criminal Court Minutes," 14 July 1862, A98 and *Star*, 15 July 1862.
1312. *Star*, 20 June 1862.
1313. "Criminal Court Minutes," 19 July 1862, A149 and *Star*, 21/30 July 1862.
1314. "Criminal Court Minutes," 17 July 1862, A117 and *Star*, 18 July 1862.
1315. "Criminal Court Minutes," 21 July 1862, A138.
1316. "Report of the Warden," Vol. 1157, 1 November 1862, 661.
1317. "Criminal Court Minutes," 24 July 1862, A134 and *Star*, 25 July 1862.
1318. "Criminal Court Minutes," 23 July 1862, A178.
1319. "Criminal Court Minutes," 26 July 1862, A190 and *Star*, 28 July 1862.
1320. "Criminal Court Minutes," 24 July 1862, T41.
1321. "Criminal Court Minutes," 26 July 1862, A166.
1322. "Criminal Court Minutes," 24July 1862, A177 and *Star*, 25 July 1862

Chapter Forty

1323. Christian Hines, *Early Recollections of Washington City*, Washington, DC: September 1866, Reprint 1981 by Junior League of Washington, 62.
1324. Ibid., 63.
1325. Ibid., 6.
1326. "Drayton and Edward Sayres." Vol. 864, (34-1), House Ex. Doc. 146, 16 August 1856.
1327. *Star*, 27 August 1853.
1328. *Star*, 29 August 1853.
1329. *Star*, 11 July 1853.
1330. *Star*, 1 September 1853.
1331. *Star*, 2 September 1853.
1332. *Star*, 2 September 1853.
1333. *Star*, 15 April 1858.

1334. *Star,* 15 April 1858.
1335. *Star,* 17 April 1858.
1336. *Star,* 17 April 1858.
1337. *Star,* 17 June 1858
1338. *Star,* 18 June 1858.
1339. *Star,* 26 June 1858.
1340. *Star,* 28 June 1858.
1341. *Star,* 13 December 1853.
1342. *Star,* 4 March 1854.
1343. "Criminal Court Minutes," 3 March 1854.
1344. *Star,* 6 March 1854.
1345. *Star,* 6 March 1854.
1346. *Star,* 2 May 1854.
1347. "Gardiner and Mears," Report by F. P. Stanton from Committee on the Judiciary, Vol. 744, (33-1), House Report 369, 3 August 1854.
1348. *Star,* 13 April 1859.
1349. Ibid., 28 February 1859.
1350. Ibid., 1 March 1859.
1351. Ibid., 28 February 1859.
1352. Ibid., 1 March 1859.
1353. Ibid., 14 April 1859.
1354. Ibid., 1 March 1859.
1355. Ibid., 13 April 1859.
1356. Ibid., 5 May 1859.
1357. Ibid., 10 May 1859.

Chapter Forty-One

1358. "Report of the Warden," Vol. 1078, (36-2), Senate Ex. Doc.1, November 1860, 505.
1359. "Eighth Annual Report of the Warden," 23 January 1837.
1360. *Star,* 5 July 1859.
1361. "Eighth Annual Report of the Warden," 23 January 1837.
1362. *Star,* 7 July 1865.
1363. Oakley, 36.
1364. "Letter from the Secretary of War relative to The Taking Down and Removal of old penitentiary in Washington Arsenal Grounds," Vol. 1567, (42-3), House Ex. Doc. 163.

1365. House Report 41 to accompany H. R. Bill 169, Vol.1206, (38-2), 2 April 1864. (Bill 169 authorized construction of a penitentiary, jail and house of corrections for the District of Columbia.)

BIBLIOGRAPHY

"A report of the Inspectors of the Penitentiary of the District of Columbia for the year 1846." Vol. 499. (29-2). H. Doc. 44. 16 Jan 1847.

Adjutant General's Report Indiana, 1861-1865. Vol. 4. Indianapolis, IN: Samuel M. Douglass State Printer, 1866.

"Annual Report of the Inspectors of the Penitentiary for the District of Columbia." Vol. 576. (31-1) H. Ex. Doc. 33. 6 February 1850.

Ashton, H., Thomas Carbery, William O'Neale, Thomson F. Mason, and James Dunlop. "Report of the Board of Inspectors of the Penitentiary for the District of Columbia." 1 February 1830.

"Charges against officers of the Penitentiary, District of Columbia." Vol. 404. (27-2) H. Doc. 174. 8 April 1842.

"Correspondence on imprisonment of soldiers and volunteers in penitentiary in the District of Columbia." Vol. 1122. (37-2) Senate Ex. Doc. 55.

Court Martial Case Files: 1809-1938. Dept of War/Dept. of Army/Office of the Judge Advocate General. Record Group 153, series PC29#15, control #NWCTB 153-PC29E15. National Archives.

Criminal Court District of Columbia Case Papers, 1838-63. Entry 45. RG 21, Stack Area 16E3, row 11, compartment 25, shelf 3. National Archives. Washington, DC.

Criminal Court Minutes: 1838-1862," RG 21, Entry 43. Washington, DC: National Archives.

"Daniel Drayton and Edward Sayres." Vol. 864. (34-1) H. Ex. Doc.146. 16 August 1856.

"D.C. Penitentiary, 1830 Report of Inspectors." Vol. 196. (21-1) House Doc. 46. 1 February 1830.

"D.C. Penitentiary, 1831 Report of Inspectors." Vol. 208. (21-2) Doc. 66. 25 January 1831.

"D.C. Penitentiary, 1832 Report of Inspectors." Vol. 217. (22-1) Doc. 80. 31 January 1832.

District of Columbia Code of Laws. Vol. 200. (21-1) House Report 269. 3 March 1830.

"Eighth Annual Report of the Warden of the Penitentiary." Vol. 303. (24-2) Doc. 97. 23 January 1837.

"Eleventh Annual Report of the Warden of the Penitentiary." Vol. 365. (26-1) H. Doc. 99. 12 February 1840.

Evening Star. Microfilm. December 1852-July 1865. Various.

"Fifteenth Annual Report of the Inspectors of the Penitentiary of the District of Columbia for the year 1843." Vol. 442. (28-1) House Doc.75. 23 January 1844.

"Fifth Annual Report of the Inspectors of the Penitentiary in the District of Columbia." Vol. 255. (23-1) Doc. 70. 28 January 1834.

"Fourteenth Annual Report of the Warden of the Penitentiary." Vol. 420. (27-3) H. Doc. 67. 17 January 1843.

Green, Constance McLaughlin. *Washington: Village and Capital, 1800-1878*. Princeton, NJ: Princeton UP, 1962.

Hines, Christian. *Early Recollections of Washington City*. Washington, DC: September 1866. Reprint 1981 by Junior League of Washington.

House Report 41 to accompany H. R. Bill 169. Vol. 1206. (38-1) 2 April 1864.

Letter from the Secretary of Interior. "List of prisoners in Penitentiary of District of Columbia by sentence of Courts-martial." Vol. 1138. (37-2) H. Ex. Doc. 127.

Letter from the Secretary of War relative to "The Taking Down and Removal of old penitentiary in Washington Arsenal Grounds." Vol. 1567. (42-3) H. Ex. Doc. 163.

Letters from the Secretary of the Interior in relation to "The Occupation of the penitentiary buildings in the District of Columbia as a place of storage for ammunition and other materials of war." Vol.1141. (37-2) H. Misdoc. 32. 14 January 1862.

List of Convictions 1831-1853. Entry 41. RG 21, Stack Area 16E3, row 11, compartment 24, shelf 1. National Archives. Washington, DC.

"Message from the President of the U.S.: Jail, Lunatic Hospital, and courthouse in the District of Columbia." Vol. 325. (25-2) House Doc. 96. 13 January 1838.

Minutes of the U.S. Circuit Court for the District of Columbia, 1801-1863. M1021. Microfilm. National Archives, Washington, DC.

Morris, J. R. "Penitentiary in the District of Columbia." (38-1) House Report 41. 2 April 1864.

"Nineteenth Annual Report of the Inspectors of the Penitentiary of the District of Columbia for the year 1847." Vol. 516. (30-1) Doc. 28. 26 January 1848.

"Ninth Annual Report of the Inspectors of the Penitentiary of Washington." Vol. 326. (25-2) House Doc.140. 2 February 1838.

Oakley, Mary Hostetler. *Journey From the Gallows: Historical Evolution of the Penal Philosophy and Practices in the Nation's Capital.* Lanham, MD: University Press of America, 1988.

"Penitentiary, District of Columbia: Fourth Annual Report." Vol. 234. (22-2) Doc. 49. 19 January 1833.

"Penitentiary District of Columbia: Report of Inspectors." Vol. 677. (32-2) Doc. 41. 12 February 1853.

"Penitentiary for the District of Columbia." Vol. 723. (33-1) Doc. 72. 3 March 1854.

Records relating to the U.S. Penitentiary for the District of Columbia. "Minute Book of the Inspectors U.S. Penitentiary, April 1829-July 1857." Entry 464. RG 48, Stack area 150, row 7, compartment 20, shelf 2. Box 1. National Archives II, College Park, MD.

Records relating to the U.S. Penitentiary for the District of Columbia. "Miscellaneous Letters." Entry 466. RG 48, Stack area 150, row 7, compartment 19, shelf 6. Box 1. National Archives II, College Park, MD.

Records relating to the U.S. Penitentiary for the District of Columbia. "Miscellaneous Records relating to the U.S. Penitentiary for the District of Columbia 1826-1865." Entry 470. RG 48, Stack area 150, Row 7, Compartment 20, shelf 1. National Archives, II, College Park, MD.

Records relating to the U.S. Penitentiary for the District of Columbia. "Register of Convicts 1831-1862." Entry 474. RG 48, Stack area 150, row 7, compartment 20, shelf 2. Box 1. National Archives II, College Park, MD.

Records relating to the U.S. Penitentiary for the District of Columbia. "Pardon papers 1832-1862." Entry 476. RG 48, Stack area 150, row 7, compartment 20, shelf 2. Box 1. National Archives II, College Park, MD.

"Registers of the Records of the Proceedings of the U.S. Army General Courts Martial 1809-1890." RG 153. Microfilm 1105. Roll 2. National Archives I.

"Report of Charles Bulfinch on the subject of Penitentiaries." Volume 152. (19-2) Report 98. 13 February 1827.

"Report of the Committee on the District of Columbia on the subject of prisons in the District." Vol. 122. (18-2) House Report 52. 1 February 1825.

"Report of the Warden of the Penitentiary." Vol. 777. (33-2) H. Ex. Doc. 1. 1 October 1854.

"Report of the Warden of the Penitentiary." Vol. 840. (34-1) H. Ex. Doc. 1. 1 October 1855.

"Report of the Warden of the Penitentiary." Vol. 893. (34-3) H. Ex. Doc. 1. 1 October 1856.

"Report of the Warden and Board of Inspectors of the U.S. Penitentiary for the District of Columbia." Vol. 942. (35-1) House Ex. Doc. 2. November 1857.

"Report of the Warden of the Penitentiary accompanying the 30th Annual Report of the Secretary of the Interior." Vol. 974. (35-2) Senate Ex. Doc. 1. 1 November 1858.

"Report of the Warden, 1859." Vol. 1023. (36-1) Senate Ex. Doc. 2. 1859.

"Report of the Warden." Vol. 1117. (37-2) S. Ex. Doc.1. 21 October 1861.

"Report of the Warden." Vol. 1078. (36-2) S. Ex. Doc.1. November 1860.

"Report of the Warden of the Penitentiary." Vol. 1157. (37-3) H. Ex. Doc.1. 1 November 62.

"Seventeenth Annual Report of the Inspectors of the Penitentiary of the District of Columbia for the year 1845." Vol. 483. (29-1) House Doc. 89. 28 January 1846.

"Seventh Annual Report of the Warden of the Penitentiary." Vol. 288. (24-1) Doc. 28. January 1836.

"Sixteenth Annual Report of the Inspectors of the Penitentiary of the District of Columbia." Vol. 465. (28-2) House Doc.115. 12 February 1845.

"Sixth Annual Report of the Warden of the Penitentiary." (23-2) Vol. 272. House Doc.75. 12 January 1835.

Stanton, F. P. "Gardiner and Mears." Report by F. P. Stanton from Committee on the Judiciary. Vol. 744. (33-1) House report 369. 3 August 1854.

Sullivan, David K. *District of Columbia Penal System, 1825-1875.* Georgetown University Thesis 4207. Washington, DC, March 1973.

"Tenth Annual Report of the Warden of the Penitentiary." (5-3) Doc.165. 7 February 1839.

"The Annual Report of the Inspectors of the Penitentiary." Vol. 599. (31-2) House Ex. Doc. 43. 3 March 1851.

"The Gardiner Investigation." Vol. 687. (32-2) H. Report 1. 7 October 1852.

"The Report of the Inspectors of the Penitentiary in the District of Columbia." Vol. 644. (32-1) Doc. 97. 3 May 1852.

"Thirteenth Annual Report of the Warden of the Penitentiary." Vol. 402. (27-2) H. Doc. 50. 20 January 1842.

"Twelfth Annual Report of the Warden of the Penitentiary." Vol. 384. (26-2) H. Doc. 92. 30 January 1841.

"Twentieth Annual Report of the Inspectors of the Penitentiary for the District of Columbia." Vol. 540. (30-2) H. Ex. Doc. 16 January 1849.

U.S. Census. District of Columbia. Washington County, 7th Ward. 21 September 1850. Microfilm M432. Roll 57. National Archives, Washington, DC.

U.S. Census. District of Columbia. Washington County, 7th Ward. 31 July 1860. Microfilm M653. Roll 104. National Archives, Washington, DC.

U.S. District Court for the District of Columbia. "Law, Appellate, Criminal Docket." RG 21, Stack 21E-4, row 14, compartment 3, shelf 2, Entry 1. Vol. 65. May 1831.

Index

Adams, 73, 101, 103, 109
Affleck, 174
Albritton, 61
Alexander, 70, 156
Allemander, 107
Allen, 100, 135
Allinger, 78
Anderson, 94, 111, 155, 178
Andree, 116
Andrews, 80
Angel, 91
Arrowsmith, 180
Arth, 142
Arthur, 145
Ashby, 80
Ashford, 27
Ashton, 19, 23, 55, 69
Atwell, 156
Atzerodt, 200
Aubert, 163
Aud, 133
Ayers, 168
Baedley, 150
Bagioli, 195
Bailey, 126
Baker, 9, 61, 90
Ball, 97
Ballard, 61
Banks, 162
Banter, 67
Baptiste, 119, 142
Barker, 57, 59, 63, 69, 84, 89
Barkman, 127
Barnes, 120, 164
Barnett, 147
Barrett, 45, 103, 141, 157
Barry, 65, 152
Bartley, 119
Barton, 125
Bartow, 50
Bashler, 124
Bateman, 103
Bates, 81, 98
Batson, 133
Baunstock, 151
Bayliss, 110, 155

Bays, 95, 99, 108
Beach, 109
Bean, 98
Beckett, 97, 104
Beckwith, 169
Beddo, 78
Bedds, 69
Beegan, 169
Beerman, 69
Bell, 56, 84, 123, 124, 130, 144, 168
Benezet, 95
Bennett, 179
Bentley, 80
Bentz, 109
Berry, 59, 139
Betz, 143
Beute, 109
Biddle, 50, 119
Biggs, 81
Bills, 133
Binnix, 146
Bird, 80
Birl, 183
Black, 85, 90
Blake, 144
Blanford, 57
Blewett, 133
Bohlayer, 149
Bohrer, 24, 28, 29
Bomford, 97
Bond, 87, 181
Bonds, 65
Bonnett, 162
Borg or Burke, 85
Boscoe, 152
Boss, 61
Boston, 145
Boswell, 178
Boucher, 162
Bowen, 156
Bowie, 115
Bowlen, 143
Boyd, 151, 162
Boyle, 36, 158
Brace, 177
Bradley, 25, 67, 88

Brady, 176
Brandt, 126
Brasey, 74
Brayley, 155
Bremline, 170
Brent, 152
Brest, 109
Brick, 143
Brieberg, 129
Brogden, 55, 59, 73
Brooders, 188
Brooke, 56
Brooks, 83, 110, 111, 136, 182
Brower, 93
Brown, 23, 34, 59, 60, 63, 65, 67, 69, 70, 77, 78, 79, 80, 83, 85, 87, 89, 91, 92, 93, 97, 101, 104, 107, 108, 116, 123, 132, 134, 135, 145, 146, 182
Browning, 155
Bryan, 183
Bryant, 35, 130, 143, 148
Buchanan, 134
Bulfinch, 3, 15
Bulger, 138
Burchell, 131
Burd, 94
Burke, 116, 127
Burnes, 59
Burnham, 136
Burns, 173
Bush, 59, 157, 173
Butler, 29, 32, 65, 70, 84, 85, 90, 91, 95, 101, 120, 124, 130, 131, 156
Butt, 55
Butterworth, 194
Byers, 55
Byrle, 123
Callahan, 65
Calvert, 113
Campbell, 44, 111, 127, 157, 167, 175
Camper, 107
Cane, 171
Cantner, 170
Carberry, 19, 23, 24, 25
Carner, 170
Carpenter, 67, 79, 92, 97, 120, 130
Carr, 51, 119

Carroll, 91
Carter, 57, 67, 143, 183, 188
Cartwright, 55
Caton, 98
Causine, 59, 85
Cavinaugh, 100
Cesalto, 150
Chandler, 148
Chase, 79, 127, 177
Chavos, 50
Childers, 98
Chisley, 171
Chollett, 94
Cisil, 87
Cissell, 73
Clark, 75, 80, 84, 87, 157
Clarke, 22, 24, 199
Clemenson, 136
Cline, 131
Clitz, 165
Clopher, 59
Clousky, 109
Cloy, 152
Coakley, 129, 149
Coale, 116
Coburn, 87
Cofen, 183
Cole, 63, 67, 85, 89, 169, 183
Coleman, 63
Colledge, 117
Collier, 93
Colligan, 172
Collins, 61, 67, 73, 77, 84, 87, 160
Coltman, 27, 28, 29
Conklin, 182
Conn, 74
Connell, 175
Connelly, 136, 178
Conner, 67
Connor, 119
Contee, 105, 127, 156
Cook, 90, 104
Cooledge, 194
Cornwell, 127
Corrigan, 143
Cosgrove, 31
Craig, 135
Crawford, 11
Croggin, 45, 53, 126

Croggins, 37
Cross, 52, 131
Cullen, 183
Culp, 74
Cummings, 177
Cunningham, 43, 44, 133, 136
Curtis, 85, 125, 175
Dade, 26
Dalman, 136
Dandridge, 142
Daniel, 61
Dant, 120
Darling, 146
Daum, 160
David, 25
Davis, 24, 57, 63, 73, 87, 89, 91, 99, 100, 111, 135, 148, 158
Davison, 129
Day, 45, 112, 113
Dayton, 172
de la Fountaine, 93
Dean, 70, 86, 87, 94
DeCamp, 155
DeFalco, 127
Delano, 160
Demaine, 125, 126
Dent, 123, 133, 143, 149, 157, 167
Devaughn, 57
DeVilliers, 160
Devlin, 139
Diggins, 183
Diggs, 63, 70, 77, 85, 95, 99, 104, 110
Dill, 151
Dix, 29
Dixon, 93
Dockhart, 31, 99
Dodson, 151
Doherty, 152
Donnelly, 51, 120, 176
Donoho, 26, 30, 183
Doras, 88
Dorey, 94
Dorrance, 35, 45, 126
Dorsey, 105
Douglas, 59
Douglass, 37, 133
Dover, 92
Dowling, 65, 90

Doyle, 146
Drayton, 186
Driscoll, 168
Driver, 150
Drury, 73
Dubois, 160
Duchanoy, 154
Ducket, 142
Duffey, 159
Duffy, 182, 194
Dunawin, 168
Dunbar, 113, 142
Dunigan, 125
Dunlop, 11, 19, 24, 81
Duvall, 113
Dyer, 89
Eagan, 63
Eaton, 103
Eberling, 153
Eckles, 101
Eckloff, 92, 94
Edes, 30, 154
Edwards, 113, 125
Effords, 63
Egan, 162
Eliason, 124
Ellis, 31, 84, 136, 152
Erb, 83
Erbach, 142
Evans, 63, 85, 103, 116, 123, 159, 167, 182
Everett, 155
Ewing, 133
Fagan, 151
Fahey, 171
Falby, 169
Farrell, 138
Fearson, 12
Feig, 160
Fenton, 99
Fenwick, 74
Ferell, 80
Ferguson, 26, 113, 159, 171
Fernandis, 120
Fey, 179
Finch, 169
Finegin, 107
Fink, 158
Finkle, 7

Finn, 162
Finnigan, 59
Fischer, 157
Fishenden, 175
Fisher, 25, 83, 145
Fitnam, 30
Fitzgerald, 168
Fleming, 8
Fletcher, 79, 130, 151, 152, 158
Foley, 111, 161
Folhouse, 78
Force, 34
Ford, 94, 97, 154
Fords, 85
Foreman, 125
Foster, 150
Fowler, 179
Fox, 65
Franck, 137, 142
Franks, 60
French, 151
Frizell, 162
Frizzell, 89
Fry, 43
Fugitt, 157
Fugleman, 137
Fuss, 159
Gaines, 91, 134
Gallagher, 172
Gant, 142, 169
Gardiner, 190, 191
Gardner, 91
Garner, 83, 87, 135
Garnett, 34, 36, 37
Garrison, 161
Gassenheimer, 143
Gautier, 156
Gavin, 130, 155
Gerholdt, 7
Getley, 163
Gibbs, 85, 115
Giles, 91
Gill, 55, 147
Glascow, 145
Glass, 154
Goddard, 74
Goddards, 61
Goetz, 99
Goldin, 100

Goldsmith, 152, 169
Gonzales, 146
Good, 84
Gordon, 157
Gorman, 116, 164
Gould, 91
Graby, 69
Graham, 79, 148
Granderson, 68
Grant, 59
Grappe, 172
Gray, 28, 32, 63, 79, 85, 116, 156
Grayson, 160
Greaves, 81
Green, 70, 77, 113, 116, 143, 177
Griffin, 174
Grimes, 91, 159
Grinder, 162
Grinnel, 157
Gunnell, 83
Gwinn, 142
Haines, 112
Hair, 155
Hale, 94
Haley, 178
Hall, 32, 57, 80, 107, 152, 169, 192
Hamelin, 150
Hamilton, 36, 158
Hanahan, 141
Hanassey, 169
Hand, 138
Handy, 35, 78, 100, 131
Haney, 100
Hanley, 93, 178
Hannchild, 109
Hanson, 94
Harbaugh, 55
Hardy, 77, 81
Harmon, 167
Harney, 151
Harper, 57, 115
Harris, 57, 156, 173, 182
Harry, 105
Harte, 74
Haveren, 170
Haw, 28, 158
Hawkins, 153, 164
Haynes, 178
Hays, 65

Heise, 38, 104
Heisler, 101, 115, 170
Heissler, 140
Hemphill, 164
Henderson, 69, 103, 171
Hendricks, 49, 50, 120
Henivery, 155
Hennessey, 168
Henning, 65
Henriques, 176
Henry, 156, 159
Hepburn, 182
Herbert, 67, 70, 77, 90
Herold, 200
Herriman, 167
Herzog, 174
Hesch, 179
Hickman, 153
Hill, 110
Hillery, 134
Hilton, 101
Hines, 57
Hinton, 126
Hobbey, 73
Hobbs, 22, 55
Hodge, 81
Hodges, 57
Hoffa, 144
Hoffman, 137, 182
Holden, 150
Holland, 116
Holloway, 120
Holly, 59, 113, 133
Holmes, 138
Homillen, 95
Homiller, 145
Hood, 164
Hooe, 25, 100
Hooker, 50
Hooper, 142
Hoot, 63
Hoover, 81, 167
Hopkins, 150
Hornsberry, 63, 67
Hornsburg, 138
House, 180
Houseman, 9
Howard, 90, 161, 167, 176
Howards, 67

Howland, 179
Hughes, 83, 100, 138
Humit, 135
Humphrey, 113
Humphreys, 97, 125, 148
Humphries, 133
Hunt, 94
Hunter, 56, 64
Hurley, 104, 156, 158
Hutchins, 145
Hutchinson, 107
Hutt, 123
Hutton, 59
Ingle, 104
Ireland, 174
Jackson, 69, 136, 148, 164
Jaeger, 154
James, 98, 175
Jasper, 78
Jenifer, 69
Jenkins, 85
Jerowitz, 154
Johnson, 36, 51, 65, 67, 80, 91, 101,
    105, 111, 115, 127, 129, 136, 140,
    158, 160, 162, 170
Johnston, 159, 178
Jones, 27, 28, 37, 45, 61, 63, 75, 84,
    103, 124, 125, 130, 132, 151, 155,
    170, 171, 174
Jordan, 172
Juley, 180
Julius, 137
Kaiser, 143
Kauffman, 152
Kays, 119
Kearney, 135
Keasbey, 37
Keen, 171
Keenan, 146, 147, 155
Keene, 63
Kein, 158
Keith, 50
Kelly, 16, 57, 89, 123, 129, 148, 171
Kelpler, 161
Kendall, 91, 112
Keppell, 135
Kernan, 113, 127
Kershner, 123
Kesley, 24

Key, 193, 194
Keyes, 39
Kidwell, 123, 154
Killian, 127
Kimberly, 169
King, 37, 73, 85, 120, 147, 150, 152, 156, 183
Kingla, 80
Kingsley, 111
Kirby, 29
Kirk, 146
Kirkley, 149
Kisfaludi, 154
Knapp, 167
Knight, 138, 169
Knott, 185
Korff, 77
Koss, 43, 129
Krauss, 134
Kreager, 45
Kreiger, 138
Kronmeyer, 176
Krouse, 121
Kurtz, 67, 74, 157
Lacey, 78, 92
Lafferty, 152
Lafontaine, 69
Lambert, 43, 133
Landvoight, 70
Lang, 177
Langster, 103
Lansdale, 116
Larkin, 59, 65
Larned, 59
Larner, 154
Laskey, 152
Latham, 126
Laurence, 24, 57
Lausman, 158
Lawn, 135
Lawrence, 109
Lawson, 108
Layland, 65
LeCompte, 144
Lee, 89, 99, 110, 111, 115, 144
Leeds, 97
Legg, 148
Leland, 69
Lewis, 115, 141

Libby, 143
Light, 170
Lightfoot, 112
Lincoln, 32
Lindsley, 89, 99, 107
Lindsly, 27, 32
Lipscomb, 148
Liscomb, 173
Lodge, 65
Lollers, 109
Lomax, 109, 157, 175
Lomman, 63, 67
Longley, 38
Looney, 146
Lord, 174
Lovett, 174
Lowe, 61
Lucas, 34, 123
Lucasey, 115
Lutz, 175, 188
Lyons, 44, 126, 133
MacDaniel, 55
Mace, 57
Mackall, 164
Mackey, 164
Mackinamer, 70
Madden, 31
Maddin, 104
Mager, 124
Magruder, 81, 113, 141
Mahar, 152
Mahon, 177
Mahoney, 129, 132, 150
Mailing, 90
Manyette, 140
Marceron, 34, 35, 36, 107, 157, 199
Marshall, 109
Martin, 77, 97
Masi, 81, 103
Mason, 19, 67, 78, 95, 107, 162
Matthews, 110, 173
Maxwell, 156, 181
McCallan, 159
McCarty, 70, 73, 135
McComb, 113
McCormick, 156, 162
McCrady, 177
McCready, 79
McDaniel, 65, 79, 83

McDonald, 36, 145
McDowell, 59
McElroy, 163
McGirk, 185
McGuire, 155
McHale, 175
McIntire, 135
McKane, 80, 88, 98
McLaughlin, 155, 161, 176
McLauglin, 56
McLellan, 178
McLoughlin, 109
McMahon, 63
McMann, 100
McMonegle, 103
McNamee, 158
McPherson, 99, 103, 104, 111, 134
Mears, 190
Meinkin, 117
Menger, 103
Merr, 176
Merriman, 156
Metternick, 183
Meyer, 109, 152, 179
Meyers, 158, 161
Michael, 69
Middleton, 83
Miles, 67, 175
Millard, 45, 141, 199
Miller, 81, 139, 145, 157, 158, 167, 169, 182, 192
Mills, 6
Minor, 25, 27
Mitchell, 55
Montgomery, 51, 120
Moody, 89, 119, 125, 155
Mooney, 115
Moore, 123
Moran, 105
Morax, 170
Mordecai, 30
Morgan, 59, 80, 88, 115, 148
Morrell, 156
Morris, 67, 80
Morsell, 60
Mortimer, 31, 32, 87, 121
Mothershead, 109
Mozine, 142
Mullet, 6

Mullin, 174
Mump, 57
Mundell, 111
Munson, 131
Murphy, 161, 162
Murtaugh, 39
Nagle, 183
Naglee, 111
Nailer, 92
Nash, 22, 60, 74
Natli, 156
Neale, 65
Needle, 156
Negro Jane, 61
Nements, 162
Nemours, 115
Nesbit, 99, 109
Netter, 119
Newcomb, 148
Newman, 157, 167
Noble, 69
Noland, 85, 104, 113
Noliean, 104
Norman, 154
Norris, 177
Northern, 163
Norton, 95
Noyes, 91
O'Bryan, 170
O'Callahan, 170
O'Dell, 174
O'Donnell, 123
O'Neale, 19, 160
O'Toole, 188
Offut, 157
Ogden, 135
Ogle, 45, 136, 183
Oswald, 182
Otis, 35, 116, 125
Ould, 34
Overton, 100
Owen, 63
Owens, 56, 59
Oxley, 111
Parker, 34, 83, 125, 136, 162
Parkes, 148
Parsons, 65, 84
Patterson, 97, 113, 143, 144
Payne, 103, 200

Peddicord, 127
Pennington, 104
Penny, 51, 113, 115, 130, 136
Peoples, 16, 56
Percall, 180
Perez, 156
Peters, 68
Pettis, 56
Pfeifer, 151
Phillips, 27, 28, 132
Pierce, 180
Piggott, 23, 25
Pilling, 101
Platz, 157
Plume, 169
Plummer, 66, 167
Poe, 144
Pope, 144
Pormley, 142
Porter, 159
Posey, 65
Potentini, 146
Potts, 158
Powell, 91
Powers, 188
Pratt, 150
Prentiss, 93
Price, 133, 147, 155
Prine, 94
Proctor, 107
Prosser, 116
Quail, 111
Queen, 73, 74, 83
Quinn, 145
Radcliffe, 158
Rady, 108
Raglan, 125
Rainey, 113
Randall, 73
Rankin, 162, 169
Ratcliff, 25
Rawlings, 138
Ray, 144
Rea, 168
Redlon, 172
Reed, 119, 172
Regalan, 110
Reswick, 25
Reutzell, 157

Reynolds, 59, 143
Rhens, 165
Rhodes, 181
Richards, 131
Richardson, 136
Rickets, 83
Rickman, 107
Rifford, 169
Rigart, 61
Riley, 77, 164
Ring, 160
Rinsey, 180
Roach, 113, 141
Robbins, 78, 150, 157
Robbisin, 68
Robertson, 129
Robinson, 125, 135, 162
Rodgers, 77
Rollins, 121
Rosa, 120
Rose, 97, 132
Rothpitz, 85
Rounds, 56, 63, 89
Rowe, 35, 161
Rowles, 87, 109
Runnells, 116
Russell, 125
Ryan, 178
Ryder, 56
Safford, 123
Sager, 177
Samstag, 135
Savoy, 65, 84, 101
Sayres, 186
Schmidt, 137
Schwingman, 152, 154
Scott, 24, 69, 84, 87, 91, 103
Scribner, 157
Scrivener, 64
Searchfield, 144
Seaton, 93
Seitz, 100
Selby, 158
Seldner, 169
Semmes, 136, 148
Sengstack, 28, 29, 30, 36, 37, 44, 130, 133
Sewall, 26
Sewalls, 83

About the author

Mary C. Thornton

A former writing instructor at the University of North Florida and Florida Community College, I have an M.A. in English from the University of North Florida where I also minored in Criminal Justice.

In May 1999, "Placing Blame," an article I wrote about the Columbine High School murders, was published in the Jacksonville Florida, *Folio Weekly*. *A Complete Guide to the History and Inmates of the U.S. Penitentiary, District of Columbia, 1829-1862* is my first book.

In 2000, I moved to Alexandria, Virginia, where I currently live with my husband Tom. I continue to research and write on the lesser known people, places, and events that occurred in nineteenth century D.C. history.

www.ingramcontent.com/pod-product-compliance
Lightning Source LLC
Chambersburg PA
CBHW061954180426
43198CB00036B/883